Civilization on Trial

and

The World and the West

CIVILIZATION ON TRIAL

and

THE WORLD AND THE WEST

by ARNOLD TOYNBEE

MERIDIAN BOOKS, INC. *New York*

Published by Meridian Books, Inc. May 1958
First printing April 1958
Second printing August 1959

Civilization on Trial, *Copyright 1948 by Oxford University Press, Inc., Seventh Printing 1955*

The World and the West, *Copyright 1953 by Oxford University Press, Inc., Second Printing 1953*

A Summary of the Argument of A Study of History *by D. C. Somervell from the Abridgment of Volumes VII-X Copyright 1957 by Oxford University Press, Inc.*

All three works reprinted in this volume appear by arrangement with Oxford University Press, Inc.

Library of Congress Catalog Card Number: 58-8525

Manufactured in the United States of America

Arnold Toynbee

Arnold Toynbee, universally acknowledged as one of the greatest historians writing at the present time, is the author of the following works:

A Study of History Volumes I-VI, boxed
Volumes VII-X, boxed
Volumes I-X, boxed

Abridgment of Volumes I-VI by D. C. Somervell
Abridgment of Volumes VII-X by D. C. Somervell

The World and the West

Civilization on Trial

An Historian's Approach to Religion

War and Civilization: Selected by A. V. Fowler from *A Study of History*

All of these works by or concerning Arnold Toynbee are available in cloth editions published by Oxford University Press. Prices available on request.

CONTENTS

ACKNOWLEDGMENTS

Ten out of the thirteen essays in this book were published separately before being brought together here, and the writer and the publishers take this opportunity of thanking the original publishers for their courteous permission to reprint:

"My View of History" was first published in England in the Contact publication *Britain between East and West;* "The Present Point in History," copyright 1947 by *Foreign Affairs;* "Does History Repeat Itself?", copyright 1947 by *The New York Times;* "The International Outlook," copyright 1947 by *International Affairs,* is based on addresses given at Harvard University on 7 April 1947, at the Montreal, Ottawa, and Toronto Branches of the Canadian Institute of International Relations during the following week, and at the Royal Institute of International Affairs in London on 22 May of the same year; "Civilization on Trial," copyright 1947 by *The Atlantic Monthly,* is based on a lecture delivered at Princeton University on 20 February 1947; "Russia's Byzantine Heritage," published in *Horizon* of August 1947, is based on a course of two lectures delivered in April 1947 at the University of Toronto on the Armstrong Foundation; "Encounters between Civilizations," published in *Harper's Magazine* of April 1947, is based on the first lecture in a series delivered at Bryn Mawr College in February and March 1947 on the Mary Flexner Foundation; "Christianity and Civilization," copyright 1947 by Arnold J. Toynbee (Pendle Hill

9

Publications), is based on the Burge Memorial Lecture for that year, which was delivered in the Sheldonian Theatre at Oxford on 23 May 1940—at a critical moment, as it happened, in the history of both the lecturer's own country and the world. "The Meaning of History for the Soul," copyright 1947 by *Christianity and Crisis,* is based on a lecture delivered at Union Theological Seminary, New York, on 19 March 1947; "The Graeco-Roman Civilization" is based on a lecture delivered at Oxford University in the summer term of one of the interwar years, in a course, organized by Professor Gilbert Murray, of prolegomena to various subjects studied in the Oxford School of *Literae Humaniores;* "The Dwarfing of Europe" is based on a lecture delivered in London on 27 October 1926, with Dr. Hugh Dalton in the chair, in a series organized by the Fabian Society on "The Shrinking World: Dangers and Possibilities"; "The Unification of the World and the Change in Historical Perspective" is based on the Creighton Lecture delivered at the University of London in 1947.

A. J. TOYNBEE

January 1948

PREFACE

Although the essays collected in this volume have been written at different dates—several as long as twenty years ago, the majority within the last fifteen months—the book has, in the writer's mind, a unity of outlook, aim, and idea which, he hopes, will be felt by his readers. The unity of outlook lies in the standpoint of a historian who sees the Universe and all that therein is—souls and bodies, experience and events—in irreversible movement through time-space. The common aim that runs through this series of papers is to gain some gleam of insight into the meaning of this mysterious spectacle. The governing idea is the familiar one that the universe becomes intelligible to the extent of our ability to apprehend it as a whole. This idea has practical consequences for the historical method. An intelligible field of historical study is not to be found within any national framework; we must expand our historical horizon to think in terms of an entire civilization. But this wider framework is still too narrow, for civilizations, like nations, are plural, not singular; there are different civilizations which meet and, out of their encounters, societies of another species, the higher religions, are born into this world. That is not, however, the end of the historian's quest, for no higher religion is intelligible in terms of this world only. The mundane history of the higher religions is one aspect of the life of a Kingdom of Heaven, of which this world is one province. So history passes over into theology. "To Him return ye every one."

CIVILIZATION ON TRIAL

1

MY VIEW OF HISTORY

My view of history is itself a tiny piece of history; and this mainly other people's history and not my own; for a scholar's life-work is to add his bucketful of water to the great and growing river of knowledge fed by countless bucketfuls of the kind. If my individual view of history is to be made at all illuminating, or indeed intelligible, it must be presented in its origin, growth, and social and personal setting.

There are many angles of vision from which human minds peer at the universe. Why am I a historian, not a philosopher or a physicist? For the same reason that I drink tea and coffee without sugar. Both habits were formed at a tender age by following a lead from my mother. I am a historian because my mother was one before me; yet at the same time I am conscious that I am of a different school from hers. Why did I not exactly take my mother's cue?

First, because I was born by my mother into the next generation to hers, and my mind was, therefore, not yet set hard when history took my generation by the throat in 1914; and, secondly, because my education was more old-fashioned than my mother's had been. My mother—belonging as she did to the first generation, in England, of university women—had obtained an up-to-date education in modern Western history, with the national history of England itself as the principal guide-line. Her son, being a boy, went to an old-fashioned English public school and was educated, both there and at Oxford, almost entirely on the Greek and Latin Classics.

For any would-be historian—and especially for one born into these times—a classical education is, in my belief, a priceless boon. As a training-ground, the history of the Graeco-Roman world has its conspicuous merits. In the first place, Graeco-Roman history is visible to us in perspective and can be seen by us as a whole, because it is over—in contrast to the history of our own Western world, which is a still-unfinished play of which we do not know the eventual ending and cannot even see the present general aspect from our own position as momentary actors on its crowded and agitated stage.

In the second place, the field of Graeco-Roman history is not encumbered and obscured by a surfeit of information, and so we can see the wood—thanks to a drastic thinning of the trees during the interregnum between the dissolution of the Graeco-Roman society and the emergence of our own. Moreover, the conveniently manageable amount of evidence that has survived is not overweighted by the state papers of parochial principalities, like those which, in our Western world, have accumulated, ton upon ton, during the dozen centuries of its pre-atomic-bomb age. The surviving materials for a study of Graeco-Roman history are not only manageabale in quantity and select in quality; they are also well-balanced in their character. Statues, poems, and works of philosophy count here for more than the texts of laws and treaties; and this breeds a sense of proportion in the mind of a historian nursed on Graeco-Roman history; for—as we can see in the perspective given by lapse of time more easily than we can see it in the life of our own generation—the works of artists and men of letters outlive the deeds of business men, soldiers, and statesmen. The poets and the philosophers outrange the historians; while the prophets and the saints overtop and outlast them all. The ghosts of Agamemnon and Pericles haunt the living world of to-day by grace of the magic words of Homer and Thucydides; and, when Homer and Thucydides are no longer read, it is safe to prophesy that Christ and the Buddha and Socrates will still be fresh in the memory of (to us) almost inconceivably distant generations of men.

The third, and perhaps greatest, merit of Graeco-Roman history is that its outlook is oecumenical rather than parochial. Athens may have eclipsed Sparta and Rome Samnium, yet Athens in her youth made herself the education of all Hellas, while Rome in her old age made the whole Graeco-Roman world into a single commonwealth. In Graeco-Roman history, surveyed from beginning to end, unity is the dominant note; and, when once I had heard this great symphony, I was no longer in danger of being hynotized by the lone and outlandish music of the parochial history of my own country, which had once enthralled me when I listened to my mother telling it to me in instalments, night by night, as she put me to bed. The historical pastors and masters of my mother's generation, not only in England but in all Western countries, had been eagerly promoting the study of national history in the mistaken belief that it had a closer bearing on their countrymen's lives and was, therefore, somehow more readily accessible to their understanding than the history of other places and times (although it is surely evident that, in reality, Jesus' Palestine and Plato's Greece were more potently operative than Alfred's or Elizabeth's England in the lives of English men and women of the Victorian age).

Yet, in spite of this misguided Victorian canonization —so alien from the spirit of the father of English history, the Venerable Bede—of the history of the particular country in which one happened to have been born, the unconscious attitude of the Victorian Englishman towards history was that of someone living outside history altogether. He took it for granted—without warrant—that he himself was standing on *terra firma,* secure against being engulfed in that ever-rolling stream in which Time had borne all his less privileged sons away. In his own privileged state of being emancipated, as he supposed, from history, the Victorian Englishman gazed with curiosity, condescension, and a touch of pity, but altogether without apprehension, at the spectacle of less fortunate denizens of other places and periods struggling and foundering in history's flood—in much the same way as, in a mediaeval Italian picture, the saved lean over the balustrade of Heaven to look down complacently at the torments of the damned in Hell. Charles the First—worse luck for him—had been in history, but Sir Robert Walpole, though threatened with impeachment, had just managed to scramble out of the surf, while we ourselves were well beyond high-water mark in a snug coign of vantage where nothing could happen to us. Our more backward contemporaries might, perhaps, still be waist-high in the now receding tide, but what was that to us?

I remember, at the beginning of a university term during the Bosnian crisis of 1908-9, Professor L. B. Namier, then an undergraduate at Balliol and back from spending a vacation at his family home just inside the Galacian frontier of Austria, saying to us other Balliol men, with (it seemed to us) a portentous air: "Well, the Austrian army is mobilized on my father's estate and the Russian army is just across the frontier, half-an-hour away." It sounded to us like a scene from *The Chocolate Soldier,* but the lack of comprehension was mutual, for a lynx-eyed Central European observer of international affairs found it hardly credible that these English undergraduates should not realize that a stone's-throw away, in Galacia, their own goose, too, was being cooked.

Hiking round Greece three years later on the trail of Epaminondas and Philopoemen and listening to the talk in the village cafés, I learnt for the first time of the existence of something called the foreign policy of Sir Edward Grey. Yet, even then, I did not realize that we too were still in history after all. I remember feeling acutely homesick for the historic Mediterranean as I walked, one day in 1913, along the Suffolk coast of a grey and uneventful North Sea. The general war of 1914 overtook me expounding Thucydides to Balliol undergraduates reading for *Literae Humaniores,* and then suddenly my understanding was illuminated. The experience that we were having in our world now had been experienced by Thucydides in his world already. I was re-reading him now with a new perception—perceiving meanings in his words, and feelings behind his phrases, to which I had been insensible until I, in my turn, had run into that historical crisis that had inspired him to write his work. Thucydides, it now appeared, had been over this ground before. He and his generation had been ahead of me and mine in the stage of historical experience that we had respectively reached; in fact, his present had been my future. But this made nonsense of the chronological notation which registered my world as "modern" and Thucydides' world as "ancient." Whatever chronology might say, Thucydides' world and my world had now proved to be philosophically contemporary. And, if this were the true relation between the Graeco-Roman and the Western civilizations, might not the relation between all the civilizations known to us turn out to be the same?

This vision—new to me—of the philosophical contemporaneity of all civilizations was fortified by being seen against a background provided by some of the discoveries of our modern Western physical science. On the time-scale now unfolded by geology and cosmogony, the five or six thousand years that had elapsed since the first emergence of representatives of the species of human society that we label "civilizations" were an infinitesimally brief span of time compared to the age, up to date, of the human race, of life on this planet, of the planet itself, of our own solar system, of the galaxy in which it is one grain of dust, or of the immensely vaster and older sum total of the stellar cosmos. By comparison with these orders of temporal magnitude, civilizations that had emerged in the second millennium B.C. (like the Graeco-Roman), in the fourth millennium B.C. (like the Ancient Egyptian), and in the first millennium of the Christian era (like our own) were one another's contemporaries indeed.

Thus history, in the sense of the histories of the human societies called civilizations, revealed itself as a sheaf of parallel, contemporary, and recent essays in a new enterprise: a score of attempts, up to date, to transcend the level of primitive human life at which man, after having become himself, had apparently lain torpid for some hundreds of thousands of years—and was still, in our day, so lying in out-of-the-way places like New Guinea, Tierra del Fuego and the north-eastern extremity of Siberia, where such primitive human communities had not yet been pounced upon and either exterminated or assimilated by the aggressive pioneers of other human societies that, unlike these sluggards, had now, though this only recently, got on the move again. The amazing present difference in cultural level between various extant societies was brought to my attention by the works of Professor Teggart of the University of California. This far-going differentiation had all happened within these brief last five or six thousand years. Here was a promising point to probe in investigating, *sub specie temporis,* the mystery of the universe.

What was it that, after so long a pause, had so recently set in such vigorous motion once again, towards some new and still unknown social and spiritual destination, those few societies that had embarked upon the enterprise called civilization? What had roused them from a torpor that the great majority of human societies had never shaken off? This question was simmering in my mind when, in the summer of 1920, Professor Namier—who had already put Eastern Europe on my map for me—placed in my hands Oswald Spengler's *Untergang des Abendlandes.* As I read those pages teeming with firefly flashes of historical insight, I wondered at first whether my whole inquiry had been disposed of by Spengler before even the questions, not to speak of the answers, had fully taken shape in my own mind. One of my own cardinal points was that the smallest intelligible fields of historical study were whole societies and not arbitrarily insulated fragments of them like the nation-states of the modern West or the city-states of the Graeco-Roman world. Another of my points was that the histories of all societies of the species called civilizations were in some sense parallel and contemporary; and both these points were also cardinal in Spengler's system. But when I looked in Spengler's book for an answer to my question about the geneses of civilizations, I saw that there was still work for me to do, for on this point Spengler was, it seemed to me, most unilluminatingly dogmatic and deterministic. According to him, civilizations arose, developed, declined, and foundered in unvarying conformity with a fixed time-table, and no explanation

was offered for any of this. It was just a law of nature
which Spengler had detected, and you must take it on trust
from the master: *ipse dixit*. This arbitrary fiat seemed disappointingly unworthy of Spengler's brilliant genius; and
here I became aware of a difference in national traditions.
Where the German *a priori* method drew blank, let us
see what could be done by English empiricism. Let us
test alternative possible explanations in the light of the
facts and see how they stood the ordeal.

Race and environment were the two main rival keys that
were offered by would-be scientific nineteenth-century
Western historians for solving the problem of the cultural
inequality of various extant human societies, and neither
key proved, on trial, to unlock the fast-closed door. To
take the race theory first, what evidence was there that the
differences in physical race between different members of
the *genus homo* were correlated with differences on the
spiritual plane which was the field of history? And, if the
existence of this correlation were to be assumed for the
sake of argument, how was it that members of almost all
the races were to be found among the fathers of one or
more of the civilizations? The black race alone had made
no appreciable contribution up to date; but, considering
the shortness of the time during which the experiment of
civilization had been on foot so far, this was no cogent
evidence of incapacity; it might merely be the consequence
of a lack of opportunity or a lack of stimulus. As for environment, there was, of course, a manifest similiarity between the physical conditions in the lower Nile valley
and in the lower Tigris-Euphrates valley, which had been
the respective cradles of the Egyptian and Sumerian civilizations; but, if these physical conditions were really the
cause of their emergence, why had no parallel civilizations
emerged in the physically comparable valleys of the Jordan
and the Rio Grande? And why had the civilization of
the equatorial Andean plateau had no African counterpart in the highlands of Kenya? The breakdown of these
would-be scientific impersonal explanations drove me to
turn to mythology. I took this turning rather self-consciously and shamefacedly, as though it were a provoca-
tively retrograde step. I might have been less diffident if

I had not been ignorant, as I was at that date, of the new ground broken by psychology during the war of 1914-18. If I had been acquainted at the time with the works of C. G. Jung, they would have given me the clue. I actually found it in Goethe's *Faust,* in which I had fortunately been grounded at school as thoroughly as in Aeschylus' *Agamemnon.*

Goethe's "Prologue in Heaven" opens with the archangels hymning the perfection of God's creation. But, just because His works are perfect, the Creator has left Himself no scope for any further exercise of His creative powers, and there might have been no way out of this *impasse* if Mephistopheles—created for this very purpose—had not presented himself before the throne and challenged God to give him a free hand to spoil, if he can, one of the Creator's choicest works. God accepts the challenge and thereby wins an opportunity to carry His work of creation forward. An encounter between two personalities in the form of challenge and response: have we not here the flint and steel by whose mutual impact the creative spark is kindled?

In Goethe's exposition of the plot of the *Divina Commedia,* Mephistopheles is created to be diddled—as the fiend, to his disgust, discovers too late. Yet if, in response to the Devil's challenge, God genuinely puts His created works in jeopardy, as we must assume that He does, in order to win an opportunity of creating something new, we are also bound to assume that the Devil does not always lose. And thus, if the working of challenge-and-response explains the otherwise inexplicable and unpredictable geneses and growths of civilizations, it also explains their breakdowns and disintegrations. A majority of the score of civilizations known to us appear to have broken down already, and a majority of this majority have trodden to the end the downward path that terminates in dissolution.

Our *post mortem* examination of dead civilizations does not enable us to cast the horoscope of our own civilization or of any other that is still alive. *Pace* Spengler, there seems to be no reason why a succession of stimulating challenges should not be met by a succession of victorious responses *ad infinitum.* On the other hand, when we make an empirical comparative study of the paths which the dead civilizations have respectively travelled from breakdown to dissolution, we do here seem to find a certain measure of Spenglerian uniformity, and this, after all, is not surprising. Since breakdown means loss of control, this in turn means the lapse of freedom into automatism, and, whereas free acts are infinitely variable and utterly unpredictable, automatic processes are apt to be uniform and regular.

Briefly stated, the regular pattern of social disintegration is a schism of the disintegrating society into a recalcitrant proletariat and a less and less effectively dominant minority. The process of disintegration does not proceed evenly; it jolts along in alternating spasms of rout, rally, and rout. In the last rally but one, the dominant minority succeeds in temporarily arresting the society's lethal self-laceration by imposing on it the peace of a universal state. Within the framework of the dominant minority's universal state the proletariat creates a universal church, and after the next rout, in which the disintegrating civilization finally dissolves, the universal church may live on to become the chrysalis from which a new civilization eventually emerges. To modern Western students of history, these phenomena are most familiar in the Graeco-Roman examples of the *Pax Romana* and the Christian Church. The establishment of the *Pax Romana* by Augustus seemed, at the time, to have put the Graeco-Roman world back upon firm foundations after it had been battered for several centuries by perpetual war, mis-government, and revolution. But the Augustan rally proved, after all, to be no more than a respite. After two hundred and fifty years of comparative tranquility, the Empire suffered in the third century of the Christian era a collapse from which it never fully recovered, and at the next crisis, in the fifth and sixth centuries, it went to pieces irretrievably. The true beneficiary of the temporary Roman Peace was the Christian Church. The Church seized this opportunity to strike root and spread; it was stimulated by persecution until the Empire, having failed to crush it, decided, instead, to take it into partnership. And, when even this reinforcement failed to save the Empire from destruction, the Church took over the Empire's heritage. The same relation between a declining civilization and a rising religion can be observed in a dozen other cases. In the Far East, for instance, the Ts'in and Han Empire plays the Roman Empire's part, while the rôle of the Christian Church is assumed by the Mahayana school of Buddhism.

If the death of one civilization thus brings on the birth of another, does not the at first sight hopeful and exciting quest for the goal of human endeavours resolve itself, after all, into a dreary round of vain repetitions of the Gentiles? This cyclic view of the process of history was taken so entirely for granted by even the greatest Greek and Indian souls and intellects—by Aristotle, for instance, and by the Buddha—that they simply assumed that it was true without thinking it necessary to prove it. On the other hand, Captain Marryat, in ascribing the same view to the ship's carpenter of HMS *Rattlesnake,* assumes with equal assurance that this cyclic theory is an extravaganza, and he makes the amiable exponent of it a figure of fun. To our Western minds the cyclic view of history, if taken seriously, would reduce history to a tale told by an idiot, signifying nothing. But mere repugnance does not in itself account for effortless unbelief. The traditional Christian beliefs in hell fire and in the last trump were also repugnant, yet they continued to be believed for generations. For our fortunate Western imperviousness to the Greek and Indian belief in cycles we are indebted to the Jewish and Zoroastrian contributions to our *Weltanschauung.*

In the vision seen by the Prophets of Israel, Judah, and Iran, history is not a cyclic and not a mechanical process. It is the masterful and progressive execution, on the narrow stage of this world, of a divine plan which is revealed to us in this fragmentary glimpse, but which transcends our human powers of vision and understanding in every dimension. Moreover, the Prophets, through their own experience, anticipated Aeschylus' discovery that learning comes through suffering—a discovery which we, in our time and circumstances, have been making too.

Shall we opt, then, for the Jewish-Zoroastrian view of history as against the Graeco-Indian? So drastic a choice may not, after all, be forced upon us, for it may be that the two views are not fundamentally irreconcilable. After all, if a vehicle is to move forward on a course which its driver has set, it must be borne along on wheels that turn monotonously round and round. While civilizations rise and fall and, in falling, give rise to others, some purposeful enterprise, higher than theirs, may all the time be making headway, and, in a divine plan, the learning that comes through the suffering caused by the failures of civilizations may be the sovereign means of progress. Abraham was an émigré from a civilization *in extremis;* the Prophets were children of another civilization in disintegration; Christianity was born of the sufferings of a disintegrating Graeco-Roman world. Will some comparable spiritual enlightenment be kindled in the "displaced persons" who are the counterparts, in our world, of those Jewish exiles to whom so much was revealed in their painful exile by the waters of Babylon? The answer to this question, whatever the answer may be, is of greater moment than the still inscrutable destiny of our world-encompassing Western civilization.

2

THE PRESENT POINT IN HISTORY

Where does mankind stand in the year 1947 of the Christian era? This question no doubt concerns the whole living generation throughout the world; but, if it were made the subject of a world-wide Gallup Poll, there would be no unanimity in the answer. On this matter, if any, *quot homines, tot sententiae;* so we must ask ourselves in the same breath: To whom is our question being addressed? For example, the writer of the present paper is a middle-class Englishman of fifty-eight. Evidently his nationality, his social milieu, and his age, between them, will in large measure determine the standpoint from which he views the world panorama. In fact, like each and all of us, he is more or less the slave of historical relativity. The only personal advantage that he can claim to possess is that he happens also to be a historian, and is therefore at least aware that he himself is a piece of sentient flotsam on the eddying surface of the stream of time. Realizing this, he knows that his fleeting and fragmentary vision of the passing scene is no more than a caricature of the surveyor's chart. God alone knows the true picture. Our individual human *aperçus* are shots in the dark.

The writer's mind runs back fifty years, to an afternoon in London in the year 1897. He is sitting with his father at a window in Fleet Street and watching a procession of Canadian and Australian mounted troops who have come to celebrate Queen Victoria's Diamond Jubilee. He can still remember his excitement at the unfamiliar, pic-

26

turesque uniforms of these magnificent "colonial" troops, as they were still called in England then: slouch hats instead of brass helmets, grey tunics instead of red. To an English child, this sight gave a sense of new life astir in the world; a philosopher, perhaps, might have reflected that, where there is growth, there is likely also to be decay. A poet, watching the same scene, did, in fact, catch and express an intimation of something of the kind. Yet few in the English crowd gazing at that march past of overseas troops in London in 1897 were in the mood of Kipling's *Recessional*. They saw their sun standing at its zenith and assumed that it was there to stay—without their even needing to give it the magically compelling word of command which Joshua had uttered on a famous occasion.

The author of the tenth chapter of the Book of Joshua was at any rate aware that a stand-still of Time was something unusual. "There was no day like that before it or after it, that the Lord hearkened unto the voice of a man." Yet the middle-class English in 1897, who thought of themselves as Wellsian rationalists living in a scientific age, took their imaginary miracle for granted. As they saw it, history, for them, was over. It had come to an end in foreign affairs in 1815, with the Battle of Waterloo; in home affairs in 1832, with the Great Reform Bill; and in imperial affairs in 1859, with the suppression of the Indian Mutiny. And they had every reason to congratulate themselves on the permanent state of felicity which this ending of history had conferred on them. "The lines are fallen unto me in pleasant places; yea, I have a goodly heritage."

Viewed from the historical vantage point of A.D. 1947, this *fin de siècle* middle-class English hallucination seems sheer lunacy, yet it was shared by contemporary Western middle-class people of other nationalities. In the United States, for instance, in the North, history, for the middle class, had come to an end with the winning of the West and the Federal victory in the Civil War; and in Germany, or at any rate in Prussia, for the same class, the same permanent consummation had been reached with the overthrow of France and foundation of the Second Reich in 1871. For these three batches of Western middle-class people fifty years ago, God's work of creation was com-

pleted, "and behold it was very good." Yet, though in
1897 the English, American, and German middle class,
between them, were the political and economic masters
of the world, they did not amount, in numbers, to more
than a very small fraction of the living generation of mankind, and there were other people abroad who saw things
differently—even though they might be impotent and in-
articulate.

In the South, for example, and in France, there were in
1897 many people who agreed with their late conquerors
that history had come to an end: The Confederacy would
never rise from the dead; Alsace-Lorraine would never be
recovered. But this sense of finality, which was so gratify-
ing to top dog, did not warm a defeated people's heart.
For them it was nothing but a nightmare. The Austrians,
still smarting from their defeat in 1866, might have felt
the same if the stirrings of submerged nationalities inside
an Empire whose territory Bismarck had left intact had
not begun, by this time, to make the Austrians feel that
history was once more on the move and might have still
worse blows than Königgratz in store for them. English
liberals at the time were indeed talking freely, and with
approval, of a coming liberation of subject nationalities in
Austria-Hungary and the Balkans. But, in spite of the
spectre of Home Rule and the stirrings of "Indian unrest,"
it did not occur to them that, in South-Eastern Europe,
they were greeting the first symptoms of a process of
political liquidation which was to spread, in their lifetime,
to both India and Ireland and, in its irresistible progress
round the world, was to break up other empires besides
the Hapsburg Monarchy.

All over the world, in fact, though at that time still
under the surface, there were peoples and classes who were
just as discontented as the French or the Southerners were
with the latest deal of history's cards, but who were quite
unwilling to agree that the game was over. There were
all the subject peoples and all the depressed classes, and
what millions they amounted to! They included the whole
vast population of the Russian Empire of the day, from
Warsaw to Vladivostok: Poles and Finns determined to
win their national independence; Russian peasants deter-

mined to gain possession of the rest of the land of which they had been given so meagre a slice in the reforms of the eighteen-sixties; Russian intellectuals and business men who dreamed of one day governing their own country through parliamentary institutions, as people of their kind had long been governing the United States, Great Britain, and France; and a young and still small Russian industrial proletariat that was being turned revolutionary-minded by living conditions that were grim enough, though perhaps less so than those of early nineteenth-century Manchester. The industrial working class in England had, of course, improved their position very notably since the opening of the nineteenth century, thanks to the factory acts, the trades unions, and the vote (they had been enfranchised by Disraeli in 1867). Still, in 1897, they could not, and did not, look back on the Poor Law Act of 1834, as the middle class did look back on the Reform Bill of 1832, as history's last word in wisdom and beneficence. They were not revolutionary, but, on constitutional lines, they were resolved to make the wheels of history move on. As for the Continental European working class, they were capable of going to extremes, as the Paris Commune of 1871 had shown in an ominous lightning flash.

This deep desire for changes and the strong resolve to bring them about by one means or another were not, after all, surprising in the underdog, as represented by under-privileged classes and defeated or unliberated peoples. It was strange, though, that the apple-cart should be upset, as it was in 1914, by the Prussian militarists' (who in truth had as little to gain and as much to lose as the German, English, and American middle class) deliberately tearing open again history's insecurely closed book.

The subterranean movements that could have been detected, even as far back as 1897, by a social seismologist who put his ear to the ground, go far to explain the upheavals and eruptions that have signalized the resumption of history's Juggernaut march during the past half-century. To-day, in 1947, the Western middle class which, fifty years ago, was sitting carefree on the volcano's crust, is suffering something like the tribulation which, a hundred to a hundred and fifty years ago, was inflicted by Jugger-

naut's car on the English industrial working class. This is
the situation of the middle class to-day not only in Germany, France, the Low Countries, Scandinavia, and Great
Britain, but also in some degree in Switzerland and Sweden,
and even in the United States and Canada. The future of
the Western middle class is in question now in all Western
countries; but the outcome is not simply the concern of
the small fraction of mankind directly affected; for this
Western middle class—this tiny minority—is the leaven
that in recent times has leavened the lump and has thereby
created the modern world. Could the creature survive its
creator? If the Western middle class broke down, would
it bring humanity's house down with it in its fall? Whatever the answer to this fateful question may be, it is clear
that what is a crisis for this key-minority is inevitably also
a crisis for the rest of the world.

It is always a test of character to be baffled and "up
against it," but the test is particularly severe when the
adversity comes suddenly at the noon of a halcyon day
which one has fatuously expected to endure to eternity.
In straits like these, the wrestler with destiny is tempted
to look for bugbears and scapegoats to carry the burden
of his own inadequacy. Yet to "pass the buck" in adversity
is still more dangerous than to persuade oneself that prosperity is everlasting. In the divided world of 1947, Communism and Capitalism are each performing this insidious
office for one another. Whenever things go awry in circumstances that seem ever more intractable, we tend to
accuse the enemy of having sown tares in our field and
thereby implicitly excuse ourselves for the faults in our
own husbandry. This is, of course, an old story. Centuries
before Communism was heard of, our ancestors found
their bugbear in Islam. As lately as the sixteenth century,
Islam inspired the same hysteria in Western hearts as Communism in the twentieth century, and this essentially for
the same reasons. Like Communism, Islam was an anti-
Western movement which was at the same time a heretical
version of a Western faith; and, like Communism, it
wielded a sword of the spirit against which there was no
defence in material armaments.

The present Western fear of Communism is not a fear

of military aggression such as we felt in face of a Nazi Germany and a militant Japan. The United States, at any rate, with her overwhelming superiority in industrial potential and her monopoly of the "know-how" of the atom bomb, is at present impregnable against military attack by the Soviet Union. For Moscow, it would be sheer suicide to make the attempt, and there is no evidence that the Kremlin has any intention of committing such a folly. The Communist weapon that is making America so jumpy (and, oddly enough, she is reacting more temperamentally to this threat than the less sheltered countries of Western Europe) is the spiritual engine of propaganda. Communist propaganda has a "know-how" of its own for showing up and magnifying the seamy side of our Western civilization and for making Communism appear a desirable alternative way of life to a dissatisfied faction of Western men and women. Communism is also a competitor for the allegiance of that great majority of mankind that is neither Communist nor Capitalist, neither Russian nor Western, but is living at present in an uneasy no-man's-land between the opposing citadels of the two rival ideologies. Both non-descripts and Westerners are in danger of turning Communist to-day, as they were of turning Turk four hundred years ago, and, though Communists are in similar danger of turning Capitalist—as sensational instances have shown —the fact that one's rival witch-doctor is as much afraid of one's own medicine as one is afraid, oneself, of his, does not do anything to relieve the tension of the situation.

Yet the fact that our adversary threatens us by showing up our defects, rather than by forcibly suppressing our virtues, is proof that the challenge he presents to us comes ultimately not from him, but from ourselves. It comes, in fact, from that recent huge increase in Western man's technological command over non-human nature—his stupendous progress in "know-how"—which was just what gave our fathers the confidence to delude themselves into imagining that, for them, history was comfortably over. Through these triumphs of clockwork the Western middle class had produced three undesigned results—unprecedented in history—whose cumulative impetus has set Juggernaut's car rolling on again with a vengeance. Our

Western "know-how" has unified the whole world in the literal sense of the whole habitable and traversable surface of the globe; and it has inflamed the institutions of War and Class, which are the two congenital diseases of civilization, into utterly fatal maladies. This trio of unintentional achievements presents us with a challenge that is formidable indeed.

War and Class have been with us ever since the first civilizations emerged above the level of primitive human life some five or six thousand years ago, and they have always been serious complaints. Of the twenty or so civilizations known to modern Western historians, all except our own appear to be dead or moribund, and, when we diagnose each case, *in extremis* or *post mortem,* we invariably find that the cause of death has been either War or Class or some combination of the two. To date, these two plagues have been deadly enough, in partnership, to kill off nineteen out of twenty representatives of this recently evolved species of human society; but, up to now, the deadliness of these scourges has had a saving limit. While they have been able to destroy individual specimens, they have failed to destroy the species itself. Civilizations have come and gone, but Civilization (with a big "C") has succeeded, each time, in re-incarnating itself in fresh exemplars of the type; for, immense though the social ravages of War and Class have been, they have not ever yet been all-embracing. When they have shattered the top strata of a society, they have usually failed to prevent the underlying strata from surviving, more or less intact, and clothing themselves with spring flowers on exposure to the light and air. And when one society has collapsed in one quarter of the world it has not, in the past, necessarily dragged down others with it. When the early civilization of China broke down in the seventh century B.C., this did not prevent the contemporary Greek civilization, at the other end of the Old World, from continuing to rise towards its zenith. And when the Graeco-Roman civilization finally died of the twin diseases of War and Class in the course of the fifth, sixth, and seventh centuries of the Christian era, this did not prevent a new civilization from successfully coming to birth in the Far East during those same three hundred years.

Why cannot civilization go on shambling along, from failure to failure, in the painful, degrading, but not utterly suicidal way in which it has kept going for the first few thousand years of its existence? The answer lies in the recent technological inventions of the modern Western middle class. These gadgets for harnessing the physical forces of non-human nature have left human nature unchanged. The institutions of War and Class are social reflexions of the seamy side of human nature—or what the theologians call original sin—in the kind of society that we call civilization. These social effects of individual human sinfulness have not been abolished by the recent portentous advance in our technological "know-how," but they have not been left unaffected by it either. Not having been abolished, they have been enormously keyed up, like the rest of human life, in respect of their physical potency. Class has now become capable of irrevocably disintegrating Society, and War of annihilating the entire human race. Evils which hitherto have been merely disgraceful and grievous have now become intolerable and lethal, and, therefore, we in this Westernized world in our generation are confronted with a choice of alternatives which the ruling elements in other societies in the past have always been able to shirk—with dire consequences, invariably, for themselves, but not at the extreme price of bringing to an end the history of mankind on this planet. We are thus confronted with a challenge that our predecessors never had to face: We have to abolish War and Class—and abolish them now—under pain, if we flinch or fail, of seeing them win a victory over man which, this time, would be conclusive and definitive.

The new aspect of war is already familiar to Western minds. We are aware that the atom bomb and our many other new lethal weapons are capable, in another war, of wiping out not merely the belligerents but the whole of the human race. But how has the evil of class been heightened by technology? Has not technology already notably raised the minimum standard of living—at any rate in countries that have been specially efficient or specially fortunate in being endowed with the riches of nature and being spared the ravages of war? Can we not look forward to seeing this rapidly rising minimum standard raised to so high a level, and enjoyed by so large a percentage of the human race, that the even greater riches of a still more highly favoured minority will cease to be a cause of heartburning? The flaw in this line of reasoning is that it leaves out of account the vital truth that man does not live by bread alone. However high the minimum standard of his material living may be raised, that will not cure his soul of demanding social justice; and the unequal distribution of this world's goods between a privileged minority and an underprivileged majority has been transformed from an unavoidable evil into an intolerable injustice by the latest technological inventions of Western man.

When we admire aesthetically the marvellous masonry and architecture of the Great Pyramid or the exquisite furniture and jewelry of Tut-ankh-Amen's tomb, there is a conflict in our hearts between our pride and pleasure in such triumphs of human art and our moral condemnation of the human price at which these triumphs have been bought: the hard labour unjustly imposed on the many to produce the fine flowers of civilization for the exclusive enjoyment of a few who reap where they have not sown. During these last five of six thousand years, the masters of the civilizations have robbed their slaves of their share in the fruits of society's corporate labours as cold-bloodedly as we rob our bees of their honey. The moral ugliness of the unjust act mars the aesthetic beauty of the artistic result; yet, up till now, the few favoured beneficiaries of civilization have had one obvious common-sense plea to put forward in their own defence.

It has been a choice, they have been able to plead, between fruits of civilization for the few and no fruits at all. Our technological command over nature is severely limited. We have at our command neither sufficient musclepower nor sufficient labour to turn out our amenities in more than minute quantities. If I am to deny these to myself just because you cannot all have them too, we shall

have to shut up shop and allow one of the finest talents
of human nature to rust away buried in a napkin; and,
while that is certainly not in my interest, it is surely not
in yours either on a longer view. For I am not enjoying
this monopoly of amenities exclusively for my own benefit.
My enjoyment is at least partly vicarious. In indulging
myself at your expense, I am in some sense serving as a
kind of trustee for all future generations of the whole
human race. This plea was a plausible one, even in our
technologically go-ahead Western world, down to the
eighteenth century inclusive, but our unprecedented technological progress in the last hundred and fifty years has
made the same plea invalid to-day. In a society that has
discovered the "know-how" of Amalthea's cornucopia, the
always ugly inequality in the distribution of this world's
goods, in ceasing to be a practical necessity, has become
a moral enormity.

Thus the problems that have beset and worsted other
civilizations have come to a head in our world to-day. We
have invented the atomic weapon in a world partitioned
between two supremely great powers; and the United
States and the Soviet Union stand respectively for two
opposing ideologies whose antithesis is so extreme that,
as it stands, it seems irreconcilable. Along what path are
we to look for salvation in this parlous plight, in which
we hold in our hands the choice of life or death not only
for ourselves but for the whole human race? Salvation perhaps lies, as so often, in finding a middle way. In politics,
this golden mean would be something that was neither the
unrestricted sovereignty of parochial states nor the unre-
lieved despotism of a centralized world government; in
economics it would be something that was neither unrestricted private enterprise nor unmitigated socialism. As
one middle-aged middle-class West European observer sees
the world to-day, salvation cometh neither from the East
nor from the West.

In A.D. 1947, the United States and the Soviet Union
are alternative embodiments of contemporary man's tremendous material power; "their line is gone out through
all the Earth, and their words to the end of the World,"

but in the mouths of these loud-speakers one does not hear the still small voice. Our cue may still be given us by the message of Christianity and the other higher religions, and the saving words and deeds may come from unexpected quarters.

3

DOES HISTORY REPEAT ITSELF?

Does history repeat itself? In our Western world in the
eighteenth and nineteenth centuries, this question used to
be debated as an academic exercise. The spell of well-being
which our civilization was enjoying at the time had dazzled
our grandfathers into the quaint pharisaical notion that
they were "not as other men are"; they had come to believe
that our Western society was exempt from the possibility
of falling into those mistakes and mishaps that have been
the ruin of certain other civilizations whose history, from
beginning to end, is an open book. To us, in our generation, the old question has rather suddenly taken on a new
and very practical significance. We have awakened to the
truth (how, one wonders, could we ever have been blind
to it?) that Western man and his works are no more in-
vulnerable than the now extinct civilizations of the Aztecs
and the Incas, the Sumerians and the Hittites. So to-day,
with some anxiety, we are searching the scriptures of the
past to find out whether they contain a lesson that we
can decipher. Does history give us any information about
our own prospects? And, if it does, what is the burden of
it? Does it spell out for us an inexorable doom, which we
can merely await with folded hands—resigning ourselves,
as best we may, to a fate that we cannot avert or even
modify by our own efforts? Or does it inform us, not of
certainties, but of probabilities, or bare possibilities, in our
own future? The practical difference is vast, for, on this
second alternative, so far from being stunned into passivity,

we should be roused to action. On this second alternative, the lesson of history would not be like an astrologer's horoscope; it would be like a navigator's chart, which affords the seafarer who has the intelligence to use it a much greater hope of avoiding shipwreck than when he was sailing blind, because it gives him the means, if he has the skill and courage to use them, of steering a course between charted rocks and reefs.

It will be seen that our question needs defining before we plunge into an attempt to answer it. When we ask ourselves "Does history repeat itself?" do we mean no more than "Does history turn out to have repeated itself, on occasions, in the past?" Or are we asking whether history is governed by inviolable laws which have not only taken effect in every past case to which they have applied but are also bound to take effect in every similar situation that may arise in the future? On this second interpretation, the word "does" would mean "must"; on the other interpretation it would mean "may." On this issue, the writer of the present article may as well put his cards on the table at once. He is not a determinist in his reading of the riddle of human life. He believes that where there is life there is hope, and that, with God's help, man is master of his own destiny, at least to some extent in some respects.

But as soon as we have taken our stand on this issue between freedom and necessity that is raised by the ambiguous word "does," we find ourselves called upon to define what we mean by the word "history." If we have to limit the field of history to events that are wholly within the control of human wills, then, to be sure, for a non-determinist no difficulty would arise. But do such events ever actually occur in real life? In our personal experience, when we are making a decision, do we not always find ourselves only partly free and partly bound by past events and present facts in our own life and in our social and physical environment? Is not history itself, in the last analysis, a vision of the whole universe on the move in the four-dimensional framework of space-time? And, in this all-embracing panorama, are there not many events that the most staunch believer in the freedom of the human will would admit, as readily as the most thorough-going determinist, to be inexorably recurrent and precisely predictable?

Some events of this undisputedly recurrent predictable order may have little apparent bearing upon human affairs —as, for example, the repetitions of history in nebulae outside the system of the Milky Way. There are, however, some very obvious cyclic movements in physical nature that do affect human affairs in the most intimate fashion— as, for example, the recurrent predictable alternations of day and night and of the seasons of the year. The day-and-night cycle governs all human work; it dictates the schedules of the transportation systems of our cities, sets the times of their rush hours, and weighs on the minds of the commuters whom it shuttles to and fro, twice in every twenty-four hours, between "dormitory" and "workshop." The cycle of the seasons governs human life itself by governing our food supply.

It is true that man, by taking thought, can win a measure of freedom from these physical cycles that is beyond the reach of birds and beasts. Though the individual cannot break the tyranny of the day-and-night cycle by leading a waking life for twenty-four hours in the day, like the legendary Egyptian Pharaoh Mycerinus, human society can achieve Mycerinus' mythical feat collectively by a planned co-operation and a division of labour. Industrial plants can be operated for twenty-four hours in the day by successive shifts of workers, and the labours of workers who work by day can be prepared for and be followed up by the labours of other workers who rest by day and work by night. The tyranny of the seasons, again, has been broken by a Western society that has expanded from the northern temperate zone into the tropics and the southern temperate zone and has devised a technique of refrigeration. Nevertheless, these triumphs of man's mind and will over the tyranny of the two physical cycles of the day and the year are comparatively small gains for human freedom, remarkable though these triumphs are. On the whole, these recurrent predictable events in physical nature remain masters of human life—even at the present level of Western man's technology—and they show their mastery by subduing human affairs, as far as their

empire over them extends, to their own recurrent predictable pattern.

But are there, perhaps, human acts, in other fields of
action, that are not—or, at any rate not so completely—
under physical nature's control? Let us examine this question in a familiar concrete case. When, in the last days of
April 1865, the horses that, in the first days of that month,
had been the cavalry and artillery horses of the Army of
Northern Virginia, were being driven behind the plough
by the men who, at the beginning of that April, had been
General Lee's cavalrymen and artillerymen, those men and
horses were once again performing an annually recurrent
agricultural operation which they themselves had performed a number of times before in their lives and which
predecessors of theirs, in the Old World before Europeans
discovered the New World, and in other societies before
our Western society's birth, had been performing, year by
year, for some five or six thousand years past. The invention of ploughing is coeval with the species of society
that we call civilizations, and pre-plough methods of agriculture—likewise governed by the year cycle—were already in use for perhaps an equal length of time before
that, during the neolithic dawn by which the sunrise of
civilization was heralded. In the spring of 1865, agriculture
in the ex-Confederate States of North America was governed by the seasons very rigidly. A few weeks' delay,
and the season would have been too late—with the disastrous consequence that the food-producing capacities of
those horses and men would have been lost to the community for a whole year longer.

Thus, in the last days of April 1865, the horses and men
of the former Army of Northern Virginia were performing a historical act—the spring ploughing—which had repeated itself, by that date, some five or six thousand times
at least, and was still repeating itself in 1947. (In that year
the writer of this article witnessed the spring ploughing
in Kentucky, and noted the farmers' anxiety when, in
the middle of that April, their work was interrupted by
heavy rainfall.)

But what about the history that General Lee's horses
and men were making, not at the end of April, but at the

beginning? Is the kind of history that is represented by
the last act of the Civil War a kind that repeats itself—as
ploughing and commuting repeat themselves owing to their
close and obvious dependence on recurrent predictable
cycles in physical nature? Are we not confronted here
with a kind of human action that is more or less independent of physical cycles and is capable of overriding
them? Suppose that General Lee had not found himself
constrained to capitulate till June 1865? Or suppose that,
General Lee having capitulated when he did, General
Grant had not been moved to make his celebrated concession of allowing the Confederate soldiers who had just
laid down their arms to take their horses back with them
to their farms, notwithstanding the contrary provision in
the terms of surrender that had just been agreed upon.
Would not either of these hypothetical man-made variations on the actual course of historical events have prevented history from repeating itself in the Southern States
in the spring ploughing of 1865?

The province of history that we are considering now
is one that used to be treated as the whole field of history
before the provinces of economic and social history were
opened up. In this old-fashioned field of battles and policies,
captains and kings, does history turn out to have repeated
itself as it does in fields of human activity that are manifestly governed by cycles in the movement of physical
nature? Was the Civil War, for instance, a unique event,
or do we find other historical events that display sufficient
similarity and affinity to it to warrant us in treating it
and them as so many representatives of a class of events
in which history has repeated itself at least to some extent?
The present writer inclines to this latter view.

The crisis represented in American history by the Civil
War was, surely, repeated in a significant sense in the contemporary crisis in German history that is represented
by the Bismarckian wars of 1864-71. In both cases, an
imperfect political union had threatened to dissolve altogether. In both cases, the issue between the dissolution
of the union and its effective establishment was decided
by war. In both cases, the partisans of effective union won,
and, in both, one of the causes of their victory was their

technological and industrial superiority over their opponents. In both, finally, the victory of the cause of union was followed by a great industrial expansion which turned both the post-bellum United States and the Second German Reich into formidable industrial competitors of Great Britain. And here we have hit upon another repetition of history; for throughout the century ending about 1870, the industrial revolution in Great Britain might have appeared to be a unique historical event, whereas, since 1870, it has come to appear, in its true light, as simply the earliest instance of an economic transformation which was eventually to occur likewise in a number of other Western countries and in some non-Western countries too. Moreover, if we shift our attention from the economic common feature of industrialization to the political common feature of federal union, we shall see the history of the United States and Germany at this point repeating itself once again in the history of a third country—in this case not Great Britain but Canada, whose constituent provinces entered into their present federation in 1867, two years after the *de facto* re-establishment of the unity of the United States in 1865 and four years before the foundation of the Second German Reich in 1871.

In the formation, in the modern Western world, of a number of federal unions, and in the industrialization of these and other countries, we see history repeating itself in the sense of producing a number of more or less contemporary examples of the same human achievement. The contemporaneity of the different instances is, however, no more than approximate. The industrial revolution occurred as an apparently unique event in Great Britain at least two generations before its occurrence in America, and Germany proved it to be a repetitive phenomenon. The insecurely welded pre-Civil-War United States had existed for "four score and seven years," and the ramshackle post-Napoleonic German Confederation for half a century, before the crucial events of the eighteen-sixties proved that federal union was a repetitive pattern which was to recur not only in Canada but in Australia, South Africa, and Brazil. Contemporaneity is not an essential condition for the repetition of history on the political and cultural plane of human affairs. The historical events that repeat themselves may be strictly contemporary or they may overlap in time or they may be entirely non-contemporaneous with one another.

The picture remains the same when we turn to the consideration of the greatest human institutions and experiences that are known to us: the civilizations in their births and growths, their breakdowns, declines, and falls; the higher religions in their foundation and evolution. Measured by our subjective personal measuring rod of the average span of the memory of a single human being who lives to a normal old age, the time interval that divides our present generation from the date of the emergence of the Sumerian civilization in the fourth millennium B.C. or from the date of the beginning of the Christian era itself seems, no doubt, a very long one. Yet it is infinitesimally small on the objective time scale that has recently been given to us by the discoveries of our geologists and astronomers. Our modern Western physical science tells us that the human race has been in existence on this planet for at least 600,000 and perhaps a million years, life for at least 500 million and perhaps 800 million years, and the planet itself for possibly 2000 million years. On this time scale the last five or six thousand years that have seen the births of civilizations, and the last three or four thousand years that have seen the births of higher religions are periods of such infinitesimal brevity that it would be impossible to show them, drawn to scale, on any chart of the whole history of this planet up to date. On this true time scale, these events of "ancient history" are virtually contemporary with our own lifetime, however remote they may appear to be when viewed through the magnifying lens of the individual human midget's subjective mental vision.

The conclusion seems to be that human history does turn out, on occasions, to have repeated itself up to date in a significant sense even in spheres of human activity in which the human will is at its nearest to being master of the situation and is least under the domination of cycles in physical nature. Must we go on to conclude that, after all, the determinists are right and that what looks like free will is an illusion? In the present writer's opinion, the correct conclusion is just the opposite. As he sees it, this tendency towards repetition, which thus asserts itself in human affairs, is an instance of one of the well-known devices of the creative faculty. The works of creation are apt to occur in bunches: a bunch of representatives of a species, a bunch of species of a genus. And the value of such repetitions is, after all, not difficult to discern. Creation could hardly make any headway at all if each new form of creature were not represented by numerous eggs distributed among numerous baskets. How else could a creator, human or divine, provide himself with sufficient materials for bold and fruitful experiment and with effective means of retrieving inevitable failures? If human history repeats itself, it does so in accordance with the general rhythm of the universe; but the significance of this pattern of repetition lies in the scope that it gives for the work of creation to go forward. In this light, the repetitive element in history reveals itself as an instrument for freedom of creative action, and not as an indication that God and man are the slaves of fate.

What is the bearing of these conclusions about history in general on the particular question of the prospects of our Western civilization? As we observed at the beginning of this paper, the Western world has become rather suddenly very anxious about its own future, and our anxiety is a natural reaction to the formidableness of the situation in which we now find ourselves. Our present situation is formidable indeed. A survey of the historical landscape in the light of our existing knowledge shows that, up to date, history has repeated itself about twenty times in producing human societies of the species to which our Western society belongs, and it also shows that, with the possible exception of our own, all these representatives of the species of society called civilizations are already dead or moribund. Moreover, when we study the histories of these dead and moribund civilizations in detail, and compare them with one another, we find indications of what looks like a recurring pattern in the process of their breakdowns, declines, and falls. We are naturally asking ourselves to-day whether this particular chapter of history is bound to re-

peat itself in our case. Is that pattern of decline and fall
in store for us in our turn, as a doom from which no
civilization can hope to escape? In the writer's opinion,
the answer to this question is emphatically in the negative.
The effort to create a new manifestation of life—be it a
new species of mollusc or a new species of human society
—seldom or never succeeds at the first attempt. Creation
is not so easy an enterprise as that. It wins its ultimate successes through a process of trial and error; and accordingly
the failure of previous experiments, so far from dooming
subsequent experiments to fail in their turn in the same
way, actually offers them their opportunity of achieving
success through the wisdom that can be gained from suffering. Of course a series of previous failures does not
guarantee success to the next comer, any more than it
condemns him to be a failure in his turn. There is nothing
to prevent our Western civilization from following historical precedent, if it chooses, by committing social suicide.
But we are not doomed to make history repeat itself; it is
open to us, through our own efforts, to give history, in
our case, some new and unprecedented turn. As human
beings, we are endowed with this freedom of choice, and
we cannot shuffle off our responsibility upon the shoulders
of God or nature. We must shoulder it ourselves. It is up
to us.

What shall we do to be saved? In politics, establish a
constitutional co-operative system of world government. In
economics, find working compromises (varying according
to the practical requirements of different places and times)
between free enterprise and socialism. In the life of the
spirit, put the secular super-structure back onto religious
foundations. Efforts are being made in our Western world
to-day to find our way towards each of these goals. If
we have arrived at all three of them, we might fairly feel
that we had won our present battle for our civilization's
survival. But these are, all of them, ambitious undertakings,
and it will call for the hardest work and the highest courage
to make any progress at all towards carrying any one of
them through to achievement.

Of the three tasks, the religious one is, of course, in
the long run by far the most important, but the other two

are the more urgent, because, if we were to fail in these in the short run, we might lose for ever our opportunity of achieving a spiritual rebirth which cannot just be whistled for at our convenience, but will only come, if it comes at all, at the unhurrying pace at which the deepest tides of spiritual creation flow.

The political task is the most urgent of all. The immediate problem here is a negative one. Faced, as we are, with the prospect that—given our present interdependence and present weapons—the world is now on the eve of being unified politically by one means or another, we have to stave off the disastrous dénouement of unification by force of arms: the familiar method of the forcible imposition of a *Pax Romana* which is probably the line of least resistance for the resolution of the formidable political forces in whose grip our own world finds itself to-day. Can the United States and the other Western countries manage to co-operate with the Soviet Union through the United Nations? If the United Nations organization could grow into an effective system of world government, that would be much the best solution of our political crux. But we have to reckon with the possibility of this enterprise's failing, and to be ready, should it fail, with an alternative to fall back upon. Could the United Nations split, *de facto,* into two groups without a breach of the peace? And, supposing that the whole face of the planet could be partitioned peacefully into an American and a Russian sphere, could two worlds on one planet live side by side on a footing of "non-violent non-co-operation" for long enough to give a chance for a gradual mitigation of the present differences in their social and ideological climates? The answer to this question would depend on whether, on these terms, we could buy the time needed to carry out our economic task of finding a middle way between free enterprise and socialism.

These riddles may be hard to read, but they do tell us plainly what we most need to know. They tell us that our future largely depends upon ourselves. We are not just at the mercy of an inexorable fate.

4

THE GRAECO-ROMAN CIVILIZATION

I am going to start from a point that has been made by Professor Gilbert Murray.[1] His point is that, in the Graeco-Roman world, the written word had a function that was not unlike that of the typescript which a speaker is required to have in front of him at Broadcasting House when he is talking over the radio. Like the present-day broadcaster's typescript, the Graeco-Roman "book" was really a system of mnemonics for conjuring up winged words, and not a book in our sense of something intended for reading to oneself, like the ordinary printed volume that is produced nowadays by publishers.

However, the Graeco-Roman world did not include the whole of mankind at any time in its history. There were always other worlds in existence side by side with it; and some of these other worlds had the extreme opposite way of looking at a book. In the Syrian world, for instance, to which the Jews belonged, a book was certainly not regarded as a mere mnemonic aid to human

[1] Sec Murray, G. G. A.: *Greek Studies* (*Oxford* 1946 Clarendon Press): "Prolegomena to the Study of Greek Literature." This paper of Professor Murray's was originally delivered as a lecture in a course of "prolegomena" organized by him for undergraduates of the University of Oxford who were just starting to read for the School of *Literae Humaniores.* The lecture on which the present paper is based was the next after Professor Murray's in this course.

discourse. It was revered as the revealed word of God: a sacred object, in which every jot and title on the written page had a magical potency and therefore an immeasurable importance.

It is one of the curiosities of history that our own traditional way of studying the Greek and Latin classics is derived from the Jewish way of studying the Law and the Prophets. In other words, we handle these Greek and Latin books in an utterly different way from that in which they were used, and were meant to be used, by their authors and their broadcasters at the time when they were made.

Our Jewish Rabbinical way of studying a book has merits which are so obvious that one need not dwell on them. When once one has been drilled into this discipline, one continues, for the rest of ones life, to read everything with a closeness and thoroughness which is, most certainly, much better than the way in which one reads a newspaper *en route* to one's office. This is a lesson which is never to be forgotten, but it is not the last lesson to be learnt from a study of the Graeco-Roman civilization. We cannot resign ourselves to that drastic and misleading limitation of outlook which is the defect of the virtue of the microscopic, intensive Rabbinical study of a sacred book or a classic. The Rabbinical outlook has two vices. It inclines one to think of a book as a thing in itself—something static and dead—instead of seeing it, for what it is, as the material track or echo or *débris* of human action (for intellectual acts are as authentic a form of action as exertions of will power or of physical energy). The second vice is really the same thing stated in more general or philosophic terms. The Rabbinical method of study makes one inclined to think of life in terms of books instead of *vice versa*. The opposite method—which is the Greek line of approach—is to study books not just for their own sake, but also because they are the key to the life of the people who wrote them.

If, following the Rabbinical rather than the Hellenic line, one were to concentrate his attention upon some particular period of Greek or Roman history for the sake of some famous literary work of that age which happens to have survived to the present day, one's historical vision might be very badly distorted; because the survival of certain portions of Greek and Latin literature, and the loss of other parts, has been determined by known historical causes; and these causes, in themselves, have nothing to do with the question whether the ages that produced the surviving literature were historically important and the ages that produced the lost literature were historically of no account.

To show what I mean, I shall put the surviving Latin books aside for a moment and take the surviving Greek books first. If one runs through a list of surviving Greek books, one finds that the vast majority of them were written in either one or the other of two periods which are separated from one another by a gap of some three centuries. The most famous—"the classics" *par excellence* —were written within a period extending over not more than five of six generations and ending in the generation of Demosthenes (i.e. approximately between 480 and 320 B.C.). But there is another surviving group which begins in the last century B.C. with writers like Diodorus Siculus and Strabo. This later group of surviving Greek authors is perhaps larger in bulk than the earlier group, and it contains such famous names as Plutarch and Lucian and Arrian and Epictetus and Marcus Aurelius. Substantially, our surviving Greek literature dates either from the "Classical" or from the "Imperial" age. The surviving works of the intervening "Hellenistic age" are either short or fragmentary.

Why is this? The selection looks odd and arbitrary at first sight, but we happen to know the reason for it. The reason is that, in the generation of Augustus, the Graeco-Roman world, which had been going to pieces during the four centuries ending in the year 31 B.C.—the year of the Battle of Actium—made a desperately earnest, and temporarily successful, effort to pull itself together. Psychologically, this effort took the form of a sort of homesickness for what now looked like a golden age in the past, an age in which Greek life had apparently been a happier and more spendid thing than it was in the last century B.C. And the people who felt like this in that later age sought salvation in archaism: in a deliberate attempt at an artificial resurrection of past happiness and beauty and greatness. One can study this archaistic movement of the "Imperial age" in religion and in literature. In literature, it led people to repudiate the modern "Hellenistic" style," to admire and study the mediaeval Attic style, and to become indifferent to the preservation of Greek books which were not either the Attic originals themselves or else ultra-modern neo-Attic imitations of them.

Now this does explain why our surviving Greek literature represents the "Imperial age" and the "Classical age" almost exclusively, and why the literature of the intervening "Hellenistic age" has mostly dropped out. But, if one is a historian, this does not make one feel: "Well then, the 'Hellenistic age' cannot be worth studying." On the contrary, the historian thinks to himself: "This difference in the degree of happiness and success and civilization between the Graeco-Roman world in the last century B.C. and the Greek world in the fifth century B.C. is something extraordinary—and something terrible; for the people in the last century B.C. were plainly right. In the intervening age there had been an enormous regression, an immense set-back. How and why did that set-back take place?" The historian sees that the Graeco-Roman world achieved a rally in the generation of Augustus after the Battle of Actium. He also sees that the preceding breakdown began with the outbreak of the Peloponnesian War, four centuries earlier. For him, the vitally interesting problem is: What was it that went wrong in the fifth century and continued to go wrong until the last century B.C.? Now, the solution of this problem can only be found by studying Greek and Roman history as a continuous story with a plot that is one and indivisible. And, therefore, from the historian's point of view, it is a defect in our traditional curriculum that, while it makes sure that one shall study the first chapter of this story by reading Thucydides and study the last chapter by reading Cicero, it gives one very little encouragement to study the intervening chapters because these do not happen to be recorded in any consecrated and canonical "classical" work of either Greek or Latin literature. And yet, if these middle chapters are left out, the Thucydidean and the Ciceronian chapters, left stranded at either end of the story, become shapeless bits of wreckage out of which it is impossible to reconstruct either the true build of the ship or the true story of the wreck.

Let us imagine a hypothetical parallel in the history of our own world. Let us anticipate the situation after the next war,[2] when Great Britain, as well as Continental Europe, will have been bombed to bits, and our Western civilization quite destroyed in its original European home, with the consequence that nothing is ever going to happen in Europe any more. That hypothetical picture of Europe as she may be before the end of the twentieth century corresponds, of course, to the real picture of Greece as she actually was by the last century B.C. Then, let us suppose to ourselves that the "Anglo-Saxon" variety of our Western civilization has just managed to survive—maimed and stunted and barbarized—in the overseas English-speaking countries. After that, let us picture the Americans and Australians making a great effort to salvage the remnants of their hereditary European culture, and, in particular, to recover and safeguard the purity of their English speech and English literary style. Well, what, in these circumstances, will they do? They will decree that the only "classical" English is the English of Shakespeare and Milton; they will teach nothing but this English henceforward in their schools and write nothing but this English —or what they fancy to be the Shakespearian and Miltonic idiom—in their newspapers and magazines. And, as life will have become rather nasty and brutish, and the market for books will have very much fallen off, they will allow all the intervening literature in the English language, from Dryden to Masefield inclusive, to go out of print.[3] That, I think, is an accurate analogy, in our own terms, of what actually happened to Greek literature. But, suppose this did happen in our own case; suppose that, for some reason or

[2] The lecture on which this paper is based was delivered in the inter-war period 1918-39.

[3] At the time when these words were written, the author did not foresee that he himself would live to witness the partial translation of his fancy into fact.

other, the whole of English literature, from the Restoration to the post-Victorians inclusive, were discredited and forgotten, would it be wise to infer from this that the eighteenth and nineteenth centuries, in which the bulk of this lost literature had been written, were centuries of no consequence in the history of our Western world?

Let us now turn to the Latin books. And I will ask my readers to think of these Latin "classics"—though the conception of them that I am going to suggest may seem rather surprising at first thoughts—as an appendage to the surviving Greek works of the "Imperial age"; as a version of Greek literature in a Latin dress. The earliest complete extant works in Latin, the surviving plays of Plautus and Terence, are undisguised translations of "Hellenistic" Greek originals. And I should say that, in a rather subtler sense, the whole of Latin literature—including even such masterpieces as the poems of Virgil—is in essence a version of Greek originals translated into the Latin. After all, I can quote the second most famous of all the Latin poets for my purpose. Indeed, the tag is so well worn that I hardly dare bring it out.

Conquered Greece took her savage conqueror captive, and introduced the arts into rustic Latium:
Graecia capta ferum victorem cepit, et artes intulit agresti Latio.

We all know the passage, and we all know that it is true. The mere linguistic difference between the Latin and Greek languages creates no division of literary style and no break in literary history. After all, our own modern Western literature is conveyed in a dozen different vernacular languages—Italian, French, Spanish, English, German, and the rest—yet no one would dream of saying that these were really all separate literatures or that any of them would or could be what it actually is if there had not been a perpetual give-and-take between all these modern Western vernaculars for centuries. Dante, Shakespeare, Goethe, and the other giants—they are all exponents of a literature that is one and indivisible. The difference between these different linguistic vehicles is of minor importance. Latin literature stands, I should say, to Greek as English literature stands to Italian and French.

Or let us look at the relation between Latin literature and Greek literature in another way. Let us employ the simile of a wave and think of the Graeco-Roman civilization as a movement in a spiritual medium—an emission of spiritual energy—which wells up from a spring of original inspiration in Greece and radiates its influence outwards from Greece in all directions in concentric waves. It is in the nature of a wave, when it is passing through a resistant medium, to become weaker and fainter the farther it travels outwards from its point of emission until, eventually, at a certain distance, it dies away. And now let us follow the course of the wave of Greek literature as it travels outwards from Greece.

At the outset, near home, the wave is so powerful that it carries along with it the use of the Greek language. When Xanthus the Lydian takes to writing history in the Greek style in the fifth century B.C., he employs not only the Greek style but the Greek language as well; and, as far afield in this direction as Cappadocia in the fourth century of the Christian era, the wave of Greek literature is still strong enough to carry the Greek language with it. This foreign Greek is used by the Cappadocians—Gregory of Nazianzus and the rest—when they are roused into literary activity in the fourth century after Christ because the wave of Greek influence has now just reached them. But, a century or so later, when the same wave, travelling still farther afield, reaches Syria and Armenia, it has become so weak that it has had to leave the Greek language behind; and the literature which is now produced, under Greek influence, by Syrians and Armenians is written not in Greek, but in the Syriac and Armenian languages.

And now let us follow the same wave as it travels in the opposite direction—not eastwards but westwards. In this direction, when it reaches Sicily it is still so strong that it simply sweeps away the non-Greek local language of the native Sicilians. So far as we know, no literary works were ever written in this Sikel language in Sicily, any more than any were ever written in Lydian in Asia Minor.

The Greek language was overpowering at this short range. I have already referred to the work written in the Greek language by a historian who lived in the last century B.C.: Diodorus Siculus. This Diodorus was a genuine Sikel and not a Siceliot or Greek colonist on Sicilian soil. His native city, Agyrium, was a Sikel city, in the interior of the island, where no Greek colony had ever been planted. Yet Diodorus writes in Greek as a matter of course. All the same, there was, in Diodorus's day, a version of the Greek literature in the Sikels' native language which was beginning to produce great works of art. But this was happening farther afield, half way up the Italian peninsula, in Latium, at a range at which the wave of Greek influence, expanding from Greece, was weaker. This continental Italian version of Greek literature was being produced in Latium in the living local Latin language of the country, with which the extinct Sikel language of Sicily seems to have been almost identical. When the wave of Greek literary influence got as far as Latium, travelling westwards, it dropped the Greek language and took to the local vernacular—just as it dropped Greek and took to Syriac and Armenian after it had travelled about the same distance eastwards.

This conception of the Greek civilization as a kind of radiation out of Greece—a four-dimensional radiation in space-time—may also be illustrated from the history of coinage. In the fourth century B.C. King Philip of Macedon opened up a number of gold and silver mines in the Thracian territories which he conquered and annexed in the neighbourhood of Mount Pangaeus. And he used the proceeds to issue a copious coinage. This coinage not only served to corrupt the politicians in the city-states of the Greek peninsula; it also spread north-westwards into the interior of Continental Europe. Philip's coins passed from hand to hand and were imitated in one barbarian mint after another, until this coinage-wave actually crossed the Channel and spread into the island of Britain. The numismatists have been able to put together an almost continuous series, ranging from Philip's original issues of the fourth century B.C. to the British imitations which were struck two or three centuries later. (It took this wave several centuries to travel that far.) There are sets of this series in our museums, and a feature which we have already observed in our literature-wave comes out in the coinage-wave still more strongly. As the wave moves farther and farther away in space from its original place of emission, and farther and farther away in time from its original date of issue, it grows weaker and weaker. The Latin version of Greek literature is palpably inferior to the Greek original; and similarly, but to a far more grotesque degree, the British imitations of King Philip's coins are inferior to the original mintage. In the latest and remotest coins of the series, the Macedonian King's image, and the superscription in Greek characters in the Greek language, have degenerated into a meaningless pattern. If we did not happen to possess examples of the intermediate terms in the series, we should never have known that there was any line of artistic affiliation between these later British coins and their Macedonian original. One could not have guessed that the pattern on the British coins was derived historically from an inscription in Greek, surrounding a human face.

Before we throw aside this simile of radiation, we may remind ourselves of another wave of Greek civilization which has had a different and more surprising—and to my mind much more interesting—outcome. When one looks at a modern Japanese print or at a mediaeval Chinese painting —dating, say, from the period of the Sung Dynasty—one is not immediately reminded of the Greek style of art. Indeed, one's first impression is that he is face to face here with an art that is even more foreign from the Greek than it is from our own. And yet, if we take some Far Eastern work of art from the Far Eastern artistic golden age—say, the fifth to the thirteenth centuries of the Christian era —we can do the same thing that we have done already with those British coins of the last century B.C. We can bring together a continuous series of works of art which stretches backwards in time from the second millennium of the Christian era, and westwards in space from China through the Tarim Basin and the Oxus and Jaxartes Basin and Afghanistan and Persia and "Iraq and Syria and Asia Minor, until we arrive at the same point in space and time to which we are led back in our series of coin types: that is to say, back to the "classical" art of Greece in the age before the generation of Alexander. As we travel back over the wake of this wave, a Japanese portrayal of the Buddha melts into a Greek portrayal of Apollo by insensible degrees.

But there is, of course, one obvious difference between the wave which begins in classical Greece and ends in a British coin and this other wave which likewise begins in classical Greece but ends in a Japanese painting of a landscape or statue of a Bodhisattva. In both cases, the historical connexion between the last term in the series and the first is unrecognizable until the intermediate terms have been fitted into their places; but the two curves—to think in a mathematical image—are quite different in character. In the series of coin types, we have a simple instance of degeneration. The art becomes poorer and poorer, steadily, as it recedes farther in space and in time from the Greece of the fourth century B.C. In the other curve, which ends not in Gaul and Britain but in China and Japan, the beginning is the same. As the Greek art of the "Hellenistic" and the early "Imperial" age spreads eastward, across the dead body of the defunct Persian Empire, until it reaches Afghanistan, it becomes more and more conventional and commercial and lifeless. And then something like a miracle happens. This fast degenerating Greek art collides in Afghanistan with another spiritual force which is radiating out of India: the Mahayana form of Buddhism. And the degenerating Greek art unites with the Mahayana to produce a distinctively new and intensely creative civilization: the Mahayanian Buddhist civilization which has travelled north-eastward across Asia to become the civilization of the Far East.

Here we have stumbled upon a wonderful property of these spiritual waves of radiation. Though their natural tendency is to weaken as they travel outwards, this tendency may be overcome and counteracted if two waves, travelling outwards from two different centres, happen to collide and coalesce. The coalescence of a Greek wave with an Indian wave has generated the Buddhist civilization of the Far East. But there is, of course, another instance of the same miracle which is much more familiar to us. The same Greek wave has also coalesced with a Syrian wave, and it is this union that has generated the Christian civilization of our Western world.

So much for this simile of waves of radiation. It is an illuminating way of looking at the histories of civilizations up to a point—but only up to a point. If we take it too seriously and do not discard it when we have made the most of it, it may become an obstacle to our seeing farther still. These metaphorical applications of the processes of inanimate nature to the delineation of life, and particularly human life, are perhaps peculiarly dangerous nowadays just because they are so much in fashion. Not so long ago, the danger was all the other way. We used to think of the processes of inanimate nature anthropomorphically, and the progress of physical science was seriously hindered until this anthropomorphic, mythological habit of looking at physical nature was broken. We have, I think, broken it effectively. In our physical science, we are thoroughly on our guard nowadays against the so-called "pathetic fallacy." But perhaps, in extricating ourselves from the "pathetic fallacy," we have fallen unawares into an opposite "apathetic fallacy"—which is every bit as fallacious. We tend, because this feels and sounds "scientific," and because science nowadays enjoys prestige, to think and talk about human beings as though they were sticks and stones and about life as though it were a stream of radiation or a constellation of protons and electrons. This may be a convenient simile, but it is, I am sure, a false route. Let us step out of this rut and set ourselves to think and speak of human civilizations in human terms.

In human terms, how are we to describe the Greek civilization, or our own Western civilization, or any other of the ten or twenty civilizations which we can count up on our fingers? In human terms, I should say that each of these civilizations is, while in action, a distinctive attempt at a single great common human enterprise, or, when it is seen in retrospect, after the action is over, it is a distinctive instance of a single great common human experience. This enterprise or experience is an effort to perform an act of creation. In each of these civilizations, mankind, I think, is trying to rise above mere humanity—above primitive humanity, that is—towards some higher kind of spiritual life. One cannot depict the goal because it has never been reached—or, rather, I should say that it has never been reached by any human society. It has, perhaps, been reached by individual men and women. At least, I can think of certain saints and sages who seem to me, in their personal lives, to have reached the goal, at least in so far as I myself am able to conceive what the goal may be like. But if there have been a few transfigured men and women, there has never been such a thing as a civilized society. Civilization, as we know it, is a movement and not a condition, a voyage and not a harbour. No known civilization has ever reached the goal of civilization yet. There has never been a communion of saints on earth. In the least uncivilized society at its least uncivilized moment, the vast majority of its members have remained very near indeed to the primitive human level. And no society has ever been secure of holding such ground as it has managed to gain in its spiritual advance. All the civilizations that we know of, including the Greek, have already broken down and gone to pieces with the single possible exception of our own Western civilization—and no child of this civilization who has been born into our generation can easily imagine that our own society is immune from the danger of suffering the common fate.

Now civilizations, I believe, come to birth and proceed to grow by successfully responding to successive challenges. They break down and go to pieces if and when a challenge confronts them which they fail to meet. Not unnaturally there are challenges that present themselves in the histories of more than one civilization. And the peculiar interest of Graeco-Roman history for us lies in the fact that the Greek civilization broke down in the fifth century B.C. through failing to find a successful response to the very challenge which is confronting our own Western civilization in our own lifetime.

If we unwind the scroll of Greek history, we find ourselves studying both the presentation of this fateful challenge and the disastrous failure to discover an answer to it. In order to suggest what this challenge was, I must

recall the salient events in the history of the Greek world
before the outbreak of the Peloponnesian War in 431 B.C.
The first event is the creation of the city-states that brought
law and order out of a social interregnum in the coast-
lands of the Aegean Sea which had followed the downfall
of the Minoan maritime empire. The next event is a pressure of population upon means of subsistence in the home
of the new civilization in Ionia and in continental European Greece. The third event is an easing of this pressure
by a colonial expansion all over the Mediterranean: the
foundation of colonial Greek city-states on barbarian
ground. The fourth event is the stoppage of this Greek
colonial expansion, in the course of the sixth century B.C.,
partly through the successful resistance of the native victims and partly through the political consolidation of the
Greeks' own rivals in the competitive colonization of the
western Mediterranean from the Levant: the Carthaginian
and Etruscan powers on the west and the Lydian Empire,
succeeded by the much greater Persian Empire, on the
east. (From the Greek standpoint the Persian Empire
meant not so much the Persians as the Phoenicians of the
Phoenician homeland in Syria, whose hands were strengthened by Persian support.)

In what we think of as the most brilliant age of the
Greek civilization—the late sixth and early fifth centuries
B.C.—the Greeks themselves had the feeling of being
hemmed in and hampered and hard pressed. As Thucydides saw it, from the age of Cyrus and Darius onwards

Hellas was repressed from all sides over a long period of time,
with the consequence that, in this period, she neither performed
any great co-operative achievement nor showed any enterprise
in the parochial life of the individual city-state communities.
[Thucydides, Book I, chap. 17]

As Herodotus saw it,

The three successive generations covered by the reigns of
Darius Hystaspes-son and Xerxes Darius-son and Artaxerxes
Xerxes-son saw Hellas overwhelmed by more troubles than
she had had to suffer from first to last during the twenty
generations preceding Darius' accession. [Herodotus, Book VI,
chap. 98]

But, as a matter of fact, this was the very age in which the Greek society succeeded in solving the new economic problem which had been presented to it by the stoppage of its geographical expansion. The problem now was how to obtain an increasing amount of subsistence for a still growing population out of a geographical area which had become stationary instead of continuing to expand. In Greek history, this problem was solved by a successful change-over from a merely extensive to a more or less intensive economic system: from mixed farming for mere local subsistence to specialized farming for export. And this revolution in agriculture produced a general revolution in Greek economic life, since the new specialized agriculture called for complementary developments in commerce and manufacture. One is studying this Greek economic revolution when one studies the history of Athens in the two generations of Solon and Peisistratus. This Attic economic revolution corresponds, historically, to the English industrial revolution at the turn of the eighteenth and nineteenth centuries of our era, and it solved the Greek economic problem of the sixth century B.C. But the solution of the economic problem raised, in turn, a political problem which the Greek civilization failed to solve; and this political failure was the cause of its breakdown.

The new political problem may be stated in the following way. So long as the economic life of each city-state remained parochial, they could all still afford to be parochial in their political life as well. The parochial sovereignty of each city-state, *vis-à-vis* every other, might and did breed perpetual petty wars, yet, in the economic circumstances of the age, these wars were not deadly in their social effects. But the new economic system, introduced by the Attic economic revolution under the spur of the stoppage of Greek colonial expansion, was based on local production for international exchange. It could only work successfully if, on the economic plane, the city-states gave up their parochialism and become interdependent. And a system of international economic interdependence could only be made to work if it could be brought within the framework of a system of international political interdependence: some international system of political law and order which would place a restraint upon the anarchic parochial sovereignty of the local city-states.

An international political order was offered, ready-made, to the Greek city-states of the sixth and fifth centuries B.C. by the Lydian and Persian and Carthaginian Empires. The Persian Empire systematically imposed orderly political relations upon the Greek city-states which it subjugated; and Xerxes attempted to complete this work by proceeding to subjugate the still independent remnant of the Greek world. These still unconquered Greek city-states resisted Xerxes desperately—and successfully—because they rightly believed that a Persian conquest would take the life out of their civilization. They not only saved their own independence but they also liberated the previously subjugated city-states of the Archipelago and the Asiatic mainland. But, having rejected the Persian solution to a Greek political problem, the Greek victors were confronted with the task of finding some other solution. And it was here that they failed. Having defeated Xerxes in the years 480 and 479 B.C., they were defeated between 478 and 431 B.C. by themselves.

The Greeks' attempt at an international political order was the so-called Delian League founded in 478 B.C. by Athens and her allies under Athenian leadership. And it is worth noticing, in passing, that the Delian League was modelled on a Persian pattern. One sees this if one compares the accounts of the system which the Athenian statesman Aristeides induced the liberated cities to accept in 478 B.C. with the account—in Herodotus Book VI, chapter 42—of the system which had been imposed upon these self-same cities by the Persian authorities after the suppression of the so-called "Ionian Revolt" some fifteen years before. But the Delian League failed to achieve its purpose. And the old political anarchy in the relations between the sovereign independent Greek city-states broke out again under new economic conditions which made this anarchy not merely harmful but deadly.

The destruction of the Graeco-Roman civilization through the failure to replace an international anarchy by some kind of international law and order occupies the history of the four hundred years from 431 to 31 B.C. After these four centuries of failure and mistery there came, in the generation of Augustus, a partial and temporary rally. The Roman Empire—which was really an international league of Greek and other, culturally related, city-states—may be regarded as a tardy solution of the problem which the Delian League had failed to solve. But the epitaph of the Roman Empire is "too late." The Graeco-Roman society did not repent until it had inflicted mortal wounds on itself with its own hands. The *Pax Romana* was a peace of exhaustion, a peace which was not creative and therefore not permanent. It was a peace and an order that came four centuries after its due time. One has to study the history of those four melancholy intervening centuries in order to understand what the Roman Empire was and why it failed.

My conclusion is that we should look at this story as a whole. It is only when it is viewed as a whole that it throws its light upon our own situation in our own world in our day. But, if one does succeed in obtaining this light from it, it proves, *experto crede,* to be most amazingly illuminating.

5

THE UNIFICATION OF THE WORLD AND THE CHANGE IN HISTORICAL PERSPECTIVE

Familiarity is the opiate of the imagination; and, just because every Western schoolboy knows that the oceanic voyages of discovery made by West European mariners some four and a half centuries ago were an epoch-making historical event, adult Western minds are apt to take the consequences for granted. In addressing myself to a Western public I shall therefore make no apology for pointing out how dramatic and how revolutionary the effect of our ocean-faring ancestors' exploit has been. It has produced nothing less than a complete transformation of the map of the world—not, of course, the physical map, but the human "lay-out" of that portion of the surface of our planet that is traversable and habitable by mankind and that the Greeks used to call the οἰκουμένη.

This Western-made change in man's human environment will be my first topic, but it leads on to two others. External changes of this magnitude usually evoke corresponding re-adjustments in people's attitudes; and, sure enough, when we look around us, we can see that, among the great majority of mankind, the effects of those Western voyages of discovery—recent though they are on even the shortest-sighted historical time-scale—have in fact already brought about a drastic change in historical outlook. This will be my second topic, but it will bring up a third by laying bare a paradox. The majority of mankind that I here have in mind is, of course, the non-Western part, and the paradox is that to-day we Westerners are the only people in the world whose outlook on history still remains pre-da Gaman. Personally, I do not believe that this antediluvian Western traditional historical outlook is going to last much longer. I have no doubt that a re-orientation is in store for us in our turn, and in our case, I fancy, it will be one in the literal meaning of the word. But why should we wait for History, like some eighteenth-century Prussian drill-sergeant, to take us by the scruff of the neck and twist our heads straight for us? Though our neighbours have recently been re-educated in this un-pleasant and humiliating way, we ought surely to do better, for we cannot plead that we have been taken by sur-prise, as they were. The facts stare us in the face, and, by exercising our historical imagination, we can perhaps an-ticipate the compulsory education that is already on its way to us. The Greek Stoic philosopher Cleanthes prays Zeus and Fate for grace to follow their lead of his own will without flinching; "for if," he adds, "I quail and rebel, I shall have to follow just the same."

Let us now plunge into our subject by reminding our-selves of the revolutionary change in the map.

One knows that mankind, being human, is always and everywhere in danger of exaggerating the historical im-portance of contemporary events because of their personal importance to the particular generation that happens to be overtaken by them. All the same, I will hazard the guess that, when the age in which we ourselves are living has been left sufficiently far behind to be seen by future historians in a revealingly remote perspective, the particu-lar contemporary event with which we are now concerned will stand out like a mountain peak on the horizon of the past. By "the age in which we are living" I mean the last five or six thousand years within which mankind, after having been human for at least six hundred thousand years before that, attained the modest level of social and moral achievement that we call "civilization." I call the recent change in the map "contemporary" because the four or five centuries during which it has been taking place are a twinkling of an eye on the time-scale that our geologists and astronomers have now revealed to us. And, when I am trying to picture to myself the perspective in which the events of these last few thousand years will appear to future historians, I am thinking of historians living 20,000 or 100,000 years later than the present date—taking it on faith from our modern Western scientists that there has been life on this planet for about eight hundred million years already, and that the planet will continue to be habitable for at least as long again (unless Western man's precocious technological "know-how" cuts the story short).

If the claim that I am making for the historic importance of our subject seems a large one, let us recall how extraordinary an event this change in the map has been. It has, I suggest, two aspects, of which the second is the more sensational. In the first place, since about A.D. 1500 (to reckon in terms of our Western parochial era), mankind has been gathered into a single world-wide society. From the dawn of history to about that date, the earthly home of man had been divided into many isolated mansions; since about A.D. 1500, the human race has been brought under one roof. This has been accomplished, under God, by human action, and here we come to the really sensational point. The agent of this revolutionary change in the affairs of men might have been any one of the divers parochial societies that were on the map when the revolution was put in hand, but the particular parochial society that has actually done the deed is the one that, of all of them, was the most unlikely candidate.

In an effort to jump clear of my native Western standing-ground and to look at this question from a less eccentric point of view, I have asked myself who was the most centrally placed and most intelligent observer that I could think of among notable non-Westerners who were alive at the moment when a few ships' companies of Western mariners embarked on the enterprise of unifying the world, and I have found my man in the Emperor Babur. Babur was a descendant, in the fifth generation, of Tamerlane, the Transoxanian conqueror who made the last attempt to unify the world by land operations from a continental centre. Within Babur's lifetime—A.D. 1483-1530—Columbus reached America by sea from Spain and da Gama

India from Portugal. Babur started his career as prince of
Farghana in the upper valley of the Jaxartes: a small country which had been the centre of the οἰκουμένη since the
second century B.C. Babur invaded India overland twenty-
one years after da Gama had arrived there by sea. Last
but not least, Babur was a man-of-letters whose brilliant
autobiography in his Turkish mother-tongue reveals a
spirit of outstanding intelligence and perceptiveness.

What was Babur's horizon? To the east of Farghana it
included both India and China, and to the west it extended
to Babur's own distant kinsmen, the Ottoman Turks. Babur
took lessons from the 'Osmanlis in military technique,
and he admired them for their piety and prowess in extending the bounds of Islam. He refers to them as "the
Ghāzis of Rum": the happy warriors who had succeeded,
where the primitive Muslim Arabs had signally failed, in
conquering for Islam the homeland of Eastern Orthodox
Christendom. I could not recollect any mention of Western
Christendom in Babur's memoirs, and I have found none
in the exhaustive geographical index of Mrs. Beveridge's
magnificent English translation. Of course Babur was aware
of the existence of the Franks, for he was a cultivated man
and he knew his Islamic history. If he had had occasion to
allude to them, he would probably have described them
as ferocious but frustrated infidels living in a remote
corner of the world at the extreme western tip of one of
the many peninsulas of the Continent of Asia. About four
hundred years before his time, he would have gone on to
relate, these barbarians had made a demonic attempt to
break out of their cramped and uninviting corner into the
broader and richer domains of Rum and Dar-al-Islam. It
had been a critical moment for the destinies of civilization,
but the uncouth aggressors had been foiled by the genius
of Saladin, and their military reverses had been capped
by a crushing moral defeat when the Christians of Rum,
faced with a choice between two alternative future masters,
chose the side of the angels by opting for "the Prophet's
turban" in preference to "the Pope's tiara," and accepted
the boon of an Ottoman Peace.

The arrival of Frankish ships in India in A.D. 1498,
twenty-one years before Babur's own first descent upon

India in A.D. 1519, seems to have escaped Babur's attention —unless his silence is to be explained not by ignorance of the event, but by a feeling that the wanderings of these water-gypsies were unworthy of a historian's notice. So this allegedly intelligent Transoxanian man-of-letters and man-of-action was blind to the portent of the Portuguese circumnavigation of Africa? He failed to perceive that these ocean-faring Franks had turned the flank of Islam and taken her in the rear? Yes, I believe Babur would have been utterly astonished if he had been told that the empire which he was founding in India was soon to pass from his descendants to Frankish successors. He had no inkling of the change that was to come over the face of the world between his generation and ours. But this, I submit, is not a reflection on Babur's intelligence; it is one more indication of the queerness of the major event in the history of the world in our time.

Since A.D. 1500 the map of the οἰκουμένη has indeed been transformed out of all recognition. Down to that date it was composed of a belt of civilizations girdling the Old World from the Japanese Isles on the north-east to the British Isles on the north-west: Japan, China, Indo-China, Indonesia, India, Dar-al-Islam, the Orthodox Christendom of Rum, and another Christendom in the West. Though this belt sagged down, in the middle, from the North Temperate Zone to the Equator and thus ran through a fairly wide range of climates and physical environments, the social structure and cultural character of these societies was singularly uniform. Each of them consisted of a mass of peasants, living and working under much the same conditions as their forefathers on the morrow of the invention of agriculture some six to eight thousand years back, and a small minority of rulers enjoying a monopoly of power, surplus wealth, leisure, knowledge, and skill which in turn enhanced their power. There had been one or two earlier generations of civilizations of the same type in the Old World. In A.D. 1500 some of these were still remembered, while others (since brought to light by modern Western archaeologists) had been forgotten. There were two of the same type in existence at this date in the New World, unknown to those of the Old World and barely known even to each other. The living civilizations of the Old World were in touch with each other, though not so closely as to be, or feel themselves to be, members of a single society.

Their contact, such as it was, down to A.D. 1500, had been established and maintained along two different lines of communication. There was a maritime line which will be familiar to latter-day Westerners as the Peninsular and Oriental Steamship Company's route to Kobe from Tilbury. In A.D. 1500, and indeed as recently as the time of a great-uncle of mine (a vivid memory of my childhood) who commanded one of the Honourable East India Company's passenger sailing ships and retired from the sea before the cutting of the Suez Canal without ever having served on board a steamer, this waterway through a chain of inland seas was broken by a portage between the Mediterranean and the Red Sea, with an alternative portage between the Mediterranean and the Persian Gulf. In the Mediterranean and Japanese sections of this maritime route, traffic had frequently been lively, and, from about 120 B.C. onwards, an infectious wave of maritime enterprise, set in motion by Greek mariners from Alexandria who found their way to Ceylon, had travelled on eastwards through Indonesia till it had carried Polynesian canoes to Easter Island. Yet, adventurous and romantic as these pre-Western seafarers were, the water-route that they opened up never came to be of more than secondary importance as a line of communication between the civilizations. The main line was provided by the chain of steppes and deserts that cut across the belt of civilizations from the Sahara to Mongolia.

For human purposes, the Steppe was an inland sea which, in virtue of happening to be dry, was of higher conductivity for human intercourse than the salt-water sea ever was before the close of the fifteenth century of the Christian era. This waterless sea had its dry-shod ships and its quayless ports. The steppe-galleons were camels, the steppe-galleys horses, and the steppe-ports "caravan cities" —ports of call on oasis-islands and termini on the coasts where the sand-waves of "the Desert" broke upon "the Sown": Petra and Palmyra, Damascus and Ur, Tamerlane's Samarkand and the Chinese emporia at the gates of the Great Wall. Steppe-traversing horses, not ocean-traversing sailing ships, were the sovereign means of locomotion by which the separate civilizations of the world as it was before A.D. 1500 were linked together—to the slight extent to which they did maintain contact with each other.

In that world, as you see, Babur's Farghana was the central point, and the Turks were, in Babur's day, the central family of nations. A Turco-centric history of the world has been published in our lifetime by the latest in the series of the great Ottoman Turkish Westernizers, President Mustafa Kemal Atatürk. It was a brilliant device for restoring the *morale* of his fellow-countrymen, but it was a still more brilliant feat of genuine historical intuition; for, from the fourth century of the Christian era, when they pushed the last of their Indo-European-speaking predecessors off the Steppe, down to the seventeenth century, which witnessed the collapse of the Ottoman, the Safawi, and the Timurid Turkish dynasties in their respective domains of Rum, Iran, and India, the Turkish-speaking peoples really were the keystone of the Asiatic arch from which the pre-da Gaman belt of civilizations hung suspended. During those twelve hundred years, the overland link between the separate civilizations was commanded by Turkish steppe-power, and, from their central position in this pre-da Gaman world, the Turks rode out, conquering and to conquer, east and west and south and north: to Manchuria and Algeria, to the Ukraine and the Deccan.

But now we come to the great revolution: a technological revolution by which the West made its fortune, got the better of all the other living civilizations, and forcibly united them into a single society of literally world-wide range. The revolutionary Western invention was the substitution of the Ocean for the Steppe as the principal medium of world-communication. This use of the Ocean, first by sailing ships and then by steamships, enabled the West to unify the whole inhabited and habitable world, including the Americas. Babur's Farghana had been the central point of a world united by horse-traffic over the Steppe; but in Babur's lifetime the centre of the world made a sudden big jump. From the heart of the Con-

tinent it jumped to its extreme western verge, and, after
hovering round Seville and Lisbon, it settled for a time in
Elizabeth's England. In our own lifetime we have seen this
volatile world-centre flit again from London to New York,
but this shift to a still more eccentric position on the far
side of the "herring pond" is a local movement, not comparable in magnitude to the jump, in Babur's day, from the
steppe-ports of Central Asia to the ocean-ports of the Atlantic. That huge jump was caused by a sudden revolution
in the means of locomotion. The steppe-ports were put out
of action when the ocean-going sailing-ship superseded the
camel and the horse; and now that, under our eyes, the
ocean-going steamship is being superseded by the aeroplane
we may ask ourselves whether the centre of the world is
not likely to jump again—and this time as sensationally as
in the sixteenth century—under the impetus of a technological revolution that is at least as radical as the sixteenth-
century substitution of da Gama's caravel for Babur's
tipuchaq. I will recur to this possibility before I conclude.
Meanwhile, before we roll up Babur's overland map of
the world and unfurl the maritime map that has held the
field from Babur's day to ours, let us call the roll of the
separate civilizations among which the human race was
partitioned down to Babur's day and interrogate them
briefly about their historical outlook.

The uniformity which these separate civilizations display
in their cultural character and their social structure extends
to their historical outlook as well. Every one of them was
convinced that it was the only civilized society in the
world, and that the rest of mankind were barbarians, un-
touchables, or infidels. In holding this view, it is evident
that at least five out of the six pre-da Gaman civilizations
must have been in error, and the sequel has shown that
actually not one of them was right. All variants of a fallacy
are no doubt equally untrue, but they may not all be
equally preposterous, and it is instructive to run through
these half-dozen rival and mutually incompatible versions
of a common "Chosen People" myth in an ascending order
of their defiance of common sense.

For the Chinese, their compartment of the surface of
the Earth was "All that is under Heaven," and the territory

under the Imperial Government's immediate rule was "the Middle Kingdom." This point of view is expressed with a serene assurance in the celebrated reply of the great Emperor Ch'ien Lung (*imperabat* A.D. 1735-95) to a letter from King George the Third of Great Britain proposing that the two potentates should enter into diplomatic and commercial relations with each other.

As to your entreaty to send one of your nationals to be accredited to my Celestial Court and to be in control of your country's trade with China, this request is contrary to all usage of my dynasty and cannot possibly be entertained. . . Our ceremonies and code of laws differ so completely from your own that, even if your envoy were able to acquire the rudiments of our civilization, you could not possibly transplant our manners and customs to your alien soil . . . Swaying the wide world, I have but one aim in view, namely to maintain a perfect governance and to fulfill the duties of the State . . . I set no value on objects strange or ingenious, and have no use for your country's manufactures.[1]

If the barbarian envoy Lord Macartney had divulged the awkward fact that his royal master periodically went out of his mind, the Emperor would not have been surprised. No sane barbarian princeling would have had the audacity to address the Son of Heaven as though he were his equal; and the tone, taken in all innocence, by the draftsman of the British missive was indeed bound to appear outrageous in the light of history as known to Ch'ien Lung and his entourage.

Ch'ien Lung himself had made history by subjugating the last wild nomads of the Eurasian Steppe and thereby bringing to an end a duel between "the Desert" and "the Sown" that had been one of the main threads in the weft of human history for the past three thousand years. "The Son of Heaven" had achieved this historic feat virtually single-handed. The only other party that could claim any share in the honours was the Caesar at Moscow. "The South Sea Barbarians" (as the Chinese called the Western water-gypsies who had been washed up against the south coast of China from that direction) had had no hand at all

[1] For the full text see Whyte, Sir F.: *China and Foreign Powers,* Oxford University Press, London, 1927, Appendix.

in this great victory for the cause of sedentary civilization. But the personal achievements of the statesman and warrior Ch'ien Lung could add little to the effulgence radiating from the Son of Heaven *ex officio*. The empire over which he ruled was the oldest, most successful, and most beneficent of all living political institutions. Its foundation in the third century B.C. had given a civilized world a civilized government conducted by a competitively recruited and highly cultivated civil service, in place of an international anarchy in which a number of parochial states, dominated by a hereditary feudal nobility, had plagued mankind by waging perpetual wars with one another. During the twenty intervening centuries, this carefully ordered world peace had occasionally lapsed, but such lapses had always been temporary, and, at the close of Ch'ien Lung's reign, the latest restoration of "the Middle Kingdom" was in its heyday. This political casket had preserved an intellectual treasure: the findings of schools of philosophy which had explored all the alternative answers to the fundamental questions of metaphysics and ethics. And the children of "the Middle Kingdom" had shown that their inborn intelligence and statesmanship were matched by their broadmindedness when they had adopted a great alien religion —the Indian-born Mahayana—to meet any spiritual needs that their secular civilization might not be able to meet entirely out of its own resources.

On the strength of this historical background, was Ch'ien Lung right in answering George III as he did? Doubtless some of my Western readers smiled as they read his answer. They smiled, of course, because they knew the sequel; but what does the sequel prove? It proves, no doubt, that the Emperor Ch'ien Lung and his advisers were unaware of the overwhelming physical power which "the South Sea Barbarians" had acquired from their practical applications of new discoveries in physical science. At the date of Lord Macartney's mission there were Chinese men-of-letters, already in the flower of their age and holding responsible positions in the imperial service, who were to live to see Great Britain make war on China and dictate terms of peace to her at the cannon's mouth. But does not this very sequel also prove that Ch'ien Lung was as wise in nis policy of non-intercourse as he was out-of-date in his information about "the South Sea Barbarians' " military calibre? His intuition had warned him against trafficking in "strange or ingenious" British wares, and one very strange ware that British merchants offered to the Imperial Government's subjects was opium. When the imperial authorities banned the traffic, as a respectable government was bound to do, the barbarians took advantage of their unsuspected military superiority to blast an entry by naval gunfire for British trade in China on British terms. I know this is a simplification of the story of "the Opium War," but in essence it is the truth, and the best that can be said for the perpetrators of this international crime is that they have, ever after, been ashamed of it. I well remember this, I hope, redeeming sense of shame being communicated to me as a child by my mother when I asked her about "the Opium War" and she told me the facts.[2]

The siren voice of History, which lured "the Son of Heaven" at Peking into fancying himself to be the unique representative of Civilization with a capital "C," was playing the same trick, in A.D. 1500, on his counterpart the Caesar at Moscow. He too was the ruler of the latest avatar of a world-empire that had occasionally lapsed but, so far, had never failed to recover itself. The universal peace radiated by Augustus from a First Rome on the banks of the Tiber had been re-established by Constantine round a Second Rome on the shores of the Bosphorus; and, when the Constantinopolitan Empire, after dying and rising again three times over—in the seventh, the eleventh, and the thirteenth centuries of the Christian era—had fallen to the infidel Turks in A.D. 1453, the sceptre had passed to a Third Rome at Moscow whose kingdom was to have no end (so all pious Muscovites must believe). The Muscovite heir of Roman world power had inherited, by the same token, the cultural achievements of Rome's Greek predecessors; and, as if that was not enough, he was also God's chosen defender of the great alien religious faith— Christianity—which had been adopted by the pagan

[2] For a summary of the facts, see note at the end of this essay.

Graeco-Roman world to make good its own spiritual short-
comings. The heir of Greece, Rome, and Christ, and,
through Christ, of God's Chosen People Israel! The title
of Muscovy appeared, in Muscovite eyes, to be as conclusive as it was unique.

If the Czar's pretension had come to the Son of Heaven's
notice, he would perhaps have treated it with a certain
leniency. When, fifteen hundred years or so before the
da Gaman revolution in the map of the world, the first
empire of Ts'in had made an adventurous voyage of exploration into the waterless sea of the Steppe and had just
brushed against the first Empire of Rome with the tips of
its antennae, the Chinese desert-mariners had generously
labelled this surprising discovery "Ta Ts'in": "the Great
China" in the Far West. But Ts'in and Ta Ts'in had always
been insulated from one another by intervening neighbours
who challenged the claims of both. In Hindu eyes, for
instance, the Buddhism that China had so reverently
adopted from India was nothing better than a deplorable
aberration (happily abandoned at home) from Hindu
orthodoxy. It was the Brahmans who held a monopoly of
right ritual, inspired scriptures, and correct theology.
Much of the population even of India, and every man,
woman, and child in the world beyond the bounds of
the Aryan Holy Land, were untouchable outcasts. India's
Muslim conquerors might wield irresistible material power,
but they could not cleanse themselves from their ritual
leprosy.

The Muslims, for their part, were as hard on the Hindus
and Christians as the Hindus were on the Muslims and
Chinese. As the Muslims saw it, the Prophets of Israel
were all right, and Jesus was God's last and greatest
prophet before His final messenger Muhammad. The Muslims' quarrel was not with the Prophet Jesus but with the
Christian Church, which had captivated Rum by capitulat-
ing to pagan Greek polytheism and idolatry. From this
shameful betrayal of the revelation of the One True God,
Islam had retrieved the pure religion of Abraham. Between
the Christian polytheists on the one side and the Hindu
polytheists on the other there again shone the light of

monotheism; and in Islam's survival lay the hope of the world.

This traditional Islamic scale of values comes out sharply in the closing sentence of the great Egyptian historian Al-Gabarti's narrative of the events of the year of the Hijrah 1213.

So this year reached its close. Among the unprecedented events that occurred in it, the most portentous was the cessation of the Pilgrimage from Egypt [to the Holy Cities of the Hijaz]. They did not send the Holy Draperies (*Kiswah*) for the Ka'bah and they did not send the Purse (*surrah*). The like of this had never happened in the present age, and never during the rule of the Banu 'Osman. [Truly,] the ordering of events lies with God alone.[8]

Which was this exciting year? In our Western notation, the twelve months corresponding to A.H. 1213 run from June A.D. 1798 to June 1799. It was, you see, the year in which Napoleon descended upon Egypt, and the sentence that I have quoted is Al-Gabarti's *grand finale* to a most vivid and penetrating account of this supremely dramatic "war of the worlds." Being a Martian myself, I was pulled up short, as I well remember, the first time I read those concluding words. Yet one cannot read Al-Gabarti without taking him seriously. He would undoubtedly figure on a list of candidates for the distinction of ranking as leading historians of civilized society up to date. I shall revert to this passage and try to persuade my fellow-Westerners that our philistine inclination to laugh at it ought to move us to laugh, instead, at our own unconscionable parochial-mindedness.

For now we come to the two really laughably fantastic cases of a local civilization's fancying itself to be the only civilization in the world.

The Japanese actually believed that their country was "the Land of the Gods" and in consequence inviolable to invaders (though the Japanese themselves had in recent

[8] Shaykh 'Adb-ar-Rahmān Al-Gabarti: *Ajā'ib-al-Áthār fi't-Tarājim wa'l-Ahbar* (Cairo, A.H. 1322, 4 vols.), vol. III, p. 63; French translation (Cairo, Imprimerie Nationale, and Paris, Leroux, A.D. 1888-96, 9 vols.), vol. VI, p. 121.

times successfully invaded it to the cost of their unlucky Nordic predecessors "the Hairy Ainu"). Japan "the Middle Kingdom"! Why, Japan in A.D. 1500 was still a feudal society in the unedifying state of anarchy from which China had been salvaged by Ts'in She Hwangti in 221 B.C. What China, so long ago, had achieved for herself unaided, Japan had failed to accomplish after having enjoyed for nearly a thousand years the blessings of a borrowed Chinese secular civilization and an Indian higher religion passed on to her by Chinese good offices. Could folly fly farther? Why, yes, it would seem that it could, for the Western variant of the universal fallacy surely outfooled the Japanese. The Franks were solemnly asserting in A.D. 1500 that the true heir of Israel, Greece, and Rome was not the Orthodox Eastern Christendom but theirs, and that it was not the Western but the Orthodox Church that was schismatic! To listen to the Frankish theologians you might have imagined that it was the four Eastern Patriarchates, and not the Patriarchate of Rome, that had doctored the Creed by slipping a *filioque* into it. And, to listen to the "Roman Emperors of the German Nation" in their political controversies with the Greek and Russian successors of Augustus and Constantine, you might have imagined that it was the Greek and Oriental provinces and not the Latin provinces in which the Roman Imperial Government had perished, never to revive, in the fifth century after Christ. In A.D. 1500 the audacity of these Frankish pretensions to be "the Chosen People" was enough to take away the breath of any rightly informed and properly impartial arbitrator. But a more astonishing fact remains to be recorded. Since then, four centuries and a half—and what centuries! —have rolled by and the Franks are still singing the same old song to-day: singing it solo now, too; for the other voices in the chorus of civilizations that were chanting a fallacious creed in unison in A.D. 1500 have, one by one, changed their tune between that year and this.

The success of the non-Western majority of mankind in re-educating themselves, while Western minds have been sticking in archaic mud, is not, of course, in itself a proof of innately superior acumen or virtue. The beginning of wisdom is a salutory shock, and the non-Western societies have had a tremendous shake-up administered to them by the Western civilization's boisterous impact. The West alone has so far escaped this unceremonious treatment. Unshattered, up till now, by an upheaval of its own making, our local civilization is still hugging the smug and slovenly illusion in which its "opposite numbers" indulged till they took their educative toss from the levelled horns of an unintentionally altruistic Western bull. Sooner or later, the repercussions of this collision will assuredly recoil upon the West herself; but for the present this Janus-like figure slumbers on—abroad a charging bull, at home a now solitary Sleeping Beauty.

The shocks which the other civilizations have received have indeed been severe enough to wake even the Seven Sleepers of Ephesus. Imagine the psychological effect of the British *diktat* of A.D. 1842 on some Chinese scholar-statesman who was old enough to remember the Emperor Ch'ien Lung's handling of Lord Macartney's embassy forty-nine years earlier! Read Al-Gabarti! I have only space to quote his account of one incident that followed the sudden appearance, on Friday the 8th Muharram, A.H. 1213, of twenty-five foreign ships off the Egyptian port of Alexandria.

The townspeople were wondering what the foreigners could have come for, when a little boat stood in and landed ten persons. . . These foreigners said that they were Englishmen, and they added that they were on the look-out for some Frenchmen, who had started with a considerable fleet for an unknown destination. They were afraid, they said, of seeing these Frenchmen make a surprise attack on Egypt, because they knew that the people of Egypt would not be able to repel the invaders or to prevent them from landing . . . The foreigners went on to say: "We shall be content to keep the sea with our ships, in order to defend the city and patrol the coast; we shall ask you for nothing but water and provisions, and for these we will undertake to pay." The notables of the city refused, however . . . to enter into relations with the English, and said to them: "This country belongs to the Sultan, and neither the French nor any other foreigners have any business here; so be good enough to leave us." At these words the English messengers returned to their ships and went off to look for their provisions somewhere else instead of at

Alexandria, "in order that God might accomplish the work that was preordained in His decree." [4]

When one reads on, one finds that these latter-day *gesta Dei per Francos* stimulated the receptive doctor of the University of Al-Azhar to begin his own personal re-education immediately. One of the first acts of the French after occupying Cairo was to stage there a scientific exhibition, with practical demonstrations, and our historian was among the visitors. After remarking that the French evidently mistook the Muslims for children who could be impressed by monkey-tricks, and that this was really rather childish of the French themselves, Al-Gabarti frankly records his admiration for the demonstrated achievements of Frankish science.[5] He notices that, among the damage suffered by the French in a revolt which they had provoked by their high-handed behaviour at the outset, the loss which they appeared to mind the most was that of some scientific instruments that had been destroyed in the house of the savant Cafarelli.[6] But Al-Gabarti's interest in French science is surpassed by his sensitiveness to French justice. French soldiers are convicted of house-breaking with violence, and, on Napoleon's personal orders, they pay for their crime with their lives.[7] Napoleon's successor in command of the French army of occupation, General Kléber, is assassinated by a Muslim fanatic, and the murderer is given a genuine fair trial. This trial wins Al-Gabarti's enthusiastic admiration, and, frank as always, he records his opinion that the Muslims would not, in corresponding circumstances, have risen to that moral level. He is so intensely interested in the proceedings and so eager to preserve a record of them, that he incorporates the *dossier* of the trial in his narrative, reproducing the documents *verbatim* in the French military chancery's defective Arabic.[8]

When one observes how quickly and readily the Egyp·

[4] French translation, vol. VI, *ad init.*
[5] French translation, vol. VI, p. 75; cp. pp. 70-71,
[6] Ibid. p. 66.
[7] Ibid. pp. 82-3.
[8] Ibid. pp. 223, 251.

tian Muslim scholar Al-Gabarti learnt a French lesson that was very far from being "without tears," one's mind turns to the series of great Ottoman Turkish westernizing statesmen: Mehmed 'Ali of Kavalla, the Macedonian battalion-commander who came and saw what the French had been doing in Egypt and who carried on Napoleon's revolutionary work there after Napoleon had come and gone;[9] Sultan Selīm III, who lost his life at Constantinople, nine years before Napoleon's disembarkation at Alexandria, in a pioneer attempt to westernize the Ottoman Army; Sultan Mahmud II, who succeeded, after half a lifetime of patient waiting, in executing his martyr-cousin's political testament; and, last but not least, President Mustafa Kemal Atatürk, who completed, in our lifetime, the totalitarian revolution in Ottoman Turkish life that Sultan Selīm had initiated some six generations earlier. These Ottoman names recall their counterparts elsewhere: the arch-westernizer Peter the Great and his Bolshevik executors; the shrewd architects of the Meiji "Restoration" in Japan; the Bengali syncretist Ram Mohan Roy, who, by carrying the issue onto the *terrain* of religion, showed the characteristic Hindu feeling for the true relative values of matter and spirit—however indignantly the orthodox Hindu pandits of the day might shake the dust of this heresiarch's defiling threshold from off their own unprofitably unsullied feet.

At the inspiration or behest of these mighty "Herodians" —and the driving force has usually been a cross between persuasion and compulsion—a younger generation of non-Westerners from all the once-separate societies which the West has now swept together in its world-enveloping net

[9] In proceeding with the writing of his history of his own times, Al-Gabarti dealt as faithfully with Mehmed 'Ali as with Napoleon or 'Abdallah Menou. In an evil hour for the historian, the dictator heard of his work and instituted inquiries into its contents, and, after that, Al-Gabarti's record of Mehmed 'Ali's deeds was abruptly terminated. Riding home on his ass one dark night (to be exact, it was the night of the 27th Ramadan, A.H. 1237, alias 22nd June 1822), our too truthful informant "softly and silently vanished away." His adverse judgment on Islamic justice had been prophetic.

has literally been coming to school in the West in our day. They are taking Western lessons at first-hand in the universities of Paris and Cambridge and Oxford; at Columbia and at Chicago; and, as I was scanning the faces of my audience in the Senate House of the University of London, I saw to my pleasure a contingent of their representatives there. An élite in all the non-Western societies has in fact by now successfully re-educated itself out of its traditional self-centred parochial point of view. Some of them, alas, have caught, instead, the Western ideological disease of Nationalism, but even Nationalism has, for non-Westerners, at least the negative merit of being an exotic infirmity. It, too, draws them out of their ancestral shell. In short, by one road or another, the emotionally upsetting but intellectually stimulating experience of being taken by storm by the West has educated these non-Western students of human affairs into realizing (and what an effort of imagination this implies!) that the past history of the West is not just the West's own parochial concern but is *their* past history too. It is theirs because the West—like those house-breaking French soldiers at Cairo whose execution by Napoleon Al-Gabarti records—has thrust its way into its defenceless neighbours' lives; and these neighbours must therefore familiarize themselves with Western history if they are to learn how to take their bearings in a new world-wide society of which we Westerners have made them members by main force.

The paradox of our generation is that all the world has now profited by an education which the West has provided, except (as we have observed already) the West herself. The West to-day is still looking at history from that old parochial self-centred standpoint which the other living societies have by now been compelled to transcend. Yet, sooner or later, the West, in her turn, is bound to receive the re-education which the other civilizations have obtained already from the unification of the world by Western action.

What is the probable course of this coming Western mental and moral revolution? Wending our way, as we have to do, with our noses up against an iron curtain that debars us from foreseeing our own future, we may per-

haps gain some illuminating side-lights from the histories
of older contemporaries where we know the whole story
because the *dramatis personae* have already departed this
life. What, for instance, was the sequel to the impact of the
Graeco-Roman civilization on its neighbours? If we follow
the thread through sixteen or seventeen centuries, from
the catabasis of Xenophon's ten thousand companions-in-
arms to the latest achievements of Greek-inspired Muslim
science and philosophy before the Mongol cataclysm, we
shall see an apparently irresistible Greek offensive on the
military, political, economic, intellectual, and artistic
planes being progressively contained, halted, and thrown
into reverse by the counter-measures of its non-Greek
victims. On all the planes on which they had been attacked,
the Orientals' counter-offensive was successful on the
whole, but it was chequered in its fortunes and sometimes
ironical in its consequences. There is, however, one point
—religion, the Greeks' Achilles' heel—at which the Oriental counter-stroke went home and made history.

This fully told yet all but contemporary tale has an
evident bearing on our own prospects; for a spiritual
vacuum like the hollow place at the heart of that Hellenic
culture which the Greeks temporarily imposed on the
world has latterly made its appearance in the culture of
our Western Christendom in the form in which this culture has been "processed" for export. For some two hundred years, dating from the beginning of the da Gaman
era, our world-storming Western forefathers made a valiant
attempt to propagate abroad the whole of our Western
cultural heritage, including its religious core as well as
its technological rind; and in this they were surely well-
inspired; for every culture is a "whole" whose parts are
subtly interdependent, and to export the husk without the
grain may be as deadly as to radiate the satellite electrons
of an atom without the nucleus. However, about the turn
of the seventeenth and eighteenth centuries of our Western
Christian era, something happened which, I venture to
prophesy, is going to loom out in retrospect as one of the
epoch-making events of our modern Western history when
this local history is seen in its true light as an incident in
the general history of mankind. This portent was a double

event, in which the Jesuits' failure was accentuated by the Royal Society's simultaneous success. The Jesuits failed to convert the Hindus and Chinese to the Roman Catholic form of Western Christianity. They failed, though they had discovered the psychological "know-how," because, when it came to the point, neither the Pope nor the Son of Heaven nor the Brahmans would have it. In the same generation, these tragically frustrated Jesuit missionaries' fellow-Western Catholics and Protestants at home came to the hazardous conclusion that a religion in whose now divided and contentious name they had been fighting an inconclusive fratricidal hundred years' war was an inopportune element in their cultural heritage. Why not tacitly agree to cut out the wars of religion by cutting out religion itself and concentrate on the application of physical science to practical affairs—a pursuit which aroused no controversy and which promised to be lucrative? This seventeenth-century turning in the road of Western progress was big with consequences; for the Western civilization that has since run like wildfire round the world has not been the whole of the seamless web; it has been a flare of cotton-waste: a technological selvage with the religious centre-piece torn out. This "utility" pattern of Western civilization was, of course, comparatively easy to take; Peter the Great revealed his genius by instantly pouncing on it as soon as it was displayed in the West's shop window. A hundred years later, the subtler and more spiritual Al-Gabarti showed a nicer discrimination. French technology hit him in the eye, but he persisted in waiting for a sign. For him, the touchstone of Western civilization, as of his own, was not technology but justice. This Cairene scholar had apprehended the heart of the matter, the issue which the West had still to fight out within itself. "And though I . . . understand all mysteries and all knowledge . . . and have not charity, I am nothing" [10]—"Or what man is there of you whom, if his son ask bread, will he give him a stone? Or, if he ask a fish, will he give him a serpent?" [11]

This brings us back to a question, raised by a sentence

[10] I Cor. xiii. 2.
[11] Matt. vii. 9-10.

of Al-Gabarti's, which is still awaiting our answer. Which really *was* the most important event of A.H. 1213? Napoleon's invasion of Egypt or the intermission of the annual pilgrimage from Egypt to the Holy Cities in the Hijaz?

The Islamic institution of the pilgrimage is of course, in itself, nothing more than an exacting external observance, but, as a symbol, it stands for the fraternal spirit that binds all Muslims together. Islam is therefore in danger when the pilgrimage falls off, as we have learnt by experience in our own lifetime; and Al-Gabarti was sensitive to this danger because he valued the spiritual treasure with which his ancestral religion was freighted. What value are we to place on Islam ourselves? In a chapter of world history in which the mastery of the world seems likely to lie in the hands of the conspicuously infra-pigmented and notoriously race-conscious transmarine English-speaking peoples, can mankind afford to do without the social cement of Islamic fraternity? Yet this social service, valuable and noble though it be, is not the essence of Islam—as Al-Gabarti would have been quick to point out to us, though he happened, himself, to be a living embodiment of this particular virtue of his Faith. As his surname records, Al-Gabarti was hereditary master of one of those "nations" that were the constituents of the University of Al-Azhar, as they were of its contemporary, the Sorbonne. And who were his nation of the Gabart? They were the Trans-Abyssinian Gallas and Somalis: true-believing ebony-coloured children of Ham. You will perceive that our hero's surname and personal name were felicitously matched: surname Al-Gabarti "the Ethiop"; personal name 'Abd-ar-Rahmān "the Servant of the God of Mercy." Yet this worshipper of a compassionate God would have testified that, if the pilgrimage is merely the symbol of a fraternity transcending differences of colour and class, this unity between true believers is, in turn, merely a translation into action here on Earth of their true belief in the unity of God. Islam's creative gift to mankind is monotheism, and we surely dare not throw this gift away.

And what about the Battle of the Pyramids? Last year, when, for the second time in my life, I was attending a peace conference in Paris, I found myself, one Sunday morning, sitting on a temporary wooden stand and watching the French "victory march" defiling past me—spahis on dancing white horses, and Tunisian light infantry led by a sedately drilled and smartly caparisoned sheep—with the Arc de Triomphe staring me in the face on the farther side of the procession's route. Staring back at that imposing pile of masonry, my eye began to travel along the row of round shields below the cornice, each bearing the name of one of Napoleon's victories. "It is perhaps a good thing," I caught myself thinking, as my eye reached the corner, "that this monument is only four-square and not octagonal, for, if they had had more room, they would have had to come, in the end, to Sédan and the Battle of France." And then my mind flitted to the equally ironical ends of other chains of national glories: A German chain in which the Battle of France had been followed within four years by the Battle of Germany, and a British chain of victories in India beginning with Plassey and Assaye and running through the sonorous Panjabi names of stricken fields in the Anglo-Sikh Wars. What, in the final account, did these Western national victories amount to? To the same zero figure as the national victories—not less famous in their day—of those Chinese "contending states" which Ts'in She Hwangti swept off the map in the third century B.C. Vanity of vanities! But Islam remains, with a mighty spiritual mission still to carry out.

So who has the last laugh in this controversy over Al-Gabarti's sense of proportion? Al-Gabarti's Western readers or Al-Gabarti himself?

Now what must we Westerners do if we aspire, like Cleanthes, to follow the beck of Zeus and Fate by using our intelligence and exercising our free will, instead of constraining those dread deities to bring us into line by the humiliating method of compulsion?

First, I would suggest, we must readjust our own historical outlook on the lines on which the educated representatives of our sister-societies have been readjusting theirs during these last few generations. Our non-Western contemporaries have grasped the fact that, in consequence of the recent unification of the world, *our* past history has become a vital part of *theirs*. Reciprocally, we mentally still-slumbering Westerners have now to realize, on our part, that, in virtue of the same revolution—a revolution, after all, that has been brought about by ourselves—our neighbours' past is going to become a vital part of our own Western future.

In rousing ourselves to make this effort of imagination we do not have to start quite from the beginning. We have always realized and acknowledged our debt to Israel, Greece, and Rome. But these, of course, are extinct civilizations, and we have managed to pay our homage to them without budging from our traditional self-centred stand-point because we have taken it for granted—in the blind-ness of our egotism—that our noble selves are those "dead" civilizations' *raison d'être*. We imagined them living and dying for the sake of preparing the way for us — playing John the Baptist to our own role as the Christ (I apologize for the blasphemy of this comparison, but it does bring out sharply how outrageously distorted our outlook has been).

We have latterly also realized the importance, as con-tributors to our own past, of certain other civilizations which were not only extinct but which had lain buried in oblivion before we disinterred their debris. It is easy for us to be generous in our acknowledgements to Min-oans, Hittites, and Sumerians, for their rediscovery has been a feather in our Western scholar's cap, and they have made their reappearance on the stage of history under our patronage.

It will be harder for us to accept the not less plain fact that the past histories of our vociferous, and sometimes vituperative, living contemporaries—the Chinese and the Japanese, the Hindus and the Muslims, and our elder brothers the Orthodox Christians—are going to become a part of our Western past history in a future world which will be neither Western nor non-Western but will inherit all the cultures which we Westerners have now brewed together in a single crucible. Yet this is the manifest truth, when we face it. Our own descendants are not going to be just Western, like ourselves. They are going to be heirs of Confucius and Lao-Tse as well as Socrates, Plato, and Plotinus; heirs of Gautama Buddha as well as Deutero-

Isaiah and Jesus Christ; heirs of Zarathustra and Muhammad as well as Elijah and Elisha and Peter and Paul; heirs of Shankara and Ramanuja as well as Clement and Origen; heirs of the Cappadocian Fathers of the Orthodox Church as well as our African Augustine and our Umbrian Benedict; heirs of Ibn Khaldun as well as Bossuet; and heirs (if still wallowing in the Serbonian Bog of politics) of Lenin and Gandhi and Sun Yat-sen as well as Cromwell and George Washington and Mazzini.

A readjustment of historical outlook demands a corresponding revision of methods of historical study. Recapturing, if we can, an old-fashioned mode of thought and feeling, let us confess, with great humility, that, through the providence of God, the historic achievement of Western man has been to do something not simply for himself but for mankind as a whole—something so big that our own parochial history is going to be swallowed up by the results of it. By making history we have transcended our own history. Without knowing what we have been doing we have taken the opportunity offered to us. To be allowed to fulfil oneself by surpassing oneself is a glorious privilege for any of God's creatures.

On this view then—a humble view and yet a proud view too—the main strand of our modern Western history is not the parish-pump politics of our Western society as inscribed on triumphal arches in a half-dozen parochial capitals or recorded in the national and municipal archives of ephemeral "Great Powers." The main strand is not even the expansion of the West over the world—so long as we persist in thinking of that expansion as a private enterprise of the Western society's own. The main strand is the progressive erection, by Western hands, of a scaffolding within which all the once separate societies have built themselves into one. From the beginning, mankind has been partitioned; in our day we have at last become united. The Western handiwork that has made this union possible has not been carried out with open eyes, like David's unselfish labours for the benefit of Solomon; it has been performed in heedless ignorance of its purpose, like the labours of the animalculae that build a coral reef up from the bottom of the sea till at length an atoll rises above the waves. But our Western-built scaffolding is made of less durable materials than that. The most obvious ingredient in it is technology, and man cannot live by technology alone. In the fullness of time, when the oecumenical house of many mansions stands firmly on its own foundations and the temporary Western technological scaffolding falls away—as I have no doubt that it will—I believe it will become manifest that the foundations are firm at last because they have been carried down to the bedrock of religion.

We have reached the Pillars of Hercules and it is time to draw in sail, for we cannot see clearly very much farther ahead. In the chapter of history on which we are now entering, the seat of material power is moving at this moment still farther away from its pre-da Gaman locus. From the small island of Britain, lying a stone's throw from the Atlantic coast of the continent of Asia, it is moving to the larger island of North America, a bowshot farther distant. But this transfer of Poseidon's trident from London to New York may prove to have marked the culmination of the dislocating effects of our current Oceanic age of intercommunication; for we are now passing into a new age in which the material medium of human intercourse is going to be neither the Steppe nor the Ocean, but the Air, and in an air age mankind may succeed in shaking its wings free from their fledgeling bondage to the freakish configuration of the surface—solid or liquid—of the globe.

In an air age the locus of the centre of gravity of human affairs may be determined not by physical but by human geography: not by the lay-out of oceans and seas, steppes and deserts, rivers and mountain-ranges, passes and straits, but by the distribution of human numbers, energy, ability, skill, and character. And, among these human factors, the weight of numbers may eventually come to count for more than its influence in the past. The separate civilizations of the pre-da Gaman age were created and enjoyed, as we have observed, by a tiny sophisticated ruling minority perched on the back of a neolithic peasantry, as Sinbad the Sailor was ridden by the Old Man of the Sea. This neolithic peasantry is the last and mightiest sleeper, before herself, whom the West has waked.

The rousing of this passively industrious mass of humanity has been a slow business. Athens and Florence each flashed her brief candle in the sleeper's drowsy eyes, but each time he just turned onto his side and sank to sleep again. It was left for modern England to urbanize the peasantry with sufficient energy on a large enough scale to set the movement travelling round the circumference of the Earth. The peasant has not taken this awakening kindly. Even in the Americas he has contrived to remain much as he was in Mexico and the Andean Republics, and he has struck new roots on virgin soil in the Province of Quebec. Yet the process of his awakening has been gathering momentum; the French Revolution carried it on to the Continent; the Russian Revolution has propagated it from coast to coast; and, though to-day there are still some fifteen hundred million not yet awakened peasants—about three-quarters of the living generation of mankind—in India, China, Indo-China, Indonesia, Dar-al-Islam, and Eastern Europe, their awakening is now only a matter of time, and, when it has been accomplished, numbers will begin to tell.

Their gravitational pull may then draw the centre-point of human affairs away from an Ultima Thule among the Isles of the Sea to some locus approximately equidistant from the western pole of the world's population in Europe and North America and its eastern pole in China and India, and this would indicate a site in the neighbourhood of Babylon, on the ancient portage across the isthmus between the Continent and its peninsulas of Arabia and Africa. The centre might even travel farther into the interior of the Continent to some locus between China and Russia (the two historic tamers of the Eurasian Nomads), and that would indicate a site in the neighbourhood of Babur's Farghana, in the familiar Transoxanian meeting-place and debating ground of the religions and philosophies of India, China, Iran, Syria, and Greece.

Of one thing we can be fairly confident: religion is likely to be the plane on which this coming centripetal counter-movement will first declare itself; and this proba-

bility offers us a further hint for the revision of our traditional Western methods of studying history. If our first
precept should be to study our own history, not on its
own account but for the part which the West has played
in the unification of mankind, our second precept, in studying History as a whole, should be to relegate economic and
political history to a subordinate place and give religious
history the primacy. For religion, after all, is the serious
business of the human race.

NOTE ON THE PART PLAYED BY OPIUM IN SINO-BRITISH RELATIONS

The terms in which this subject has been referred to in the
foregoing essay may be supported by the following summary
of the facts, which is based on (i) Williamson, J. A., and other
members of the Historical Association: *Common Errors in
History* (London, 1945, King and Staples); (ii) Pratt, Sir J.:
War and Politics in China (London, 1943, Cape); (iii) Costin,
W. C.: *Great Britain and China, 1833-1860* (Oxford, 1937,
Clarendon Press); (iv) Morse, H. B.: *The International Rela-
tions of the Chinese Empire: The Period of Conflict, 1834-1860*
(London, 1910, Longmans, Green). None of the authors of
these works are Chinese; all are Westerners; all but one are
British subjects; the author of (iv) is a citizen of the United
States.

1. The smoking of opium, which is the most noxious way of
taking the drug, was first introduced into China by the Dutch
(from Java).

2. Addiction to opium-smoking came to be far more widespread in China than elsewhere (for example, than in British
India, which came to be the chief, though never sole, source
of opium production in the world and of opium importation
into China).

3. The British Government in India assumed a monopoly
of the sale of opium in their dominions in A.D. 1773, and of the
manufacture of it in A.D. 1797.

4. In A.D. 1800 the Chinese Government forbade both the
cultivation of the opium poppy in China and its importation
from abroad (opium smoking had long since been a penal
offence in China).

5. Before A.D. 1830, the policy of the British Indian Government was to restrict the consumption of opium, at home and
abroad, by charging a high price; from A.D. 1830 onwards they
followed the opposite policy of winning the maximum revenue

from opium by stimulating consumption through lowering the price. "This had the double effect of greatly increasing the amount of opium smuggled into China and of increasing the amount of revenue accruing to the Indian Government" (Pratt, *op. cit.,* p. 44).

6. The British Government in India were unwilling, until A.D. 1907, to make the sacrifice of revenue that would be entailed in putting an embargo on the export of opium from India to China (The British Indian Government's opium revenue rose from about £1,000,000 per annum in the years 1820-43 to over £7,000,000 in 1910-11).

7. In the period A.D. 1800-1858, during which the importation of opium into China was illegal, the lion's share of the smuggling trade was done by British ships.

8. The British Government in the United Kingdom never made this smuggling trade illegal for British subjects, and they discountenanced compliance with the Chinese Government's demand that foreign merchants should sign bonds undertaking not to smuggle opium into China and accepting a liability to suffer capital punishment for this offence at the hands of the Chinese authorities if the offenders were caught and convicted.

9. The smuggling trade would not have been (a) lucrative, if there had not been a keen demand for opium among the Chinese public, or (b) feasible, if the British and other foreign smugglers had not had energetic Chinese confederates.

10. Most Chinese officials were unwise and incompetent, and some of them corrupt, in their handling of the particular problem of opium-smuggling and the general problem of doing business with Western traders and with the representatives of Western governments:—

(a) They treated representatives of Western governments as if they were the agents of client princes and Western traders as though they were barbarians;

(b) They failed to put down the smuggling of opium into China;

(c) Some of them connived at the smuggling and participated in its profits.

11. The British Government in the United Kingdom were prevented, by the influence of the China Trade in Parliament, from giving their Superintendents of Trade in China adequate authority over British subjects there during the critical years A.D. 1834-1839.

12. The Westerners justly complained that their legitimate trade was vexatiously restricted and that they were subjected to wanton personal humiliations.

13. The Chinese justly complained (a) that the advent of Western traders had brought on China the curse of opium-smuggling on a large scale (in A.D. 1836 the value of the opium smuggled into China was greater than the combined value of the tea and silk legitimately exported); (b) that British and other Western sailors in the port of Canton were drunken, riotous, and homicidal.

14. In 1839, a Chinese Imperial Commissioner, Lin Tse-sü, succeeded, by a bloodless boycott and blockade of the Western merchants at Canton, in compelling the British Chief Superintendent of the trade of British subjects in China, Captain Charles Elliot, to co-operate with him in enforcing the surrender, by Western merchants, of 20,283 chests of opium, valued at over £11,000,000, at that time held by them on Chinese soil or in Chinese territorial waters. Commissioner Lin duly destroyed the confiscated opium, but he failed to put an end to opium-smuggling.

15. Thereafter, hostilities were started by the British, first on 4 September 1839, at Kowloon in retaliation for a refusal of permission to purchase food supplies, and then on 3 November 1839, at Chuen-pi, in retort to a Chinese demand for the surrender of the murderer of a Chinese subject, Lin Wei-hi, who had been fatally injured on 7 July, at Kowloon, in an indiscriminate assault on the Chinese civilian population by British (and perhaps also American) sailors who were trying to lay hands on intoxicating liquor.

N.B. Captain Elliot had held a judicial inquiry into this incident on 10 July and had tried, but failed, to identify the murderer.

16. The British Government in the United Kingdom had already taken steps to despatch a naval and military expeditionary force to China after being informed of the action taken by Commissioner Lin, but before receiving the news of the outbreak of hostilities.

17. The British Government met with some opposition and censure, from a minority in Parliament and among the public, for making war on China in A.D. 1839-42.

18. In the peace treaty signed at Nanking on 29 August 1842, the British compelled the Chinese to open treaty ports and to cede territory, but not to legalize the opium traffic.

19. At the instance of the British Government, the Chinese Government agreed, on 13 October 1858, to legalize the importation of opium into China after defeat in a second Sino-British war and fifty-eight years' experience of failure to prevent the smuggling traffic.

20. As between the Chinese and the British, the issue over opium was eventually closed (a) by the progressive reduction, *pari passu,* during the years 1907-1919, of opium cultivation in China and the importation of opium into China from India, by agreement between the Chinese and British Indian Governments; (b) by the total prohibition of exports of opium from British India in A.D. 1926.

N.B. As a result of political anarchy in China, followed by Japanese invasion and occupation, the cultivation of the opium poppy in China afterwards became rife again.

6

THE DWARFING OF EUROPE [1]

Before the War of 1914-18, Europe enjoyed an undisputed ascendency in the world, and the special form of
civilization which had been developing in Western Europe
during the past twelve hundred years seemed likely to
prevail everywhere.

The ascendency of Europe was marked by the fact that
five out of the eight great powers then existing—that is to
say, the British Empire, France, Germany, Austria-Hungary, and Italy—had their roots in European soil. A sixth,
the Russian Empire, lay in the immediate continental
hinterland of the European peninsula, and during the last
two and a half centuries it had become welded onto
Europe—partly by the growth of a great trade between
agrarian Russia and industrial Europe (a trade which had
developed *pari passu* with the industrialization of Western-
and-Central European countries); partly by the political
incorporation in Russia of a fringe of countries with a
Western tradition of European civilization, such as Poland,
Finland, and the Baltic Provinces; and partly by the adoption of Western technique, institutions, and ideas on the
part of the Russians themselves. The two remaining great
powers—Japan and the United States—were geographically
non-European, and for that very reason they took little

[1] This paper is based on a lecture delivered in London on
the 26th October, 1926. In the course of the intervening
twenty years, many of these possibilities have become accomplished facts.

part, before the First World War, in the play of international politics—a play which was performed at that time on a European stage. It may be pointed out, however, that Japan, like Russia, had only risen to the rank of a great power through a partial adoption of that Western civilization of which Western Europe was the home. As for the United States, she was the child of Western Europe and, down to 1914, she was still drawing heavily upon European capital—human capital in the form of immigrants and material capital in the form of goods and services financed by European loans—in order to develop her latent natural resources.

This ascendency of Europe in the world went hand in hand with the spread of Western civilization. The two movements were complementary, and it would be impossible to say that either was the cause or the effect of the other. Naturally, the spread of Western civilization was facilitated by the ascendency of Europe, because the strong and efficient are always imitated by the weak and inefficient—partly out of necessity and partly from admiration (whether this admiration is avowed or not). On the other hand, the spread of Western civilization gave those peoples among whom it was indigenous an inestimable advantage in competition with those among whom it was exotic. During the century ending in 1914, the world was conquered economically not only by the new Western industrial system but by the Western nations among whom that system had been invented; and the advantage possessed by an inventor in a battle fought with his own weapons was illustrated strikingly in the First World War itself. The fact that the War of 1914-18 was fought on the lines of Western military technique—which was of course an application of Western industrial technique—gave Germany an absolute military superiority over Russia, though German man-power was only half as great as Russian at the time. Had the Central-Asian, and not the Western, technique of warfare been predominant in the world during the years 1914-18, as it had been during the Middle Ages, the Russian Cossacks might have overwhelmed the Prussian Uhlans. (Both these types of cavalry had a Central-Asian origin which is betrayed by their Turkish names

—"Oghlan" being the Turkish for "boy," and "Qazaq" for "digger.")

The predominance of the Western civilization throughout the world, on the eve of the fateful year 1914, was, indeed, both recent and unprecedented. It was unprecedented in this sense—that, though many civilizations before that of Europe had radiated their influence far beyond their original home-lands, none had previously cast its net right round the globe.

The civilization of Eastern Orthodox Christendom, which grew up in mediaeval Byzantium, had been carried by the Russians to the Pacific; but, so far from spreading westwards, it had itself succumbed to Western influence since the close of the seventeenth century. The civilization of Islam had expanded from the Middle East to Central Asia and Central Africa, to the Atlantic coast of Morocco and the Pacific coasts of the East Indies, but it had obtained no permanent foothold in Europe and had never crossed the Atlantic into the New World. The civilization of ancient Greece and Rome had extended its political dominion into North-Western Europe under the Roman Empire and its artistic inspiration into India and the Far East, where Graeco-Roman models had stimulated the development of Buddhist art. Yet the Roman Empire and the Chinese Empire had co-existed on the face of the same planet for two centuries with scarcely any direct intercourse, either political or economic. Indeed, so slight was the contact that each of these two societies saw the other, through a glass darkly, as a half-mythical fairyland. In other words, the Graeco-Roman civilization and the contemporary Far Eastern civilization each expanded to their full capacity, in the same age, without coming into collision. It was the same with the other ancient civilizations. Ancient India radiated her religion, her art, her commerce and her colonists into the Far East and the East Indies, but never penetrated the West. The civilization of the Sumerians in the Land of Shinar exerted an influence as far afield as the Indus Valley and Transcaspia and South-Eastern Europe; but attempts to prove that it was the parent of the early Chinese civilization on the one side, or of the Egyptian on the other, have miscarried. There is a brilliant and rather militant school of English anthropologists who maintain that all known civilizations—including those of Central America and Peru—can be traced back to an Egyptian origin. And these anthropologists point to the present world-wide extension of our Western civilization as an analogy in support of their thesis. If our own civilization has become world-wide in our own time, they argue, why should not the Egyptian civilization have achieved an equal extension a few thousand years earlier? This thesis is interesting, but it is the subject of acute controversy and must be regarded as non-proven. As far as we know for certain, the only civilization that has ever yet become world-wide is ours.

Moreover, this is a very recent event. Nowadays we are apt to forget that Western Europe made two unsuccessful attempts to expand before she eventually succeeded.

The first of these attempts was the mediaeval movement in the Mediterranean for which the most convenient general name is the Crusades. In the Crusades, the attempt to impose the political and economic dominion of West Europeans upon other peoples ended in a complete failure, while, in the interchange of culture, the West Europeans received a greater impress from the Muslims and Byzantines than they imparted to them. The second attempt was that of the Spaniards and Portuguese in the sixteenth century of our era. This was more or less successful in the New World—the modern Latin American communities owe their existence to it—but, elsewhere, Western civilization, as propagated by the Spaniards and Portuguese, was rejected after about a century's trial. The expulsion of the Spaniards and Portuguese from Japan, and of the Portuguese from Abyssinia, in the second quarter of the seventeenth century, marked the failure of this second attempt.

The third attempt was begun in the seventeenth century by the Dutch, French, and English, and these three West European nations were the principal authors of the world-wide ascendency that our Western civilization was enjoying in 1914. The English, French, and Dutch peopled North America, South Africa, and Australasia with new nations of European stock which started life with the Western social heritage, and they brought the rest of the world within the European orbit. By 1914, the network of European trade and European means of communication had become world-wide. Almost the whole world had entered the Postal Union and the Telegraphic Union, and European devices for mechanical locomotion—the steamship, the railway, the motor-car—were rapidly penetrating everywhere. On the plane of politics, the European nations had not only colonized the New World but had conquered India and tropical Africa.

The political ascendency of Europe, however, though outwardly even more imposing than her economic ascendency, was really more precarious. The daughter-nations overseas had already set their feet firmly on the road towards independent nationhood. The United States and the Latin American Republics had long since established their independence by revolutionary wars; and the self-governing British Dominions were in process of establishing theirs by peaceful evolution. In India and tropical Africa, European domination was being maintained by a handful of Europeans who lived there as pilgrims and sojourners. They had not found it possible to acclimatize themselves sufficiently to bring up their children in the tropics; and this meant that the hold of Europeans upon the tropics had not been made independent of a European base of operations. Finally, the cultural influence of the West European civilization upon Russians, Muslims, Hindus, Chinese, Japanese, and tropical Africans was so recent a ferment that it was not yet possible to predict whether it would evaporate without permanent effect, or whether it would turn the dough sour, or whether it would successfully leaven the lump.

This then, in very rough outline, was the position of Europe in the world on the eve of the War of 1914-18. She was in the enjoyment of an undisputed ascendency, and the peculiar civilization which she had built up for herself was in process of becoming world-wide. Yet this position, brilliant though it was, was not merely unprecedented and recent; it was also insecure. It was insecure chiefly because, at the very time when European expansion was approaching its climax, the foundations of West European civilization had been broken up and the great deeps loosed by the release and emergence of two elemental forces in European social life—-the forces of industrialism and democracy, which were brought into a merely temporary and unstable equilibrium by the formula of nationalism. It is evident that a Europe which was undergoing the terrific double strain of this inward transformation and outward expansion—both on the heroic scale—could not with impunity squander her resources, spend her material wealth and man-power unproductively, or exhaust her muscular and nervous energy. If her total command of resources was considerably greater than that which any other civilization had ever enjoyed, these resources were relative to the calls upon them; and the liabilities of Europe on the eve of 1914, as well as her assets, were of an unprecedented magnitude. Europe could not afford to wage even one World War; and when we take stock of her position in the world after a Second World War and compare it with her position before 1914, we are confronted with a contrast that is staggering to the imagination.

In a certain sense, Europe still remains the centre of the world; and in a certain sense, again, the world is still being leavened by that Western civilization of which Western Europe is the original home; but the sense in which these two statements are still true has changed so greatly that the bare statements are misleading without a commentary. Instead of being a centre from which energy and initiative radiate outwards, Europe has become a centre upon which non-European energy and initiative converge. Instead of the world being a theatre for the play of European activities and rivalries, Europe herself—after having been the cockpit in two world wars in which the world did its fighting on European soil—is now in danger of becoming for a third time an arena for conflicts between non-European forces. An arena still may be defined as a central, public place, but it is hardly a place of honour or security.

It is true, again, that the influence of our Western civilization upon the rest of the world is still at work. Indeed, its action has become intensified, if we measure it in purely quantitative terms. For example, before the two wars, the new facilities for travel were only available for a wealthy minority of Europeans and Americans. During the wars, these facilities were turned to account to transport not only Europeans and Americans but Asiatics and Africans, *en masse,* to fight, or to labour behind the front, in war-zones all over the world. During the last twenty or thirty years, additional means of mechanical communication have been made available, not merely for a minority but for large sections of society. The motor-car has learnt to conquer the desert; the aeroplane has out-sped the motor-car; and the radio has reinforced the tele-phone and telegraph as a means of instantaneous long dis-tance intercourse. Unlike the railway and the telegraph, the motor-car and the radio-set can be owned and em-ployed by private individuals—a feature which greatly enhances their efficacy as media of communication. With the wholesale intermingling of peoples during the two wars, and with these new mechanical aids to communica-tion after them, it is not surprising to find that the leaven of Western civilization is penetrating the world more widely, deeply, and rapidly now than before.

At this moment, we see peoples like the Chinese and the Turks, who within living memory seemed bound hand and foot by the Confucian and the Islamic social heritage, adopting not merely the material technique of the West (the industrial system and all its works) and not merely the externals of our culture (trifles like felt hats and cinemas) but our social and political institutions: the Western status of women, the Western method of educa-tion, the Western machinery of parliamentary representa-tive government. In this, the Turks and Chinese are only conspicuous participants in a movement which is spreading over the whole of the Islamic world, the whole of the Hindu world, the whole of the Far East, the whole of tropical Africa; and it looks almost as though a radical Westernization of the entire world were now inevitable. Insensibly, our attitude towards this extraordinary proc-ess has changed. Formerly, it caught our attention in the two apparently isolated cases of Japan and Russia, and we thought of these two cases as "sports"—due, perhaps, to some exceptional quality in the social heritage of these two countries which made their peoples specially susceptible to Westernization; or due, perhaps, alternatively, to the personal genius and forcefulness of individual statesmen like Peter the Great and Catherine and Alexander the Liberator and that group of Japanese elder statesmen who deliberately imposed the adoption of Western ways upon the mass of their fellow-countrymen from the eighteen-sixties onwards. Now we see that Japan and Russia were simply forerunners of a movement which was to become universal. As Europeans observe this process of the Westernization of the world and watch it gathering momentum under their eyes, they may be inclined to exclaim almost in a spirit of exaltation: "What does it matter if Europe really has lost her ascendency in the world, if the whole world is becoming European? *Europae si monumentum requiris, circumspice!*"

That mood of exaltation, however, if it did for a moment capture European minds, would rapidly be dispelled by doubts. The propagation of Western culture from Europe over the world may be a great thing quantitatively, but what about quality? If at this instant Europe were to be blotted out of the book of life, would the Western civilization be able to maintain its European standard in the foreign environments to which it has been transplanted? If Europe were blotted out altogether, could the Western civilization even survive? And with Europe still alive, but deposed from her former position of supremacy— which is manifestly the fate that has overtaken her—will the Western civilization, though saved from extinction, escape degeneration?

Still more alarming doubts suggest themselves when we contemplate the modern history of Russia—and Russia is the most instructive case to consider, because in Russia the process of Westernization has had longer than elsewhere to work itself out. In Russia, the leaven of Western Europe has been at work for two centuries longer than in Japan or China, and for a century longer than among the Muslims and the Hindus. Thus, the point to which the current of Westernization has carried Russia by now enables us to foresee, by analogy, at any rate one of the possibilities that lie before the Far East, Islam, India, and Africa in the course of the next few generations. This

possibility which is revealed by the case of Russia—and
of course it is no more than one possibility among a number of alternatives—is a disconcerting one for Western
minds to contemplate.

The Europeans have regarded themselves as the Chosen
People—they need feel no shame in admitting that; every
past civilization has taken this view of itself and its own
heritage—and, as they have watched the Gentiles, one
after another, casting aside their own heritage in order to
take up Europe's instead, they have unhesitatingly con-
gratulated both themselves and their cultural converts.
"One more sinner," Europeans have repeated to themselves devoutly, "has repented of the filthy devices of the
heathen and become initiated into the True Faith."

Now the first effects of the conversion—at any rate
among the peoples converted to Western civilization before the wars—appeared to bear out this pious and opti-
mistic view. For half a century after the Revolution of
1868, Japan seemed to have come unscathed through the
tremendous transformation to which she had committed
herself; and Russia would have been pronounced by a detached observer who took stock of her in 1815, or even as
lately as 1914, to have been set by Peter the Great upon
the road of progress—though in her case the road might
have appeared to be longer, steeper, and more toilsome
than in the case of Japan. A fair-minded observer of Russia, at either of those dates, would have admitted that the
standard of Western civilization in a recently Westernized
Russia was far lower than in a Europe where that civilization was at home; but he would have pleaded that, in spite
of this backwardness, and in spite of disappointingly fre-
quent set-backs, Russia was rapidly catching up the European vanguard in the march of Western civilization.
"Remember," he would have said, "that, in this forward
march, Europe had ten centuries' start, and you will admit that the pace at which Russia is catching up to Europe
is very creditable."

But what would the same fair-minded observer say
about Russia to-day? I do not propose to speculate on the
moral judgment that he would pass—that is irrelevant to
my subject—but, whatever his judgments of value might

be, I think he could hardly avoid making the two following judgments of fact: first, that the Gospel according to
Lenin and Stalin draws its inspiration from the West every
bit as much as the Gospel according to Peter and Alexander; and, second, that the effect of the West upon Russia
has changed over from positive to negative. The Russian
prophets of the first dispensation were inspired by a set
of Western ideas which attracted them towards the social
heritage of our Western civilization; the Russian prophets
of the second dispensation have been attracted by another
set of ideas which are also of Western origin, but which
lead them to regard the West as a kind of apocalyptic
Babylon. We cannot comprehend the total effect of Westernization upon Russia up to date unless we see this Bolshevik reaction of the twentieth century and the Petrine
reaction of the seventeenth century in perspective—as successive, and perhaps inseparable, phases in a single process
which the encounter between two different civilizations
has set up. In this perspective we shall come to regard the
process of Westernization with less complacency, and shall
find ourselves reciting the parable:

When the unclean spirit is gone out of a man, he walketh
through dry places, seeking rest; and, finding none, he saith:
"I will return unto my house whence I came out." And when
he cometh he findeth it swept and garnished. Then goeth he
and taketh to him seven other spirits more wicked than himself, and they enter in and dwell there; and the last state of
that man is worse than the first.

From a Western standpoint, "the unclean spirit" which
originally possessed Russia was her Byzantine social heritage. When Peter the Great went on his pilgrimage to
Europe and beheld Solomon in all his glory, there was
no more spirit left in him. Byzantinism did not, indeed, go
out of Russia, but it did go underground, and for ten
generations the Russian people walked through dry places,
seeking rest and finding none. Unable to endure existence
in a swept and garnished house, they flung their doors
wide open and summoned all the spirits of the West to
enter in and dwell there; and in crossing the threshold
these spirits have turned into seven devils.

The moral seems to be that a social heritage will not readily bear transplantation. Culture spirits which are the tutelary geniuses, the Lares and Penates, of the house where they are at home and where there is a pre-established harmony between them and the human inhabitants, become demons of malevolence and destruction when they enter into a house inhabited by strangers; for these strangers are naturally ignorant of the subtle rites in which their new gods' souls delight. As long as the Ark of Jehovah remained in Israel among Jehovah's Chosen People, it served them as their talisman, but, when the Ark was captured by the Philistines, the hand of the Lord was heavy upon every city in which it rested, and the Chosen People themselves were infected with the plague by which the Gentiles were requited for their sacrilege.

If this analysis is right, Europeans cannot take much comfort for the dethronement of Europe in the prospect that the influence of European civilization may yet become the dominant force in the world. They will be less impressed by the fact that this mighty force has been generated in Europe than by the equally evident fact that, at a certain stage in its operation, it is apt to take a violently destructive turn. Indeed, this destructive recoil of European influence abroad upon Europe herself seems to be one of the signal dangers to which Europe is exposed in the new position in which she finds herself since the wars. In order to estimate the other principal danger to which Europe is now exposed, we must turn our attention from the relations between Europe and Russia to the relations between Europe and the United States.

The reversal in the relations between Europe and the United States since 1914 gives the measure in which the world-movement centering in Europe has become centripetal instead of centrifugal. The United States, as she was in 1914, was a monument of the outward radiation of European energies during the previous three centuries. Her population of over one hundred millions had been created by the man-power of Europe, and the volume of migration across the Atlantic was expanding, on a steeply ascending curve, down to the very year in which the First World War broke out. Again, the development of the material resources of the vast territory of the United States —a territory comparable in area to the whole of Europe, excluding Russia—was dependent not merely upon the influx of European man-power but upon the importation of European goods and the application of European services. The positive current of economic circulation, in the form of emigrants and goods and services, was flowing before 1914 from Europe into the United States; the negative current, in the form of remittances and payments of interest for goods and services supplied on credit, was flowing from the United States to Europe. As a result of the two wars, the direction of the current has been dramatically reversed.

The facts are so notorious, they are so constantly and so deeply impressed upon our consciousness, that I almost feel that I ought to apologize to my readers for recalling them. From the moment when the First World War broke out, the stream of European emigrants to America ceased to flow; and, by the time the first war was over, the United States—who had previously not only welcomed European immigrants but whose employers of labour had sought them in the highways and hedges of Europe and compelled them to come in—had learnt to feel that European immigration was not a national asset but a national danger: that it was a transaction in which the balance of advantage was with the immigrant and not with the country which received him. This momentous change of attitude in the United States towards European immigration was promptly given practical expression in the two restriction acts of 1921 and 1924. The effect upon the economic life of Europe—or, more accurately, of those European countries from which the largest contingents of emigrants to the United States had latterly been drawn—was very far-reaching.

Take the classic case of Italy. In 1914 the number of Italian immigrants into the United States was 283,738; by contrast, the Italian annual quota proclaimed by President Coolidge on the 30th June, 1924, in pursuance of the Act of that year, was 3,845. In consequence, the stream of Italian emigrants was partly dammed up and partly diverted from the vacuum in the United States—a vacuum which had existed because America was a new world in process of development—to the vacuum in France—a vacuum which had been created because Europe was an old world devastated by having been made into the battle-field of an oecumenical war. In the eighteenth century, French and English armies crossed the Atlantic in order to fight on the banks of the Ohio and the St. Lawrence for the possession of the North American continent. In the twentieth century, American armies have crossed the Atlantic in order to decide the destinies of the world on European battle-fronts. Till 1914, the fertilizing stream of European emigration to America was still increasing in volume. From 1921 onwards, this stream was being deliberately checked, and during the inter-war years it was replaced by an uneconomic trickle of American tourists to Europe.

Of course, this inter-war trickle of American tourists to Europe, though small and unproductive compared to the mighty river of emigrants which had formerly flowed from Europe to America, was very large compared to any other movement of travel for uneconomic purposes that there had ever been; and the fact that this tourist traffic could be financed brings me to the second point in which the relations between Europe and the United States have been reversed—a point which is so obvious that I shall simply state it without dwelling on it. The United States had changed, almost in the twinkling of an eye, from being the greatest debtor country in the world to being the greatest creditor country; and, in spite of their traditional aversion to European entanglements, Americans were driven, by the necessities of the new economic situation, to seek markets on credit, in Europe, for American goods and services. But there was an unfortunate difference in kind between pre-war European investment in the United States and the inter-war American investment in Europe. Before 1914, Europe provided the United States with credits for productive outlay. During the two wars, Europe borrowed from America the means of working her own destruction; and to-day she is borrowing desperately from America again, not in order to develop new European resources, but merely to repair some part of the ravages which two world wars have inflicted on her.

Confronted with this painful reversal in their relations with the United States, Europeans naturally ask themselves: "Is this an accidental, and therefore retrievable and merely temporary, misfortune—an incidental consequence of exceptional catastrophes? Or has it older and deeper causes, the effect of which it will be less easy to counteract?" I venture to suggest that this second possibility appears to be the more probable of the two—that, although the two wars have precipitated this reversal of relations and have given it a revolutionary and dramatic outward form, some such reversal was nevertheless inherent in the previous situation, and would have taken place—though no doubt more gently and gradually—even if these wars had never been fought.

In support of this view, I shall put forward two points for consideration: first, the nature of the industrial system which Europe invented a century and a half ago and which has now spread all over the world; and, second, the fate of certain earlier centres of civilization—for example, mediaeval Italy or ancient Greece—which anticipated modern Europe in propagating their own civilization beyond their borders, though never quite so far and wide as modern Europe has propagated hers.

First, let us consider the industrial system. It was invented in Great Britain at a time when parliamentary representative government within the framework of a national state had become the settled basis of English life. It immediately became apparent that a community built on the geographical scale of Great Britain, and possessing that cohesion and solidarity which the political institutions of representative government on the national scale had already given to Great Britain before the close of the eighteenth century, was the minimum unit of territory and population in which the industrial system could be operated with profit. The spread of industrialism from Great Britain across the European continent was, I should say, one of the main factors that produced the national unifications of Germany and Italy—two notable political consolidations of territory and population in Europe which were completed within a century of the Industrial Revolution in England. About the year 1875, it looked as though Europe would find equilibrium through being organized into a number of industrialized democratic national states—units of the calibre of Great Britain, France, Germany, and Italy, as they existed from 1871 to 1914. We can now see that this expectation of equilibrium, on the basis of the national unit, was illusory. Industrialism and democracy are elemental forces. In the eighteen-seventies they were still in their infancy, and we cannot yet foresee the ultimate dimensions to which they may grow or forecast the protean shapes which they may assume. What we can now pronounce with certainty is that the European national state—of the dimensions attained by France and Great Britain in the eighteenth century and by Germany and Italy in the nineteenth—is far too small and frail a vessel to contain these forces. The new wines of industrialism and democracy have been poured into old bottles and they have burst the old bottles beyond repair.

It is now hardly conceivable that the ultimate minimum effective unit of the industrial system can be anything less than the entire utilizable surface of the planet and the whole of mankind. And, on the political plane, likewise, the minimum unit is showing a tendency to increase in scale, in sympathy with the extension, to a world-wide range, of the operations of industry. That tendency in the economic field has been fully matched in the political field by the emergence of world-wide political organizations: the United Nations and its precursor the League of Nations (and in this connexion I would suggest that the economic and technical activities of the United Nations, though the least conspicuous, are not the least important). But, short of the world-wide United Nations organization, we see on the present political map certain elastic associations of self-governing nations like the British Commonwealth or the Pan American Union, in each of which a considerable number of national states are grouped together. And within these two groups we can discern a number of political entities which are smaller and more closely knit than either of the associations to which they belong, yet at the same time are not nearly so small as typical European national states like France or Italy.

These non-European polities of a supra-national calibre have discovered a new political form adapted to their scale: they have abandoned the unitary centralized organization of the French type in favour of a federalism which combines the advantages of variety and devolution with those of uniform united action for purposes common to the whole union. Up to the present moment, the United States is the only country of this new type and calibre which has come of age, and she has already given astonishing evidence of the economic power and energy which this new species of political organization is able to generate and release. We can perceive, however, that the United States is simply the first to reach maturity among a number of adolescent states which have organized themselves or are organizing themselves on a similar federal basis and on a comparable geographical scale. Apart from the United States, most of the new non-European states of this type still lack some element essential to the full exercise of their latent strength. The Commonwealth of Australia and the Argentine Federal Republic lack population; the Union of South Africa lacks population and is also confronted with the colour problem far more formidably than the United States. The rest lack either population, or education, or political experience and stability, or several of these requisites together; and some of them are doubtless so heavily handicapped that they will fail to achieve their potentialities. It is not yet possible to forecast the future of the United States of Brazil, the Republic of Mexico, the Chinese Republic, the nascent polities of India and Pakistan; and the destiny of the Union of Soviet Socialist Republics is inscrutable. Yet, even though some of these still adolescent federal states of the overseas type and calibre may fall by the wayside, it is extremely probable that, within the next generation, there will have grown to maturity, outside Europe, at least as many federal states of the type and calibre of the United States as there are national states in Europe of the type and calibre of Great Britain, France, and Italy. More than one of these non-

European states will be comparable in order of magnitude to the whole of Europe put together.

Thus Europe as a whole is in process of being dwarfed by the overseas world which she herself has called into existence, while the national states of Europe, singly, are being dwarfed by the federal states of this new world overseas. Faced with this situation, what future has Europe to expect?

Some light on her future may be afforded by analogies from the past. After all, what Europe has achieved in the world, though possibly unprecedented in scale, is not unprecedented in character. Ancient Greece and mediaeval Italy both anticipated her. Each of these earlier societies was divided into a number of city-states, which were no more diminutive, in proportion to their respective worlds, than is a European national state in proportion to the world of to-day. Each of these societies created such a noble civilization and put forth such an intense and effectively directed energy that in spite of its internal disunion —in spite of the passionate particularism of its city-states and their constant fratricidal struggles—ancient Greece and mediaeval Italy each, in its day, succeeded in establishing its political, economic, and cultural ascendency far and wide over the surrounding Gentiles. Each of them, in its great age, set at defiance the dictum that a house divided against itself cannot stand. Yet their latter end was a tragic proof that the text is true.

In either case, the Chosen People taught the Gentiles to follow their way of life, and in either case the Gentiles learnt to follow it, but on a far larger material scale. The city-states of Greece found themselves dwarfed by the greater powers—the Macedonian, Syrian and Egyptian monarchies, the Carthaginian Empire, and the Roman Confederation—which arose round the Mediterranean after the expansion of the Greek civilization in the age of Alexander; and Greece then became at once the pilgrimage resort, the university, and the battlefield of these new Hellenized powers. It was the same with mediaeval Italy—and in her case the story has a special appositeness; for the new powers which were called into existence by the spread of the Italian Renaissance beyond the Alps, and which dwarfed and dominated the city-states of Milan and Florence and Venice from the end of the fifteenth century onwards, were those European national states—such states as Spain and France—which are now being dwarfed under our eyes by the United States of America.

As we reflect on these precedents, two questions naturally suggest themselves: first, how was it that the converted Gentiles, who in all else were the passive pupils and clumsy imitators of their Greek and Italian masters, were able to solve that one vital problem of political construction on a greater scale which their masters had repeatedly attempted to solve without ever succeeding? Secondly, how was it that the Greeks and Italians went on failing to solve their problem of political consolidation after it had become fully apparent to them that the penalty of continued failure would be political and economic downfall? In the Greece of the fourth, third, and second centuries B.C., in the Italy of the fifteenth, sixteenth, and seventeenth centuries of the Christian era, everybody deplored the continuance of the old particularism, everybody tried to overcome it, and every attempt to transcend it failed until the Greeks and the Italians resigned themselves in despair to a doom which had come to seem inevitable. Why should peoples who were still resourceful and creative in other fields have remained ineffective in this one field, even under the supreme incentive of self-preservation?

The first question is comparatively easy to answer. The Gentiles in the outer court of the Temple succeeded in building up political organizations of a larger calibre than the Greek and Italian city-states, not because they had greater political ability or political experience than the Greeks and Italians—on the contrary, they had much less —but because political construction is much easier in a new country on the fringes of a civilization than in an old country at its centre. It is easier because there is less pressure, more available space, and no old buildings standing on the site to which an architect has to adjust his new designs. In the new country on the edge of the world, the political architect has a free field and no commitments. Even if he is a dull fellow, it is not difficult for him to build something more spacious and convenient than can be attempted by his highly trained and talented colleague who has to work on a cramped site in the congested heart of an ancient city, overshadowed by the monuments of the past. It is the mere advantage of the geographical situation, not the merit of the local architect, which brings it about that the new big-scale architecture is invented on the outskirts and not in the centre; but, though this is not the fault of the gifted inhabitants of the centre, the consequences which it brings upon them are not on that account the less serious.

In this attempt to answer my first question, I think I have already indicated the answer to the second—to the question, that is, why the Greeks and Italians, when their city-states were dwarfed and their independence was threatened by the construction of larger-scale states around them, still failed to throw their city-states together and consolidate them into a single political structure of the new order of magnitude. The answer seems to be that they could not escape from the toils of their own great traditions. In the great age of ancient Greece—the age in which she had created the Greek civilization which subsequently conquered the world—an independent Athens, and independent Corinth, an independent Sparta had been the outstanding features in the political landscape. Think away the independence of those great city-states in the great age, and all that was greatest in that age, and permanently great in that civilization, would threaten to fade out of the picture. The independence of the city-states had the same roots as the civilization itself—and this is another way of saying that it was ineradicable so long as that civilization lasted. Without an independent Athens and an independent Sparta there could not be a Greek world. On the other hand, the new Greek city-states founded on Asiatic soil by Alexander and his successors had no cherished tradition of independence which inhibited them from allowing themselves to be banded together, with other city-states of their kind, to form a federal organization on a larger scale. In times when salvation depends on innovation, the parvenu finds salvation more easily than the aristocrat.

I will conclude by attempting to examine how these

precedents bear upon the prospects of Europe in the new age following the two world wars—an age in which the dwarfing of Europe is one of the most striking new features. The Europeans of to-day, like the Italians of the sixteenth century of our era and like the Greeks of the third century B.C., are well aware of their peril. They fully realize how serious it is; and they understand—at least, in a general way—what it is that they have to accomplish in order to ward this danger off. Ever since 1914, Europeans have given much thought to the problem of European union; and, though the publicists may have led the way, the men of action—in industry, in finance, and even in diplomacy—have also been at work on the problem.

As the point of departure, we may take Dr. Friedrich Naumann's brilliant book *Mitteleuropa,* published in 1915. It was natural that the vision of a European political unit on a larger scale than the national state should have presented itself first in the centre of Europe, where the pressure was greatest, and in time of war, when the normal pressure of existence was so sharply intensified for the central powers by a military struggle on two fronts and a naval blockade. It was also natural that a German writer, with the history of the German Zollverein in his mind, should start from the idea of a supra-national customs-union and proceed from this starting point to schemes for co-operation in other departments of public life. Between the two wars, Naumann's conception of "Central Europe" was expanded by other continental publicists into that of "Pan-Europa"—a general European union which, like Naumann's "Central Europe," was to be based upon a Zollverein. This project of "Pan-Europa" seems first to have been ventilated in inter-war Austria—a country for whom the subdivision of Europe into a number of independent fragments, isolated from one another economically as well as politically, was hardly tolerable within the frontiers which had been assigned to Austria in the peace-settlement of 1919-20. After the Second World War, this movement for the unification of Europe has re-emerged, and it has now received powerful encouragement from America in the terms of the Marshall Plan.

The eagerness and earnestness of the response which the

Marshall Plan has evoked on the European side are indications that Europe does realize her danger, does know what are the proper measures of defence, and does desire to take these measures. But the crucial question is this: Is Europe's desire to retain, or retrieve, some vestige of her former position in the world a force that is strong enough to overcome the obstacles in the path?

The most conspicuous obstacles are perhaps the following three: first, the special problems presented by the British Commonwealth and the Soviet Union—polities on the supra-national scale which, hitherto, have been half inside Europe and half outside; second, the continuing tendency of the industrial system to enlarge the scale of its operations—a tendency which has already burst the bounds of the national state, and may very well burst the bounds of even the largest regional units, in its march towards world-unity; third, the dead-weight of European tradition, which makes a Europe without a sovereign independent Great Britain or a sovereign independent France as difficult for Englishmen and Frenchmen to love and cherish, or indeed even to imagine, as a Hellas without an independent Athens and Sparta would have been difficult to imagine for an Athenian and a Spartan of the third or second century B.C. Are any or all of these obstacles likely to be overcome?

The obstacle presented by the Soviet Union looks, it must frankly be confessed, much more difficult after the Second World War than before it. Within its inter-war frontiers, the Soviet Union, unlike the previous Russian Empire, lay virtually outside Europe, for at that stage it did not include that fringe of countries with a Western tradition of culture whose inclusion had brought the former Russian Empire into the fellowship of European states. As a result of the War of 1914-18, the successful invasion of the Russian Empire by the Germans, and the two successive Russian revolutions of 1917, these Western borderlands parted company with Russia and entered the European fellowship on their own account as the independent national states of Finland, Estonia, Latvia, Lithuania, and Poland. As a result of the War of 1939-45, however, there has been a reversion here to something much more like the pre-1914 situation. The three Baltic States have been re-annexed to Russia as constituent republics of the Soviet Union, and not only Finland and the whole of Poland (including the former Prussian and Austrian portions), but Roumania, Bulgaria, Hungary, and Czechoslovakia as well, have been brought within the Soviet sphere of influence, *de facto* though not *de jure,* as satellite states. Including the German territories, east of the Northern Neisse and the Oder, which have been assigned to Poland by the Soviet Union in compensation for the Ukrainian and White Russian provinces of interwar Poland which the Soviet Union has now taken back, and adding to all this the Soviet zones of occupation in Germany and Austria, we find the western boundary of the Soviet world now running down the middle of Europe, north and south, from the Baltic to the Adriatic.

Would the Soviet Government ever allow the Soviet half of post-war Europe to combine with the other half in anything like a Pan European association? We may guess that Moscow would allow this only on one condition, and that is that Europe should form her union round a Russian nucleus and under Russian hegemony. This is a condition which the West European countries would be altogether unwilling to accept, and that means that, if the Marshall Plan does lead to union in Europe, the union is likely to be limited to countries lying west of the western boundary of the Soviet sphere.

If, however, the Russian obstacle to European union has grown more formidable, the British obstacle has probably become easier to surmount. Any project for European union threatens to put Great Britain in a dilemma. If a Pan-European union, or even a narrower West European union, were successfully established by her continental European neighbours, Great Britain could hardly afford to stand outside it. Yet she could equally ill afford to enter a European union at the cost of breaking her links with the overseas English-speaking countries: the United States and the overseas members of the Commonwealth. This dilemma does not arise, however, when the European union which Great Britain is asked to join is sponsored by the United States and is designed as a basis for closer relations between a united Europe and America. In fact, Great Britain is relieved of embarrassment by just those intentions and assumptions of the Marshall Plan that are unpalatable to the Soviet Union. The terms of the Marshall Plan allow Great Britain to have the best of both worlds; she can enter into association with her neighbours on the European Continent without endangering her relations with her existing associates overseas; and a European union on these terms can be sure of receiving Great Britain's whole-hearted support.

But is "union" the right name for the constellation of forces that we are forecasting? Would not "partition" be a more accurate word? For if Eastern Europe is to be associated with the Soviet Union under Soviet hegemony and Western Europe with the United States under American leadership, the division of Europe between these two titanic non-European powers is the most significant feature of the new map to a European eye. Are we not really arriving at the conclusion that it is already beyond Europe's power to retrieve her position in the world by overcoming the disunity that has always been her bane? The deadweight of European tradition now weighs lighter than a feather in the scales, for Europe's will no longer decide Europe's destiny. Her future lies on the knees of the giants who now overshadow her.

The Marshall Plan also throws into relief another of those obstacles to the union of Europe that we have mentioned. The tendency of the industrial system to go on extending the scale of its operations till this scale becomes world-wide tells heavily against the prospects of a mere regional European grouping. If the Marshall Plan bears fruit, the result will be to salvage the countries of Western Europe by building them into an economic system, centering round the United States, that will embrace the whole world except for the Soviet sphere; for the West European countries will bring with them their African and Asiatic possessions and dependencies, while the United States will bring with her the Latin American countries and China, and the overseas members of the British Commonwealth may be counted on, in the circumstances, to join in. In terms of this scale of economic operations, a European union, even if it embraced the whole of Europe, would be almost as inadequate an economic unit as a national state on the scale of France or a city-state on the scale of mediaeval Venice. On the economic plane of vision it looks as though "Pan-Europa" had already become an anachronism without our ever having had an opportunity of creating her; and West Europeans need not regret that "Pan-Europa" has been still-born if they are offered the alternative of entering into an all but world-wide association. If Europe's once unquestioned ascendency in the world proves to be a passing curiosity of history that is doomed to die, the Marshall Plan gives Western Europe at least the solace of seeing her dead supremacy given Christian burial. Euthanasia, however, is neither recovery nor resurrection. On the morrow of the Second World War, the dwarfing of Europe is an unmistakably accomplished fact.

7

THE INTERNATIONAL OUTLOOK [1]

When I compare the aftermaths of the two wars, I see a number of obvious resemblances, but one outstanding difference. Last time, we believed that the War of 1914-18 had been a terrible but nevertheless non-significant interruption in the course of reasonable civilized historical progress. We thought of it as an accident like a railway collision or an earthquake; and we imagined that, as soon as we had buried the dead and cleared up the wreckage, we could go back to living the comfortable uneventful life which, at that time, had come to be taken for granted, as though it were the birthright of man, by that small and exceptionally privileged fraction of the living generation of mankind that was represented by people of the middle class in the democratic industrial Western countries. This time, by contrast, we are well aware that the end of hostilities is not the end of the story.

What is the issue that is arousing this anxiety to-day all over the world: among the Americans, the Canadians, ourselves, our European neighbours, and the Russians (for, from the glimpse of the Russians that I had at Paris this last summer, I should say that we can gauge the Russians' feelings pretty accurately by analogy with our own)?

[1] This paper is based on a lecture delivered on 22 May 1947, in London at Chatham House, on return from a visit to the United States and Canada between 8 February and 26 April 1947.

I shall give you my own personal view, which is, as you will see, a controversial one. My personal belief is that this formidable issue is a political issue, not an economic one, and I further believe that it is not the question whether the world is going to be unified politically in the near future. I believe—and this is, I suppose, my most controversial assertion, but I am simply stating what I do sincerely think —I believe it is a foregone conclusion that the world is in any event going to be unified politically in the near future. (If you consider just two things, the degree of our present interdependence and the deadliness of our present weapons, and put these two considerations together, I do not see how you can arrive at any other conclusion.) I think the big and really formidable political issue to-day is, not *whether* the world is soon going to be unified politically, but in which of two alternative possible ways this rapid unification is going to come about.

There is the old-fashioned and unpleasantly familiar way of continual rounds of wars going on to a bitter end at which one surviving great power "knocks out" its last remaining competitor and imposes peace on the world by conquest. This is the way in which the Graeco-Roman world was forcibly united by Rome in the last century B.C., and the Far Eastern world in the third century B.C. by the Roman-minded principality of Ts'in. And then there is the new experiment in a co-operative government of the world—no, not quite a new one, because there were abortive attempts at finding a co-operative way out of the troubles that were actually brought to an end by the forcible imposition of the *Pax Romana* and the *Pax Sinica;* but our own pursuit, in our own lifetime, of this happier solution has been so much more resolute and so much more self-conscious that we may perhaps fairly regard it as a new departure. Our first attempt at it was the League of Nations; our second attempt is the United Nations organization. It is evident that we are engaged here on a very difficult political pioneering enterprise over largely unknown ground. If this enterprise did succeed—even if only just so far as to save us from a repetition of "the knock-out blow"—it might open out quite new prospects for mankind: prospects that we have never sighted before during these last five or six thousand years that have seen us making a number of attempts at civilization.

After greeting this gleam of hope on our horizon we should be sinking into a fool's paradise if we did not also take note of the length and the roughness of the road that lies between our goal and the point at which we stand to-day. We are not likely to succeed in averting "the knock-out blow" unless we take due account of the circumstances that unfortunately tell in favour of it.

The first of these adverse circumstances, with which we have to contend, is the fact that, within the span of a single lifetime, the number of great powers of the highest material calibre—if we measure this calibre in terms of sheer war potential—has dwindled from eight to two. To-day, in the arena of naked power politics, the United States and the Soviet Union face one another alone. One more world war, and there might be only a solitary great power left to give the world its political unity by the old-fashioned method of the conqueror imposing his fiat.

This startlingly rapid fall in the number of great powers of the highest material calibre has been due to a sudden jump in the material scale of life, which has dwarfed powers of the dimensions of Great Britain and France by comparison with powers of the dimensions of the Soviet Union and the United States. Such sudden jumps have occurred before in history. Between five and four hundred years ago, powers of the dimensions of Venice and Florence were similarly dwarfed by the sudden emergence of powers of the dimensions of England and France.

This dwarfing of the European powers by the United States and the Soviet Union would have happened, no doubt, in any case in course of time. It is, I should say, an inevitable ultimate consequence of the recent opening-up of the vast spaces of North America and Russia, and of the still more recent development of their resources by the application there, on a massive scale, of technical methods partly invented in the laboratories of Western Europe. But the time taken by this inevitable process might have been as much as a hundred years if it had not been telescoped into a third or a quarter of that span by the cumulative effect of two world wars. If the change had not been thus accelerated, it would have been a gradual process that might have allowed all parties time to adjust themselves to it more or less painlessly. As a result of its having been speeded up by the two wars, it has been a revolutionary process which has put all parties in a quandary.

It is important for European observers to realize (as one does realize when he has been watching the reactions in the United States at first hand) that this speeding-up of the transfer of material power from the older powers of the inner ring in Europe to the younger powers of the outer ring in America and Asia is as awkward for the Americans as it is for ourselves. The Americans are homesick for their comparatively carefree nineteenth-century past. At the same time, they realize, far more clearly, and also far more generally, than either they or we realized after the War of 1914-18, that it is impossible to put the clock back to a comfortabale pre-war hour. They know that they have got to stay out in the world now, however much they may dislike the bleakness of the prospect. They are facing this unwelcome new chapter in their history with an un-enthusiastic confidence when they think of it in terms of the technical and economic jobs that they will be called upon to do in Greece and Turkey and in other foreign countries that, as the President warned them, may follow. But they express something like dismay when they are reminded that man does not live by bread alone, and that they will have to take a hand in politics as well as econom-ics if they are to succeed in acclimatizing democracy, in the Western meaning of the term, in non-Western countries where they are intervening for this purpose. "Screen" the political prisoners in Ruritania, and see to it that the Ruri-tanian government releases those who ought to be at liberty? Secure the transformation of the Ruritanian police from an agency for twisting the arms of the political op-ponents of the partisan government of the day into an agency for protecting the liberties of the subject? Bring about a corresponding reform of the Ruritanian courts of justice? If you suggest to Americans to-day that, when once they have implicated themselves in Ruritania, they will find it impossible to leave these political enterprises un-attempted, they are apt to exclaim that the United States docs not command the personnel for handling jobs of this kind abroad.

This uneasiness about incurring political responsibilities in politically backward foreign countries has aroused, in American minds, a sudden concern about the future of the British Empire. This concern, like most human feelings on most occasions, is, I should say, partly self-regarding and partly disinterested. The self-regarding consideration in American minds is the prospect that, if the British Empire were to disintegrate, it would leave a huge political vacuum—far larger and more perilous than the no-man's-land in Greece and Turkey—into which the United States might find herself constrained to step in order to forestall the Soviet Union. The Americans have become alive to the convenience, for them, of the British Empire's existence just at the moment when, as they see it, the British Empire is being liquidated. But this recently aroused American concern for the Empire is also largely disinterested and warm-hearted. The traditional American denunciation of British imperialism went hand in hand, I fancy, with an unconscious assumption that this British Empire was, for good or evil, one of the world's established and abiding institutions. Now that the Americans really believe that the Empire is in its death agony, they are beginning to regret the imminent disappearance of so prominent and familiar an object in their political landscape, and are becoming conscious of services performed by the Empire for the world, which they did not value and hardly noticed so long as they could take the continuance of those services for granted.

This abrupt change in the American attitude towards the British Empire during the winter of 1946-7 was the consequence of American interpretations of current events. At that time, two facts were striking the American imagination: the physical sufferings of the people of Great Britain, and the definite decision of the Government of the United Kingdom to withdraw from India in 1948. Taken together, these two facts made on American minds the impression that the British Empire was "down and out"; and, in their sensational way, American commentators telescoped into a single instantaneous event the whole evolution of the

British Empire since 1783, and at the same time assumed that the change had been wholly involuntary. As most Americans saw it, the United Kingdom had suddenly become too weak to hold the Empire by force any longer; few of them appeared to realize that the British people had learnt a tremendous lesson from the loss of the Thirteen Colonies and had been trying to apply that lesson ever since.

In uninstructed American minds, the impression was that the Empire of King George III had existed practically unchanged till yesterday and was suddenly crumbling today; and, however wide of the mark it may seem to us to be, this American notion is not really so surprising as it must sound to British ears. On matters which do not happen to come within the range of our adult experience, all of us are apt to retain, uncriticized and unrevised, the crude and simple-minded conceptions that were suggested to us in childhood. There is, for instance, or used to be till lately, a British schoolboy legend that the French have no capacity for governing dependencies or handlng backward peoples. The average American's notion of the British Empire is similarly based on the legend of the Revolutionary War that he learned at school, and not on any first-hand grown-up observation of present facts. Many Americans, for instance, show ignorance even of the present status of Canada, though they themselves may be in constant personal contact with Canadians and, if they are, will have recognized them instinctively as being upstanding free people of the same kind as the Americans themselves. Yet, so far from putting two and two together and looking into the facts afresh, it is as likely as not that they will have gone on imagining that Canada in their time is still being ruled from Downing Street and is paying taxes which she never paid to the Treasury in Whitehall.

This explains in large measure why both the speed and the character of the change that has taken place in the constitution of the British Empire have been misconceived by many American minds. Yet, when all due correction of such misconceptions has been made, the British critic has, in his turn, to face the fact that, in the power of the Empire, as distinct from its constitution, a change has taken place that has been not only very great but also very rapid. The truth is that in terms of pure power politics— of sheer war potential—there are now only two great powers left confronting one another: the United States and the Soviet Union. The recognition of this fact in the United States explains the heart-searching caused by the announcement of "the Truman Doctrine." Americans realize that this is a turning-point in American history for two reasons. In the first place, it brings the United States right out of her traditional isolation; and in the second place the President's move might turn out—however far this may have been from his intention—to have given the whole course of international affairs an impulsion away from the new co-operative method of trying to achieve political world unity, and towards the old-fashioned method of fighting out the last round in the struggle of power politics and arriving at the political unification of the world by the main force of a "knock-out blow."

Having now reviewed the circumstances that tell in favour of this old-fashioned solution, we must arouse ourselves to get the better of them by reminding ourselves how utterly disastrous a "knock-out blow" would be. It would condemn mankind to go through at least one more world war. A third world war would be fought with atomic and other perhaps not less deadly new weapons. Moreover, in previous cases— for example, the forcible unification of the Chinese world by the principality of Ts'in, and of the Graeco-Roman world by Rome—the achievement of a long overdue political unification through a "knock-out blow" has been purchased at the prohibitive price of inflicting mortal wounds on the society that has had unity imposed upon it by this extreme resort to force.

If we thought of these wounds in material terms, and tried to estimate the capacity of different civilizations for reconstruction as well as destruction, it might not be easy to draw up strictly comparable balance-sheets for our modern Western civilization on the one hand and for the Graeco-Roman and Chinese civilizations on the other. No doubt we have a far greater capacity to reconstruct as well as to destroy than the Chinese and the Romans had. On the other hand, a simpler social structure has a far greater spontaneous recuperative power than a more complicated one has. When I see our re-building programme in Great Britain being retarded by shortages of skilled labour and of highly processed materials, and perhaps not least by the mere complication of the administrative machine, my mind goes back to a glimpse that I had in 1923 of a Turkish village reconstructing itself after it had been devastated in the last phase of the Graeco-Turkish War of A.D. 1919-22. Those Turkish villagers were not dependent on materials or labour from outside, and they were not at the mercy of red tape. They were rebuilding their houses and replacing their household utensils and agricultural implements with their own hands, out of wood and clay within their reach. Who can estimate whether New York, after a third world war, would fare materially as well as Yeni Keui after 1922 or as badly as Carthage after 146 B.C.? The self-inflicted wounds from which civilizations die are not, however, those of a material order. In the past, at any rate, it has been the spiritual wounds that have proved incurable; and since, beneath all the variety of cultures, there is uniformity in man's spiritual nature, we may guess that the spiritual devastation produced by a "knock-out blow" is of about the same deadly degree of severity in every case.

Yet, if the coercive method of attaining political world unity is immeasurably disastrous, the co-operative method, on its side, bristles with difficulties.

At the present moment, for example, we can see the great powers trying—perhaps unavoidably—to do at the same time two things which are not only different but which militate against one another all the time and are quite incompatible in the long run. They are trying to launch a new system of co-operative world government without being able to forecast its chances of success, and they are safeguarding themselves against the possibility of its being a failure by continuing to manoeuvre against one another, in the old-fashioned way, in a game of power politics which, if persisted in, can only lead to a third world war and a "knock-out blow."

The United Nations organization may fairly be described as a political machine for putting into effect the maximum possible amount of co-operation between the United States and the Soviet Union—the two great powers who would be the principal antagonists in a final round of naked power politics. The present constitution of the U.N. represents the closest degree of co-operation that the United States and the Soviet Union can reach at present. This constitution is a very loose confederation, and the presiding genius of Chatham House, Lionel Curtis, has pointed out that political associations of this loose-knit type have never proved stable or lasting in the past.

The United Nations organization after the World War of 1939-45 is in the same stage as the United States after the War of Independence. In either case, during the war, a strong common fear of a dangerous common enemy held a loose association of states together. The existence of this common enemy was like a life-belt keeping the association afloat. When the common enemy has been removed by defeat, the association that was launched on his account has to sink or swim without the unintended but most efficacious aid which the common enemy's existence provided. In such post-war circumstances a loose confederation cannot long remain in its original state: sooner or later it must either break up or be transformed into a genuine and effective federation.

A federation, in order to be a lasting success, seems to require a high degree of homogeneity between the constituent states. It is true that in Switzerland and in Canada we see remarkable examples of effective federations that have successfully surmounted formidable differences of language and religion. But would any sober-minded observer to-day venture to name a date at which a federation between the United States and the Soviet Union might become practical politics?—and those are the two states that have to be federated if federal union is to save us from a third world war.

Yet these obvious difficulties in the path of the co-operative method of working towards the inevitable goal of world unity must not daunt us, because this method brings with it certain unique benefits that no alternative can offer.

It is only if there is some constitutional form of world

government that powers can continue to count as great powers—and really to play that part—in spite of their war potential being no longer a match for the war potential of the Soviet Union and the United States. In an even partially constitutional world community, Great Britain, the continental West European countries, and the Dominions can still have an influence in international counsels far in excess of the ratio of their war potential to that of "the Big Two." In an even semi-parliamentary international forum, the political experience, maturity, and moderation of countries like these will weigh heavily in the balance alongside of the grosser weight of Brennus' sword. In a pure power-politics world, on the other hand, these highly civilized but materially less powerful states will count for nothing compared with the United States and the Soviet Union. In a third world war, all of them—except perhaps South Africa, Australia, and New Zealand—will be battlefields. This will be especially the fate of Great Britain and Canada—a prospect of which the Canadians, as well as the English, are well aware.

As we look this dangerous situation in the face, some further questions suggest themselves.

In politics, unlike personal relations, the saying that "two is company, three is none" is the very opposite of the truth. Where eight great powers, or even three great powers, can be gathered together, it is less difficult to manage a co-operative government of the world than where we can muster no more than two. This obvious reflexion raises the question whether it is possible to call into existence a third great power which could be the peer of the United States and the Soviet Union on all planes: a match for each of them in terms of war potential in the arena of power politics, and their moral and political equal in the international council chamber in so far as mankind succeeds in its present political pioneering enterprise of substituting the humane device of constitutional government for the blind play of physical force in the conduct of international relations.

Could this role of a third great power in every sense—a role which the United Kingdom, by itself, no longer has the material strength to sustain—be filled by the British

Commonwealth collectively? The short answer to this question is, I think: "On a bare statistical test, yes; on a geographical and political test, no."

In the counsels of a constitutionally governed world, the states members of the Commonwealth will carry great weight because they are a large contingent in the small company of states that are politically mature, and also because they will be apt to speak with much the same voice —not because their policy will have been regimented, concerted, or even co-ordinated in advance, but because they have vitally important things in common in their political, social, and spiritual traditions and have not ceased to live in unusually close and friendly relations with one another since they have moved off on their separate roads towards the goal of self-government. But, in order to transform the Commonwealth into a third great power by making it as powerful collectively as its members are influential in the aggregate, the countries of the Commonwealth would have to weld themselves together into a massive military unity as highly centralized as the Soviet Union is at all times and as the United States is in time of war; and one has only to state this requirement in order to see that it is quite impracticable. It would mean reversing the direction in which the Commonwealth has been consistently and deliberately moving since 1783, and scrapping cumulative results of this evolution which are the cherished joint achievements of the people of the United Kingdom and the peoples of the other countries in the Commonwealth that have attained self-government, on a par with the United Kingdom, in the course of this last century and a half.

One cannot have one's cake and eat it. One cannot put one's treasure in progressive devolution aiming at a maximum of self-government in as many parts of the Commonwealth as may display or develop an aptitude for governing themselves, and at the same time expect to command the collective military strength which the government at Moscow—to take as an illustration the most pertinent case in point—has been consistently and deliberately building up for the last six centuries at the cost of liberty, variety, and other political and spiritual blessings which the Commonwealth countries have secured for themselves at the cost of collective power. The Commonwealth countries cannot repudiate their ideals and unravel the web of history that they have woven for themselves; they would not do this if they could; and, even if they could and would perform this left-handed miracle, they would have thrown away their birthright in vain; for, at however great a sacrifice of the Commonwealth's characteristic virtues and achievements, the Commonwealth could never be consolidated, either politically or geographically, to a degree that would make it a match for the United States or the Soviet Union in military power in terms of atomic warfare. In the game of power politics, a consolidated Commonwealth would still be a pawn, or at the most a knight, but never a queen.

If the British Commonwealth cannot fill the role of "Third Great Power" in the world after the War of 1939-45, could the part be played by a United States of Europe? This suggestion, too, wears a promising appearance at first sight; but it, in turn, fails to stand the test of examination.

Hitler once said that, if Europe seriously wanted to be a power in the world in our time (and by "power," of course, Hitler meant brute military strength), then Europe must welcome and embrace the Führer's policy; and this hard saying was surely the truth. Hitler's Europe—a Europe forcibly united by German conquest and consolidated under German domination—is the only kind of Europe that could conceivably be a match in war potential for either the Soviet Union or the United States; and a Europe united under German ascendency is utterly abhorrent to all non-German Europeans. Some of them have been subjected to the appalling experience of German conquest and domination twice in one lifetime; most of them have undergone it during the Second World War; and the handful that have escaped have been near enough to the fire and sufficiently scorched by its heat to share the feelings of those who have been burnt outright.

In a European Union excluding both the Soviet Union and the United States—and that, *ex hypothesi,* is the point of departure for trying to construct a European "Third Great Power"—Germany must come to the top sooner or later by one means or another, even if this United Europe were to be presented, at the start, with a Germany that was disarmed and decentralized or even divided. In the *Raum* that lies between the United States and the Soviet Union, Germany occupies a commanding central position; the German nation is half as numerous again as the next most numerous nation in Europe; the German-inhabited heart of Europe (not reckoning in either Austria or the German-speaking part of Switzerland) contains a preponderant proportion of Europe's total resources—in raw materials, plant, and human skill—for heavy industry; and the Germans are as efficient in organizing both human and non-human raw materials for making war as they are inept in trying to govern themselves and intolerable as rulers of other people. On whatever terms Germany were to be included, at the start, in a United Europe that did not include either America or Russia, she would become the mistress of such a Europe in the long run; and, even if the supremacy which she has failed to win by force in two wars were to come to her, this time, peacefully and gradually, no non-German European will believe that the Germans, once they realized that this power was within their grasp, would have the wisdom or self-restraint to refrain from plying the whip and digging in the spurs. This German crux would appear to be an insurmountable obstacle to the construction of a European "Third Great Power."

Nor, in the world as it is to-day, could a militarily consolidated Europe look forward with any more reasonable hope than a militarily consolidated British Commonwealth to making itself a match for the United States or the Soviet Union at the cost of sacrificing cherished liberties. In Western Europe, especially (and Western Europe is the heart of Europe), the traditions of national individuality are so strong that the closest practicable European Union would be too loosely knit to be more than a pawn in the power game, even if this United Europe included the British Isles on the west and the countries now under Russian domination on the east, and even if the peoples of Europe as a whole tried their hardest to swallow Hitler's unpalatable gospel.

Where, then, are we to find our third great power? If

not in Europe and not in the British Commonwealth, then certainly not in China or India; for, in spite of their ancient civilizations and their vast populations, territories, and resources, these two mammoths are most unlikely to prove able to exert their latent strength during the critical period of history that lies, we may guess, immediately ahead of us. We are driven to the conclusion that we cannot hope to ease the tensity of the present international situation by raising the number of powers of the highest military calibre through adding even one to the two that now confront one another. And this leads us to a final question: if we cannot see our way to any rapid attainment of the goal of world unity by constitutional co-operation, can we find some way of postponing the terrible alternative of unification by force? Could two separate political worlds be delimited—one under the hegemony of the United States and the other under the domination of the Soviet Union? And, if a demarcation line between them, encircling the globe, could be drawn without bringing the two great powers to blows, could an American world and a Russian world exist side by side, on the face of the same planet, for more than a short time without falling into war with one another, as, under different social and technological traditions, a Roman world and a Chinese world did once co-exist for several centuries without war and indeed almost without intercourse of any kind? If we could win time for peace by a provisional recourse to insulation, perhaps the social climates of the political universes on either side of the dividing line might gradually influence one another until they had become like enough to make it possible for the Soviet Union and the United States to enter, in an auspicious hour, into that effective political co-operation with one another that is at present beyond their reach by reason of the ideological and cultural gulf that now divides them.

What prospects are there of the United States' and the Soviet Union's practising "non-violent non-co-operation" towards one another over a span of thirty, fifty, a hundred years? If a dividing line could be drawn round the world, would that leave elbow-room enough for each of them in her own sphere? The answer to our question would be an encouraging one if we could render it in economic terms alone; for each of these giants has ample economic elbow-room not only within its own sphere of influence but within its own political frontiers. One of the considerations that drove the rulers of Nazi Germany and contemporary Japan into aggressive war was their inability to provide more than a minority of their young men with jobs that satisfied their expectations, or even with jobs of any kind. By contrast, both Russia and America to-day have openings enough and to spare for the rising generation for as many years as anyone can see ahead. If man were nothing more than economic man, there would be no reason in the world why Russia and America should collide with one another for generations to come. But, unfortunately, man is a political as well as an economic animal. He has to contend not only with want but with fear, and, on the plane of ideas and ideologies, Russia and America cannot so easily avoid crossing each other's path by staying at home and each cultivating her own ample garden. On this plane, the social climates of the two great powers will undoubtedly influence one another, but this mutual influence will not by any means necessarily be pacific in its effect or lead towards reciprocal assimilation; it might alternatively produce a thunderstorm or an explosion. Neither the Capitalist nor the Communist world is immune against subversive influences radiating from the other; for neither of them is the earthly paradise that it claims to be; and they reveal their fears in the measures which each takes to protect itself against the other's radiation. The iron curtain with which the Soviet Union attempts to screen off the outer world tells its own tale eloquently. But on the Capitalist side there is a corresponding, though less paralysing, fear of Communist missionary activity; and, while in democratic countries this fear does not express itself in governmental bans on personal intercourse, it does very readily become inflamed into a panic-stricken hysteria.

Fear, then, might do what want could hardly do in causing Russia and America to fall foul of one another. But how, it might be asked, could this lead to an outright ordeal by battle between antagonists of such extremely unequal strength? The United States, with her immense superiority in industrial equipment, now capped by her monopoly of the "know-how" of the manufacture of the atom bomb, is so much stronger than the Soviet Union that, short of attempting to wrench out of her rival's grip some country upon which the Soviet Union has already fastened its hold, it is apparently possible to-day for the United States to assert her own protectorate over any country she chooses in the no-man's-land between the Soviet Union and herself, with little danger of the Soviet Union's attempting to oppose her by overt force. This is illustrated by the impunity with which the United States has been able to spread her aegis over Greece and Turkey, though these two countries lie on the very threshold of the approaches to the Soviet Union's principal granary and arsenal in the Ukraine and the Caucasus. This would mean that the United States has it in her power to draw the demarcation line between an American and a Russian sphere close round the present fringes of the Soviet Union's political domain. That would give the United States the lion's share of a partitioned globe. And this—so we might be inclined, on first thoughts, to conclude the argument— would augment America's already great preponderance over Russia very notably.

This conclusion, however, is one which second thoughts might revise. On such a division of the world, the preponderance of the United States would indeed be overwhelming statistically, but that, after all, is a theoretical and possibly misleading basis of comparison. In political, social, and ideological terms, would the ratio of strength be the same as in terms of area, population, and productivity? Could an American-led three-quarters or four-fifths of the world be so closely united in itself politically, socially, and ideologically as to be impervious to Russian missionary activity? Or, to put this last question the other way round, how far would the majority of the inhabitants of our hypothetical American sphere of influence be likely to be attracted by the present rather conservative American gospel of out-and-out individualism?

The present American ideology lays great stress on the value of freedom, but seems less keenly alive to the need for social justice. This is not at all surprising in an ideology that is a home-grown product; for, in the United States to-day, the minimum standard of living is so extraordinarily high that there is not a crying need to curb the freedom of the able, the strong, and the rich in order to deal out a dole of elementary social justice to the incompetent, the weak, and the poor. But the material well-being of the people of the United States is, of course, something exceptional in the world as it is to-day. The overwhelming majority of the living generation of mankind—beginning with a foreign-born or foreign-descended underworld in the United States itself, and ending with nearly a thousand million Chinese and Indian peasants and coolies—is to-day "under-privileged," and is becoming increasingly conscious of its plight, and increasingly restive at it. In an unequally divided planet, the majority of this vast mass of primitive suffering humanity would be on the American side of the line; and to appreciate the utterly un-American problems of this miserable flock would demand an almost superhumanly imaginative and benevolent sympathy on the part of their American shepherds. Here, for the American, would be his Achilles' heel, and, for the Russian, his opportunity to sow tares in his adversary's field. To look at the situation through Russian eyes, there might seem, in these circumstances, to be quite a promising prospect of at any rate partly redressing, by propaganda, a balance that had been upset by the American discovery of the "know-how" of the atom bomb.

In a divided world in which the Americans had to fear the effects of Russian propaganda on vast non-American populations under the aegis of the United States, while the Soviet Government, on its side, was terrified of the attraction which the capitalist way of life might have for any Soviet citizens who came into personal contact with it, the prospects of stability and peace would evidently be unpromising if there were no other factor in the situation. Fortunately a third factor, and a constructive one, would be provided by Great Britain and several of the continental West European countries.

In this post-war chapter of history, these West European countries are in an intermediate position between the

United States and the overseas Dominions of the British Commonwealth on the one hand and the politically and economically backward countries on the other. Post-war conditions in Western Europe are not so bad as to give the desperate remedies prescribed by Communism that attraction for Englishmen, Dutchmen, Belgians and Scandinavians that they might have for the flagrantly "underprivileged" majority of Mexicans, Egyptians, Indians, and Chinese; but Western Europe is at the same time not so prosperous as to be able to afford the undiluted regime of private enterprise that still prevails in North America above the Rio Grande. In these circumstances, Great Britain and her West European neighbours are each trying to arrive at a working compromise—suited to their own economic conditions here and now, and subject to modification in either direction as these conditions may change for better or for worse—between unrestricted free enterprise and unlimited socialism.

If these West European social experiments achieve any measure of success, they may prove a valuable contribution to the welfare of the world as a whole. Not that they could serve as "blue prints" for automatic application elsewhere; for the different peoples of the world, who have suddenly been brought into close quarters with one another physically through the many inventions of the West, are still divided from one another politically, economically, socially, and psychologically by differences that it will take time to overcome. In a world in this stage of social evolution, a particular local and temporary solution of a world-wide problem cannot be applicable, as it stands, outside the country where it has been worked out by trial and error to fit the local conditions of the moment. But perhaps here we have put our finger on the service which the West European countries can perform for the world to-day. An awkward feature of the American ideology of free enterprise—as well as of the Russian ideology of Communism—is precisely that it presents a social "blue print" as a panacea for every conceivable social ill in every known set of social circumstances. But this does not fit the facts of real life. In real life, every social system that can be observed at first hand or reconstructed from records is

a mixed system, lying at some point between the two theoretical poles of undiluted socialism and undiluted free
enterprise. The statesman's task is to strike that note in
the gamut that tunes in with the particular social circumstances of his time and place; to find the right mixture
between free enterprise and socialism for driving his truck-
of-state on the particular gradient on which it happens to
be travelling at the moment. What the world needs above
all now is to get the issue of free enterprise versus socialism
off its ideological pedestal and to treat it, not as a matter
of semi-religious faith and fanaticism, but as a common-
sense, practical question of trial and error, of, more or less,
circumstance and adaptation.

If Western Europe could influence the rest of the world
in this direction in the chapter of history ahead of us, that
might be not only a great contribution to prosperity but
also a great service to peace. It might be one of the influences that would gradually break down the social, cultural,
and ideological barriers between the United States and the
Soviet Union. But, as has been suggested more than once
in this paper, there has to be a minimum of constitutional
co-operative government in the world to allow countries
of the material calibre of the United Kingdom or the
Netherlands to exercise influence in a world-society in
which, as a result of one of those changes in the scale of
material life that overtake us from time to time, the only
surviving great powers, in terms of sheer war potential, are
giants of the tremendous calibre of the Soviet Union and
the United States.

Could this West European influence work its beneficent
unifying effect in a world unequally divided into an American and a Russian sphere? If it could, this might be a
second line to fall back on if our second attempt at co-
operative world government were to fail like the first.
But it would, of course, be far better if the United Nations
organization could be carried through to success, and this,
I would suggest to you most earnestly, is the goal towards
which we ought still to strive with all our might, without
allowing ourselves to be dismayed or deterred by difficulties, however baffling, at a stage which is, after all, still
a very early one in the United Nations' career.

8

CIVILIZATION ON TRIAL

I

Our present Western outlook on history is an extraordinarily contradictory one. While our historical horizon has been expanding vastly in both the space dimension and the time dimension, our historical vision—what we actually do see, in contrast to what we now could see if we chose —has been contracting rapidly to the narrow field of what a horse sees between its blinkers or what a U-boat commander sees through his periscope.

This is certainly extraordinary; yet it is only one of a number of contradictions of this kind that seem to be characteristic of the times in which we are living. There are other examples that probably loom larger in the minds of most of us. For instance, our world has risen to an unprecedented degree of humanitarian feeling. There is now a recognition of the human rights of people of all classes, nations, and races; yet at the same time we have sunk to perhaps unheard-of depths of class warfare, nationalism, and racialism. These bad passions find vent in cold-blooded, scientifically planned cruelties; and the two incompatible states of mind and standards of conduct are to be seen to-day, side by side, not merely in the same world, but sometimes in the same country and even in the same soul.

Again, we now have an unprecedented power of production side by side with unprecedented shortages. We have invented machines to work for us, but have less spare labour than ever before for human service—even for such an essential and elementary service as helping mothers to look after their babies. We have persistent alternations of widespread unemployment with famines of man-power. Undoubtedly, the contrast between our expanding historical horizon and our contracting historical vision is something characteristic of our age. Yet, looked at in itself, what an astonishing contradiction it is!

Let us remind ourselves first of the recent expansion of our horizon. In space, our Western field of vision has expanded to take in the whole of mankind over all the habitable and traversable surface of this planet, and the whole stellar universe in which this planet is an infinitesimally small speck of dust. In time, our Western field of vision has expanded to take in all the civilizations that have risen and fallen during these last 6000 years; the previous history of the human race back to its genesis between 600,000 and a million years ago; the history of life on this planet back to perhaps 800 million years ago. What a marvellous widening of our historical horizon! Yet, at the same time, our field of historical vision has been contracting; it has been tending to shrink within the narrow limits in time and space of the particular republic or kingdom of which each of us happens to be a citizen. The oldest surviving Western states—say France or England—have so far had no more than a thousand years of continuous political existence; the largest existing Western State—say Brazil or the United States—embraces only a very small fraction of the total inhabited surface of the Earth.

Before the widening of our horizon began—before our Western seamen circumnavigated the globe, and before our Western cosmogonists and geologists pushed out the bounds of our universe in both time and space—our prenationalist mediaeval ancestors had a broader and juster historical vision than we have to-day. For them, history did not mean the history of one's own parochial community; it meant the history of Israel, Greece, and Rome. And, even if they were mistaken in believing that the world was created in 4004 B.C., it is at any rate better to look as far back as 4004 B.C. than to look back no farther than the Declaration of Independence or the voyages of the *Mayflower* or Columbus or Hengist and Horsa. (As a matter of fact, 4004 B.C. happens, though our ancestors did not know this, to be a quite important date: it approximately marks the first appearance of representatives of the species of human society called civilizations.)

Again, for our ancestors, Rome and Jerusalem meant much more than their own home towns. When our Anglo-Saxon ancestors were converted to Roman Christianity at the end of the sixth century of the Christian era, they learned Latin, studied the treasures of sacred and profane literature to which a knowledge of the Latin language gives access, and went on pilgrimages to Rome and Jerusalem—and this in an age when the difficulties and dangers of travelling were such as to make modern war-time travelling seem child's play. Our ancestors seem to have been big-minded, and this is a great intellectual virtue as well as a great moral one, for national histories are unintelligible within their own time limits and space limits.

II

In the time dimension, you cannot understand the history of England if you begin only at the coming of the English to Britain, any better than you can understand the history of the United States if you begin only at the coming of the English to North America. In the space dimension, likewise, you cannot understand the history of a country if you cut its outlines out of the map of the world and rule out of consideration anything that has originated outside that particular country's frontiers.

What are the epoch-making events in the national histories of the United States and the United Kingdom? Working back from the present towards the past, I should say they were the two world wars, the Industrial Revolution, the Reformation, the Western voyages of discovery, the Renaissance, the conversion to Christianity. Now I defy anyone to tell the history of either the United States or the United Kingdom without making these events the cardinal ones, or to explain these events as local American or local English affairs. To explain these major events in the history of any Western country, the smallest unit that one can take into account is the whole of Western Christendom. By Western Christendom I mean the Roman

Catholic and Protestant world—the adherents of the Patriarchate of Rome who have maintained their allegiance to
the Papacy, together with the former adherents who have
repudiated it.

But the history of Western Christendom, too, is unintelligible within its own time limits and space limits.
While Western Christendom is a much better unit than
the United States or the United Kingdom or France for a
historian to operate with, it too turns out, on inspection,
to be inadequate. In the time dimension, it goes back only
to the close of the Dark Ages following the collapse of
the western part of the Roman Empire; that is, it goes
back less than 1300 years, and 1300 years is less than a
quarter of the 6000 years during which the species of
society represented by Western Christendom has been in
existence. Western Christendom is a civilization belonging
to the third of the three generations of civilizations that
there have been so far.

In the space dimension, the narrowness of the limits of
Western Christendom is still more striking. If you look at
the physical map of the world as a whole, you will see
that the small part of it which is dry land consists of a
single continent—Asia—which has a number of peninsulas
and off-lying islands. Now, what are the farthest limits to
which Western Christendom has managed to expand? You
will find them at Alaska and Chile on the west and at Finland and Dalmatia on the east. What lies between those
four points is Western Christendom's domain at its widest.
And what does that domain amount to? Just the tip of
Asia's European peninsula, together with a couple of large
islands. (By these two large islands, I mean, of course,
North and South America.) Even if you add in the outlying and precarious footholds of the Western world in
South Africa, Australia, and New Zealand, its total habitable present area amounts to only a very minor part of
the total habitable area of the surface of the planet. And
you cannot understand the history of Western Christendom within its own geographical limits.

Western Christendom is a product of Christianity, but
Christianity did not arise in the Western world; it arose
outside the bounds of Western Christendom, in a district

that lies today within the domain of a different civilization: Islam. We Western Christians did once try to capture from the Muslims the cradle of our religion in Palestine. If the Crusades had succeeded, Western Christendom would have slightly broadened its footing on the all-important Asiatic mainland. But the Crusades ended in failure.

Western Christendom is merely one of five civilizations that survive in the world to-day; and these are merely five out of about nineteen that one can identify as having come into existence since the first appearance of representatives of this species of society about 6000 years ago.

III

To take the four other surviving civilizations first: if the firmness of a civilization's foothold on the continent—by which I mean the solid land-mass of Asia—may be taken as giving a rough indication of that civilization's relative expectation of life, then the other four surviving civilizations are "better lives"—in the jargon of the life insurance business—than our own Western Christendom.

Our sister civilization, Orthodox Christendom, straddles the continent from the Baltic to the Pacific and from the Mediterranean to the Arctic Ocean: it occupies the northern half of Asia and the eastern half of Asia's European peninsula. Russia overlooks the back doors of all the other civilizations; from White Russia and North-Eastern Siberia she overlooks the Polish and Alaskan back doors of our own Western world; from the Caucasus and Central Asia she overlooks the back doors of the Islamic and Hindu worlds; from Central and Eastern Siberia she overlooks the back door of the Far Eastern world.

Our half-sister civilization, Islam, also has a firm footing on the continent. The domain of Islam stretches from the heart of the Asiatic continent in North-Western China all the way to the west coast of Asia's African peninsula. At Dakar, the Islamic world commands the continental approaches to the straits that divide Asia's African peninsula from the island of South America. Islam also has a firm footing in Asia's Indian peninsula.

As for the Hindu society and the Far Eastern society, it

needs no demonstration to show that the 400 million Hindus and the 400 or 500 million Chinese have a firm foothold on the continent.

But we must not exaggerate the importance of any of these surviving civilizations just because, at this moment, they happen to be survivors. If, instead of thinking in terms of "expectation of life," we think in terms of achievement, a rough indication of relative achievement may be found in the giving of birth to individual souls that have conferred lasting blessings on the human race.

Now who are the individuals who are the greatest benefactors of the living generation of mankind? I should say: Confucius and Lao-tse; the Buddha; the Prophets of Israel and Judah; Zoroaster, Jesus, and Muhammad; and Socrates. And not one of these lasting benefactors of mankind happens to be a child of any of the five living civilizations. Confucius and Lao-tse were children of a now extinct Far Eastern civilization of an earlier generation; the Buddha was the child of a now extinct Indian civilization of an earlier generation. Hosea, Zoroaster, Jesus, and Muhammad were children of a now extinct Syrian civilization. Socrates was the child of a now extinct Greek civilization.

Within the last 400 years, all the five surviving civilizations have been brought into contact with each other as a result of the enterprise of two of them: the expansion of Western Christendom from the tip of Asia's European peninsula over the ocean, and the expansion of Orthodox Christendom overland across the whole breadth of the Asiatic continent.

The expansion of Western Christendom displays two special features: being oceanic, it is the only expansion of a civilization to date that has been literally world-wide in the sense of extending over the whole habitable portion of the Earth's surface; and, owing to the "conquest of space and time" by modern mechanical means, the spread of the network of Western material civilization has brought the different parts of the world into far closer physical contact than ever before. But, even in these points, the expansion of the Western civilization differs in degree only, and not in kind, from the contemporary overland expansion of Russian Orthodox Christendom, and from similar expansions of other civilizations at earlier dates.

There are earlier expansions that have made important contributions towards the present unification of mankind —with its corollary, the unification of our vision of human history. The now extinct Syrian civilization was propagated to the Atlantic coasts of Asia's European and African peninsulas westward by the Phoenicians, to the tip of Asia's Indian peninsula south-eastwards by the Himyarites and Nestorians, and to the Pacific north-eastwards by the Manichaeans and Nestorians. It expanded in two directions overseas and in a third direction overland. Any visitor to Peking will have seen a striking monument of the Syrian civilization's overland cultural conquests. In the trilingual inscriptions of the Manchu Dynasty of China at Peking, the Manchu and Mongol texts are inscribed in the Syriac form of our alphabet, not in Chinese characters.

Other examples of the expansion of now extinct civilizations are the propagation of the Greek civilization overseas westwards to Marseilles by the Greeks themselves, overland northwards to the Rhine and Danube by the Romans, and overland eastwards to the interiors of India and China by the Macedonians; and the expansion of the Sumerian civilization in all directions overland from its cradle in Iraq.

IV

As a result of these successive expansions of particular civilizations, the whole habitable world has now been unified into a single great society. The movement through which this process has been finally consummated is the modern expansion of Western Christendom. But we have to bear in mind, first, that this expansion of Western Christendom has merely completed the unification of the world and has not been the agency that has produced more than the last stage of the process; and, second, that, though the unification of the world has been finally achieved within a Western framework, the present Western ascendency in the world is certain not to last.

In a unified world, the eighteen non-Western civilizations—four of them living, fourteen of them extinct—will assuredly reassert their influence. And as, in the course of generations and centuries, a unified world gradually works its way toward an equilibrium between its diverse component cultures, the Western component will gradually be relegated to the modest place which is all that it can expect to retain in virtue of its intrinsic worth by comparison with those other cultures—surviving and extinct—which the Western society, through its modern expansion, has brought into association with itself and with one another.

History, seen in this perspective, makes, I feel, the following call upon historians of our generation and of the generations that will come after ours. If we are to perform the full service that we have the power to perform for our fellow human beings—the important service of helping them to find their bearings in a unified world—we must make the necessary effort of imagination and effort of will to break our way out of the prison walls of the local and short-lived histories of our own countries and our own cultures, and we must accustom ourselves to taking a synoptic view of history as a whole.

Our first task is to perceive, and to present to other people, the history of all the known civilizations, surviving and extinct, as a unity. There are, I believe, two ways in which this can be done.

One way is to study the encounters between civilizations, of which I have mentioned four outstanding examples. These encounters between civilizations are historically illuminating, not only because they bring a number of civilizations into a single focus of vision, but also because, out of encounters between civilizations, the higher religions have been born—the worship, perhaps originally Sumerian, of the Great Mother and her Son who suffers and dies and rises again; Judaism and Zoroastrianism, which sprang from an encounter between the Syrian and Babylonian civilizations; Christianity and Islam, which sprang from an encounter between the Syrian and Greek civilizations; the Mahayana form of Buddhism and Hinduism, which sprang from an encounter between the Indian and Greek civilizations. The future of mankind in this world—if mankind is going to have a future in this world—lies, I believe, with these higher religions that have appeared within the last

4000 years (and all but the first within the last 3000 years), and not with the civilizations whose encounters have provided opportunities for the higher religions to come to birth.

A second way of studying the history of all the known civilizations as a unity is to make a comparative study of their individual histories, looking at them as so many representatives of one particular species of the genus Human Society. If we map out the principal phases in the histories of civilizations—their births, growths, breakdowns, and declines—we can compare their experiences phase by phase; and by this method of study we shall perhaps be able to sort out their common experiences, which are specific, from their unique experiences, which are individual. In this way we may be able to work out a morphology of the species of society called civilizations.

If, by the use of these two methods of study, we can arrive at a unified vision of history, we shall probably find that we need to make very far-going adjustments of the perspective in which the histories of divers civilizations and peoples appear when looked at through our peculiar present-day Western spectacles.

In setting out to adjust our perspective, we shall be wise, I suggest, to proceed simultaneously on two alternative assumptions. One of these alternatives is that the future of mankind may not, after all, be going to be catastrophic and that, even if the Second World War prove not to have been the last, we shall survive the rest of this batch of world wars as we survived the first two bouts, and shall eventually win our way out into calmer waters. The other possibility is that these first two world wars may be merely overtures to some supreme catastrophe that we are going to bring on ourselves.

This second, more unpleasant, alternative has been made a very practical possibility by mankind's unfortunately having discovered how to tap atomic energy before we have succeeded in abolishing the institution of war. Those contradictions and paradoxes in the life of the world in our time, which I took as my starting point, also look like symptoms of serious social and spiritual sickness, and their existence—which is one of the portentous features in the landscape of contemporary history—is another indication that we ought to take the more unpleasant of our alternatives as a serious possibility, and not just as a bad joke.

On either alternative, I suggest that we historians ought to concentrate our own attention—and direct the attention of our listeners and readers—upon the histories of those civilizations and peoples which, in the light of their past performances, seem likely, in a unified world, to come to the front in the long run in one or other of the alternative futures that may be lying in wait for mankind.

V

If the future of mankind in a unified world is going to be on the whole a happy one, then I would prophesy that there is a future in the Old World for the Chinese, and in the island of North America for the *Canadiens*. Whatever the future of mankind in North America, I feel pretty confident that these French-speaking Canadians, at any rate, will be there at the end of the story.

On the assumption that the future of mankind is to be very catastrophic, I should have prophesied, even as lately as a few years ago, that whatever future we might be going to have would lie with the Tibetans and the Eskimos, because each of these peoples occupied, till quite lately, an unusually sheltered position. "Sheltered" means, of course, sheltered from the dangers arising from human folly and wickedness, not sheltered from the rigors of the physical environment. Mankind has been master of its physical environment, sufficiently for practical purposes, since the middle palaeolithic age; since that time, man's only dangers—but these have been deadly dangers—have come from man himself. But the homes of the Tibetans and the Eskimos are sheltered no longer, because we are on the point of managing to fly over the North Pole and over the Himalayas, and both Northern Canada and Tibet would (I think) be likely to be theatres of a future Russo-American war.

If mankind is going to run amok with atom bombs, I personally should look to the Negrito Pygmies of Central Africa to salvage some fraction of the present heritage of mankind. (Their eastern cousins in the Philippines and in the Malay Peninsula would probably perish with the rest of us, as they both live in what have now come to be dangerously exposed positions.)

The African Negritos are said by our anthropologists to have an unexpectedly pure and lofty conception of the nature of God and of God's relation to man. They might be able to give mankind a fresh start; and, though we should then have lost the achievements of the last 6000 to 10,000 years, what are 10,000 years compared to the 600,000 or a million years for which the human race has already been in existence?

The extreme possibility of catastrophe is that we might succeed in exterminating the whole human race, African Negritos and all.

On the evidence of the past history of life on this planet, even that is not entirely unlikely. After all, the reign of man on the Earth, if we are right in thinking that man established his present ascendency in the middle palaeolithic age, is so far only about 100,000 years old, and what is that compared to the 500 million or 800 million years during which life has been in existence on the surface of this planet? In the past, other forms of life have enjoyed reigns which have lasted for almost inconceivably longer periods—and which yet at last have come to an end. There was a reign of the giant armored reptiles which may have lasted about 80 million years; say from about the year 130 million to the year 50 million before the present day. But the reptiles' reign came to an end. Long before that —perhaps 300 million years ago—there was a reign of giant armoured fishes—creatures that had already accomplished the tremendous achievement of growing a moveable lower jaw. But the reign of the fishes came to an end.

The winged insects are believed to have come into existence about 250 million years ago. Perhaps the higher winged insects—the social insects that have anticipated mankind in creating an institutional life—are still waiting for their reign on Earth to come. If the ants and bees were one day to acquire even that glimmer of intellectual understanding that man has possessed in his day, and if they were then to make their own shot at seeing history in perspective, they might see the advent of the mammals, and the brief reign of the human mammal, as almost irrelevant episodes, "full of sound and fury, signifying nothing."

The challenge to us, in our generation, is to see to it that this interpretation of history shall not become the true one.

9

RUSSIA'S BYZANTINE HERITAGE

I

If this were a sermon, not an essay, the inevitable text would be a famous line of Horace's: *Naturam expellas furca, tamen usque recurret:* "You may throw Nature out with a pitchfork, but she will keep coming back."

The present regime in Russia claims to have made a clean cut with Russia's past—not, perhaps, in all minor externals, but at any rate in most things that matter. And the West has taken it from the Bolsheviks that they have done what they say. We have believed and trembled. Yet reflexion suggests that it is not so easy to repudiate one's heritage. When we do try to repudiate the past, it has, as Horace knew, a sly way of coming back on us in a thinly disguised form. Some familiar examples may bring the point home.

In 1763 it looked as if the British conquest of Canada had revolutionized the political map of North America by putting an end to the partition of the continent which had followed from the competitive colonization of the St. Lawrence valley by the French and the Atlantic seaboard by the English; but the appearance of this revolutionary change turned out to be illusory. The two dominions that had been united in 1763 were sundered again in 1783. It is true that, in the once-again divided continent, it was the St. Lawrence valley, now, that was British, whereas it had been the Atlantic seaboard before. But this transposition of the British domain in North America was a minor variation compared to the re-emergence, after twenty years of unity, of the original division of the continent into two politically separate fractions.

In a similar way, it looked as though the Restoration of 1660 had revolutionized the religious life of England by reuniting an English Protestant Church which had split before the close of the sixteenth century into an Episcopalian and a Presbyterian faction. Appearances, however, were illusory here again; for the sixteenth-century breakaway from Episcopalianism reasserted itself in the eighteenth century in the emergence of the new Methodist type of non-conformity.

In France, again, Roman Catholic orthodoxy has been disappointed, time and again, of the hope that it had succeeded in re-establishing religious uniformity once and for all by suppressing a heresy. The Albigenses were suppressed, only to break out again as Huguenots. When the Huguenots were suppressed in their turn, they broke out again as Jansenists, who were the nearest thing to Calvinists that Roman Catholics could be. When the Jansenists were quashed they broke out again as Deists; and to-day the division of the French into a clerical and an anti-clerical faction still reproduces the thirteenth-century division between Catholics and Adoptionists (or whatever the doctrine may have been that the Albigenses really held), in spite of repeated attempts, during the last seven centuries, to dragoon the French people into religious unity.

In the light of these obvious historical illustrations of Horace's theme, let us try to look into the relation of present-day Russia to Russia's past.

Marxism wears the appearance of being a new order in Russia because, like the new way of life introduced into Russia in an earlier chapter by Peter the Great, it came from the West. If these fits of Westernization have been spontaneous, it might be plausible to present them as genuine new departures. But has Russia been Westernizing herself voluntarily or under duress?

On this point, the present writer's personal beliefs are as follows: For nearly a thousand years past, the Russians have, as he sees it, been members, not of our Western civilization, but of the Byzantine—a sister society, of the same Graeco-Roman parentage as ours, but a distinct and different civilization from our own, nevertheless. The Russian members of this Byzantine family have always put up a strong resistance against threats of being overwhelmed by our Western world, and they are keeping up this resistance to-day. In order to save themselves from being conquered and forcibly assimilated by the West, they have repeatedly been constrained to make themselves masters of our Western technology. This *tour de force* has been achieved at least twice over in Russian history: first by Peter the Great, and then again by the Bolsheviks. The effort has had to be repeated, because Western technology has continued to advance. Peter the Great had to master the arts of the seventeenth-century Western shipwright and drill-sergeant. The Bolsheviks had to get even with our Western industrial revolution. And no sooner have they done that than the West gets ahead of Russia again by discovering the "know-how" of the manufacture of the atom bomb.

All this puts the Russians in a dilemma. In order to save themselves from being completely Westernized by force, they have to Westernize themselves partially, and in this they have to take the initiative if they are to make sure of both Westernizing in time and of keeping the repugnant process within bounds. The fateful question is, of course: Can one manage to adopt an alien civilization partially without being drawn on, step by step, into adopting it as a whole?

We may feel our way towards an answer to this question by glancing back at the principal chapters in the history of Russia's relations with the West. In the West we have a notion that Russia is the aggressor, as indeed she has all the appearance of being when looked at through Western eyes. We think of her as the devourer of the lion's share in the eighteenth-century partitions of Poland; as the oppressor of both Poland and Finland in the nineteenth century; and as the arch-aggressor in the post-war world of to-day. To Russian eyes, appearances are just the contrary. The Russians see themselves as the perpetual victims of aggression from the West, and, on a longer historical perspective, there is perhaps a greater justification than we might suppose for the Russian point of view. A detached investigator, if such could be found, might report that the Russian's eighteenth-century successes against Sweden and Poland were counter-offensives, and that their gains in territory in these counter-offensives are less characteristic of the relations between Russia and the West than the Russian losses of territory to the West both before and after.

"The Varangians," who founded the first rudiments of a Russian state by seizing command of the navigable inland waterways and thereby establishing their domination over the primitive Slav populations in the hinterland, seem to have been Scandinavian barbarians who had been stirred up and set moving—eastward as well as westward—by the northward march of Western Christendom under Charlemagne. Their descendants in their home country were converted to Western Christianity and appeared, in their turn, over Russia's western horizon as the latter-day Swedes: heathens transformed into heretics without having been cured of being aggressors. Then again, in the fourteenth century, the best part of Russia's original domain—almost the whole of White Russia and the Ukraine—was shorn away from Russian Orthodox Christendom and annexed to Western Christendom through being conquered by the Lithuanians and the Poles. (The fourteenth-century Polish conquests of originally Russian ground in Galicia were not recovered by Russia till the last phase of the War of 1939-45).

In the seventeenth century, Polish invaders penetrated the hitherto unconquered part of Russia as far as Moscow and were driven out only by a supreme effort on the Russian side, while the Swedes shut Russia off from the Baltic by annexing the whole east coast down to the northern limits of the Polish dominions. In 1812 Napoleon repeated the Poles' seventeenth-century exploit; and, after the turn of the nineteenth and twentieth centuries, blows from the West came raining down on Russia thick and fast. The Germans, invading her in the years 1915-18, overran the Ukraine and reached Transcaucasia. After the collapse of the Germans, it was the turn of the British, French, Americans, and Japanese to invade Russia from four different quarters in the years 1918-20. And then, in 1941, the Germans returned to the attack—more formidable and more ruthless than ever. It is true that, during the eighteenth and nineteenth centuries, Russian armies also marched and fought on Western ground, but they came in always as allies of one Western power against another in some Western family quarrel. In the annals of the centuries-long warfare between the two Christendoms, it would seem to be the fact that the Russians have been the victims of aggression, and the Westerners the aggressors, more often than not.

The Russians have incurred the hostility of the West through being obstinate adherents of an alien civilization, and, down to the Bolshevik revolution of 1917, this Russian "mark of the beast" was the Byzantine civilization of Eastern Orthodox Christendom. The Russians embraced Eastern Orthodox Christianity at the end of the tenth century, and it is significant that this was a deliberate choice on their part. Alternatively they might have followed the example of either their south-eastern neighbours, the Khazars, on the Steppes, who had been converted in the eight century to Judaism, or their eastern neighbours the White Bulgarians, down the Volga, who had been converted in the tenth century to Islam. In spite of these precedents, the Russians made their own distinctive choice by adopting the Eastern Orthodox Christianity of the Byzantine world; and, after the capture of Constantinople by the Turks in 1453 and the extinction of the last remnant of the East Roman Empire, the principality of Moscow, which by then had become the rallying point of Russian Orthodox Christendom against both Muslims and Latins, self-consciously took over the Byzantine heritage from the Greeks.

In 1472 the Grand Duke of Moscow, Ivan III, married Zoë Palaeológos, a niece of the last Greek wearer, at Constantinople, of the East Roman Imperial Crown. In 1547 Ivan IV ("the Terrible") had himself crowned Czar or East Roman Emperor; and, though the office was vacant, his assumption of it was audacious, considering that, in the past, Russian princes had been ecclesiastical subjects of a Metropolitan of Kiev or Moscow who had been a subordinate of the Oecumenical Patriarch of Constantinople—a prelate who, in his turn, was a political subject of the Greek Emperor at Constantinople, whose style, title, and prerogative were now being assumed by the Muscovite Grand Duke Ivan. The last and decisive step was taken in 1589, when the reigning Oecumenical Patriarch of Constantinople, now a servant of the Turks, was induced or coerced, during a visit to Moscow, to raise his former subordinate the Metropolitan of Moscow to the status of an independent Patriarch. Though the Greek Oecumenical Patriarch has continued, down to this day, to be recognised as *primus inter pares* among the heads of the Orthodox churches—which, though united in doctrine and liturgy, are independent of each other in government—the Russian Orthodox Church, from the moment when its independence was conceded to it, became the most important of all the Orthodox Churches *de facto,* since it was then by far the strongest in numbers and was also the only one that enjoyed the backing of a powerful sovereign state.

From 1453 onwards Russia was the only Orthodox Christian country of any account that was not under Muslim rule, and the capture of Constantinople by the Turks was dramatically avenged by Ivan the Terrible when he captured Qazan from the Tatars a century later. This was another step in Russia's assumption of the Byzantine heritage, and Russia was not just being cast for this role by the blind working of impersonal historical forces. The Russians knew well what they were about: in the sixteenth century, the policy was expounded with arresting clarity and confidence in a celebrated passage of an open letter addressed to the Grand Duke Basil III of Moscow, whose reign intervened between those of the third and the fourth Ivan, by the monk Theophilus of Pskov:

The Church of Old Rome fell because of its heresy; the gates of the Second Rome, Constantinople, have been hewn down by the axes of the infidel Turks; but the Church of Moscow, the Church of the New Rome, shines brighter than the Sun in the whole Universe . . . Two Romes have fallen, but the Third stands fast; a fourth there cannot be.

In thus assuming the Byzantine heritage deliberately and self-consciously, the Russians were taking over, among other things, the traditional Byzantine attitude towards the West; and this has had a profound effect on Russia's own attitude towards the West, not only before the Revolution of 1917 but after it.

The Byzantine attitude towards the West is a simple one, and it ought not to be difficult for Westerners to understand. Indeed, we ought to be able to sympathize with it, because it springs from the same extravagantly improbable belief that we happen to hold about ourselves. We "Franks" (as the Byzantines and the Muslims call us) sincerely believe that we are the chosen heirs of Israel, Greece, and Rome—the Heirs of the Promise, with whom, in consequence, the future lies. We have not been shaken out of this belief by the recent geological and astronomical discoveries that have pushed out the bounds of our universe so immensely far in time as well as in space. From the primal nebula through the protozoon, and from the protozoon through primitive man, we still trace a divinely appointed genealogy which culminates teleologically in ourselves. The Byzantines do just the same, except that they award themselves the improbable birthright that, on our Western scheme, is ours. The Heirs of the Promise, the people with the unique future, are not the Franks but the Byzantines—so runs the Byzantine version of the myth. And this article of faith has, of course, one very practical corollary. When Byzantium and the West are at odds, Byzantium is always right and the West is always wrong.

It will be evident that this sense of orthodoxy and sense of destiny, which have been taken over by the Russians from the Byzantine Greeks, are just as characteristic of the present Communist regime in Russia as they were of the previous Eastern Orthodox Christian dispensation there. Marxism is, no doubt, a Western creed, but it is a Western creed which puts the Western civilization "on the spot"; and it was, therefore, possible for a twentieth-century Russian whose father had been a nineteenth-century "Slavophil" and his grandfather a devout Eastern Orthodox Christian to become a devoted Marxian without being required to make any reorientation of his inherited attitude towards the West. For the Russian Marxian, Russian Slavophil, and Russian Orthodox Christian alike, Russia is "Holy Russia," and the Western world of the Borgias and Queen Victoria, Smiles' Self-Help and Tammany Hall, is uniformly heretical, corrupt, and decadent. A creed which allows the Russian people to preserve this traditional Russian condemnation of the West intact, while at the same time serving the Russian government as an instrument for industrializing Russia in order to save her from being conquered by an already industrialized West, is one of those providentially convenient gifts of the gods that naturally fall into the lap of the Chosen People.

II

Let us look a little further into this Byzantine heritage of Russia's which does not seem to have lost its hold on the Marxian Russia of to-day. When we turn back to the Greek first chapter of Byzantine history in Asia Minor and Constantinople in the early Middle Ages, what are our sister society's salient features? Two stand out above the rest: the conviction (mentioned already) that Byzantium is always right, and the institution of the totalitarian state.

The germ of the conviction of being always right first sprouted in the souls of the Greeks at a moment when, so far from feeling superior to the West, they were at a disadvantage that was intensely humiliating. After having made a mess of their political life for centuries, the Greeks at last had peace imposed on them by the Romans. For the Greeks, the Roman Empire was a necessity of life and, at the same time, an intolerable affront to their pride. This was, for them, a formidable psychological dilemma. They found their way out of it by making the Roman Empire a Greek affair. In the age of the Antonines, Greek men of letters took possession of the idea of the Roman Empire by presenting it as a practical realization of the ideal kingdom of Plato's philosopher king, while Greek men of action gained admission to the Roman public service. In the fourth century after Christ, the Roman Emperor Constantine planted his New Rome at Byzantium, on the site of an ancient Greek city. Constantinople was intended by its

Latin-speaking founder to be as Latin as Rome itself, but by the time of Justinian, only two hundred years later, Byzantium had become Greek again—though Justinian was a zealous champion of the Latin language that was his, as well as Constantine's, mother tongue. In the fifth century, the Roman Empire survived in its Greek and semi-Hellenized Oriental provinces when it collapsed in the West, including Italy itself. At the turn of the sixth and seventh centuries, in the time of Pope Gregory the Great, the Latin Old Rome was a derelict, neglected outpost of an Empire of which the Greek New Rome was now the centre and seat of power.

Down to this day, if you ask a Greek peasant what he is, and he forgets for a moment that he was taught at school to say "Hellene," he will tell you that he is "Romyós," meaning a Greek-speaking Eastern Orthodox Christian subject of an ideally eternal Roman Empire with its capital at Constantinople. The use of the name "Hellene" to mean "Modern Greek" is an archaistic revival; in popular usage since the sixth century of the Christian era, the antithesis between "Roman" (now meaning Greek-speaking adherent of the Orthodox Christian Church) and "Hellene" (meaning pagan) has replaced the classical antithesis between "Hellene" (meaning civilized man) and "Barbarian." That may look like a revolutionary change, yet nature *"will* keep coming back," for the one thing which, for the Greek, is of supreme importance has remained constant in spite of this change. The Greek is always right. So long as the pagan Greek culture is the hall-mark of superiority, the Greek glories in being a Hellene. But when the tables are turned and Hellenism in its turn is cast out to become barbarism's bedfellow in the outer darkness, the Greek changes his tune and now proclaims himself a subject of the Christian Roman Empire. Hellenism may lose caste, so long as the Greek does not.

Having thus adroitly vindicated his title to be the true Heir of the Kingdom, whatever kingdom it might be, the Greek Orthodox Christian went on to put Latin Christendom "on the spot." In the ninth century, the Greek Oecumenical Patriarch of Constantinople, Photius, pointed out that the Western Christians had become schismatics. They had tampered with the Creed. They had inserted an unauthorized *filioque*. Byzantium is always right, but she had a particular reason, at that moment, for putting Western Christendom in the wrong. Photius made his damaging theological discovery about the Latins during the first round of a political contest between Byzantine Christendom and Western Christendom in which Photius himself was a leading combatant.

This contest, like that between the United States and the Soviet Union to-day, was for the allegiance of a political and ideological no-man's-land lying between the two rival powers. In the ninth century the heathen, who, during "the Wandering of the Nations," had occupied South-Eastern Europe from the gates of Constantinople to the gates of Vienna, began to feel attracted by the Christian civilization of their neighbours. To which of the two Christendoms should they turn for light? To the Greek Orthodox Christendom of the Byzantines? Or to the Latin Catholic Christendom of the Franks? Prudence suggested approaching whichever of the two Christian powers was geographically the more remote and therefore politically the less dangerous; so the Moravian heathen, who were "up against" the Franks, turned to Constantinople, while the Bulgarian heathen, who were "up against" the Byzantines, turned to Rome—as Greece and Turkey to-day, lying, as they do, on Russia's and not on America's threshold, have turned to Washington, not to Moscow. When once these overtures had been made and had not been rejected, the competition between the West and Byzantium for the prize of South-Eastern Europe had begun, and the stakes were so high that the rivalry was almost bound to end in rupture. The crisis which Photius had brought to a head was unexpectedly postponed by the irruption of the Hungarians. When this fresh horde of heathen established itself astride the Danube towards the close of the ninth century, Eastern Orthodox Christendom and Catholic Christendom were opportunely insulated from one another again. But, upon the conversion of the Hungarians to Western Christianity at the end of the tenth century, the quarrel between the rival Christendoms burst out again and quickly festered into the definitive schism of 1054.

Thereafter, Byzantine pride suffered a terrible series of reverses. Frankish Christians from the west and Turkish Muslims from the east now fell upon the Byzantine world simultaneously. The interior of Russia, around Moscow, was the only part of Eastern Orthodox Christendom that did not eventually lose its political independence. The homelands of the Byzantine civilization in Asia Minor and the Balkan Peninsula were completely submerged, and, in the last phase of their discomfiture, on the eve of the second and final fall of Constantinople in 1453, the only freedom of manoeuvre that was left to the Greeks was to choose between two odious alien yokes. Faced with this grievous choice, the mediaeval Greek Orthodox Christians passionately rejected the yoke of their schismatic Western fellow Christians and with open eyes elected, as the lesser evil, the yoke of the Muslim Turks. They would "rather behold in Constantinople the turban of Muhammad than the Pope's tiara or a cardinal's hat."

The feelings that determined this significant choice are on record in the works of literature. During the Middle Ages, as to-day, the antipathy between the two rival heirs of Rome was mutual. Read the Lombard Bishop Liutprand's report to the Saxon Emperors Otto I and II of his diplomatic mission, in their service, to the Byzantine Court of Constantinople in the year 968. If you were sensitive solely to the tone and temper, and momentarily forgot the date, you might fancy that the author was an American visitor to Moscow in any year since 1917. Read the Byzantine Princess Imperial Anna Comnena's history of the reign of her father the Emperor Alexius, who had to cope with the First Crusade. You might fancy that the authoress was a cultivated twentieth-century Frenchwoman describing the invasion of Paris by a wave of Middle-Western American tourists—at least, that is what you might fancy till you lighted on her description of the cross-bow, that deadly new weapon of which the Westerners (in spite of being always wrong) had inexplicably discovered the "know-how." If only it had been discovered by the Byzantines, whose destiny is to be always right! This passage of Anna Comnena's history might be a Russian complaint in 1947 about America's monopoly of the atom bomb.

Why did Byzantine Constantinople come to grief? And why, on the other hand, has Byzantine Moscow survived? The key to both these historical riddles is the Byzantine institution of the totalitarian state.

Empires like the Roman or Chinese, which bestow peace for centuries on once war-ridden worlds, win so powerful a hold on the affections and imaginations of their subjects that these cannot imagine living without them, and, consequently, cannot believe that these supposedly indispensable institutions can ever really cease to exist. When the Roman Empire perished, neither contemporaries nor posterity acknowledged its demise, and, since their eyes refused to face the facts, they sought, at the first opportunity, to bring these facts into conformity with their fancy by conjuring the Roman Empire back into existence. In the eighth century of the Christian era, there were determined attempts to revive the Roman Empire in both East and West. In the West, Charlemagne's attempt was a fortunate failure; but the attempt made by Leo the Syrian at Constantinople, two generations earlier, was a fatal success.

The crucial consequence of this successful establishment of a mediaeval East Roman Empire in the homelands of the Byzantine civilization was that the Eastern Orthodox Church fell back into subjection to the State.

In the pagan Graeco-Roman world, religion had been part and parcel of secular public life. Christianity, springing up without the Roman Empire's leave, defended its freedom at the price of outlawry and persecution. When the Imperial Government came to terms with the Church, it seems to have expected that Christianity would slip into the dependent and subordinate position that an official paganism had previously occupied *vis-à-vis* the Roman State; and, in the Greek heart of the Empire, where the Empire continued to be a going concern for nearly three centuries after the conversion of Constantine, this expectation was more or less realized—as witness what happened to St. John Chrysostom when he fell foul of the Empress

Eudoxia, and to Pope Vigilius when he incurred the displeasure of the Emperor Justinian. Fortunately, however, for the Church, it was freed from its official cage by the Empire's collapse. Even at Constantinople, the Oecumenical Patriarch Sergius dealt with the Emperor Heraclius on equal terms in the supreme crisis of the seventh century, and in the West, where the Empire had broken down two hundred years earlier and was never successfully restored, the Church not only recovered its freedom but preserved it. In our Western world, for the most part, the Church has maintained its independence of the state and has sometimes even exercised an ascendency over it. The modern free churches in Protestant countries and the mediaeval Catholic Church in a not yet divided Western Christendom are, alike, in the main line of our Western tradition, while the modern established churches in Protestant countries have been, on the whole, something exceptional in Western history. Moreover, even where the Church has been resubjected to the secular power in a Western state, this un-Western relation between Church and State has been tempered by the climate of ecclesiastical independence which has been prevalent in Western Christendom on the whole. In the Byzantine world, on the other hand, the successful re-establishment of the Empire in the eight century deprived the Eastern Orthodox Church of the freedom that she, too, had momentarily regained. She did not re-enter the prison house without a struggle. The battle went on for about two hundred years, but it ended in the Church's becoming virtually a department of the mediaeval East Roman state; and a state that has reduced the Church to this position has thereby made itself "totalitarian"—if our latter-day term "totalitarian state" means a state that has established its control over every side of the life of its subjects.

The mediaeval Byzantine totalitarian state conjured up by the successful resuscitation, at Constantinople, of the Roman Empire had a disastrous effect on the development of the Byzantine civilization. It was an incubus that overshadowed, crushed, and stunted the society that had conjured it up. The rich potentialities of the Byzantine civilization, which the Byzantine state nipped in the bud, are revealed in flashes of originality that burst out in regions beyond the range of the East Roman Empire's effective power, or in centuries subsequent to the Empire's demise: the spiritual genius of the tenth-century Sicilian monk, Saint Nilus, who made a new Magna Graecia in Calabria out of Christian Greek refugees from his native island, or the artistic genius of the sixteenth-century Cretan painter, Theotokópoulos, whom the West admires as "El Greco." The "peculiar institution" of the Byzantine society not only blighted these brilliant capacities for creation; it brought the mediaeval Byzantine civilization itself to the premature downfall that has been mentioned above, by making it impossible for the Byzantine world to expand without precipitating a war to the death between the Greek apostles of Byzantine culture and their principal non-Greek proselytes.

The subjection of the Oecumenical Patriarch of Constantinople to the East Roman Emperor created an insoluble dilemma when a heathen prince embraced Eastern Orthodox Christianity. If the convert became the Oecumenical Patriarch's ecclesiastical subject he would be recognizing, by implication, the political sovereignty of the East Roman Emperor, which would be an intolerable consequence for the convert. On the other hand, if he vindicated his political independence by setting up a tame Patriarch of his own, he would be claiming, by implication, to be the East Roman Emperor's peer, which would be an intolerable consequence for the Emperor. This dilemma did not worry the Russian convert-prince, Vladímir, and his successors, because the remoteness of Russia from Constantinople made the theoretical political overlordship of the East Roman Emperor innocuous there. But it did worry the princes of Bulgaria, whose dominons lay at the East Roman Empire's European threshold; and, when Bulgaria finally opted for Byzantium after a preliminary flirtation with Rome, there turned out not to be room for both a Greek Orthodox Christian East Roman Empire and a Slav Orthodox Christian Bulgaria in the same Byzantine world. The result was a Graeco-Bulgarian hundred years' war which ended in the destruction of Bulgaria by the East Roman Empire in 1019 and which inflicted such deadly wounds on the victor that he succumbed, in his turn, to Frankish and Turkish attacks before the eleventh century was over. Russia alone in the Byzantine world of the day was saved by her remoteness from being engulfed in this cataclysm; and thus it was the latest convert to Byzantine Christianity that survived to become the Heir of the Promise—the destiny which, as the Byzantines believe, is not our Western birthright, but theirs.

Russia's life, however, has not been an easy one on the whole. Though she owed her survival in the early Middle Ages to a happy geographical accident, she has had, since then, as we have seen, to save herself by her own exertions. In the thirteenth century she was attacked on two fronts by the Tatars and the Lithuanians, as the Greek homelands of the Byzantine civilization had been attacked by the Turks and the Crusaders some two hundred years before; and, though she eventually got the upper hand, once for all, over her adversaries on the east, she is still having to run her arduous race against the ever-advancing technological "know-how" of the Western world.

In this long and grim struggle to preserve their independence, the Russians have sought salvation in the political institution that was the bane of the mediaeval Byzantine world. They felt that their one hope of survival lay in a ruthless concentration of political power and worked out for themselves a Russian version of the Byzantine totalitarian state. The Grand Duchy of Moscow was the laboratory of this political experiment, and Moscow's service, and reward, was the consolidation, under her rule, of a cluster of weak principalities into a single great power. This Muscovite political edifice has twice been given a new façade—first by Peter the Great and then again by Lenin—but the essence of the structure has remained unaltered, and the Soviet Union of to-day, like the Grand Duchy of Moscow in the fourteenth century, reproduces the salient features of the mediaeval East Roman Empire.

In this Byzantine totalitarian state, the church may be Christian or Marxian so long as it submits to being the secular government's tool. The issue between Trotsky, who wanted to make the Soviet Union an instrument for furthering the cause of the Communist world revolution, and Stalin, who wanted to make Communism an instrument for furthering the interests of the Soviet Union, is the old issue on which battle was once joined between Saint John Chrysostom and the Empress Eudoxia and between Theodore of Studium and the Emperor Constantine VI. In the modern, as in the mediaeval, Byzantine world the victory has fallen to the champion of the secular power—in consistent contrast to the course of history in the West, where it was the ecclesiastical power that won the day in the trails of strength between Gregory VII and Henry IV and between Innocent IV and Frederick II.

The Byzantine institution of the totalitarian state has not so far had the same fatal consequences for Russian Orthodox Christendom that it had in the homelands of the Byzantine civilization when it precipitated a war to the death between the mediaeval Greeks and Bulgars. But we do not know what effect this political heirloom in Russia's Byzantine heritage is going to have on Russia's fortunes now that she has to make the momentous choice between taking her place in a Western world or holding aloof and trying to build up an anti-Western counter-world of her own. We may guess that Russia's ultimate decision will be deeply influenced by the sense of orthodoxy and sense of destiny which she has also inherited from her Byzantine past. Under the Hammer and Sickle, as under the Cross, Russia is still "Holy Russia" and Moscow still "The Third Rome." *Tamen usque recurret.*

10

ISLAM, THE WEST, AND THE FUTURE

In the past, Islam and our Western society have acted and reacted upon one another several times in succession, in different situations and in alternating roles.

The first encounter between them occurred when the Western society was in its infancy and when Islam was the distinctive religion of the Arabs in their heroic age. The Arabs had just conquered and reunited the domains of the ancient civilizations of the Middle East and they were attempting to enlarge this empire into a world state. In that first encounter, the Muslims overran nearly half the original domain of the Western society and only just failed to make themselves masters of the whole. As it was, they took and held North-West Africa, the Iberian Peninsula, and Gallic "Gothia" (the coast of Languedoc between the Pyrenees and the mouth of the Rhône); and a century and a half later, when our nascent Western civilization suffered a relapse after the breakdown of the Carolingian Empire, the Muslims took the offensive again from an African base of operations and this time only just failed to make themselves masters of Italy. Thereafter, when the Western civilization had surmounted the danger of premature extinction and had entered upon a vigorous growth, while the would-be Islamic world state was declining towards its fall, the tables were turned. The Westerners took the offensive along a front which extended from end to end of the Mediterranean, from the Iberian Peninsula through

Sicily to the Syrian "Terre d'Outre Mer"; and Islam, attacked simultaneously by the Crusaders on one side and by the Central Asian Nomads on the other, was driven to bay, as Christendom had been driven some centuries earlier when it had been compelled to face simultaneous attacks on two fronts from the North European barbarians and from the Arabs.

In that life-and-death struggle, Islam, like Christendom before it, triumphantly survived. The Central Asian invaders were converted; the Frankish invaders were expelled; and, in territorial terms, the only enduring result of the Crusades was the incorporation in the Western world of the two outlying Islamic territories of Sicily and Andalusia. Of course, the enduring economic and cultural results of the Crusaders' temporary political acquisitions from Islam were far more important. Economically and culturally, conquered Islam took her savage conquerors captive and introduced the arts of civilization into the rustic life of Latin Christendom. In certain fields of activity, such as architecture, this Islamic influence pervaded the entire Western world in its so-called "mediaeval" age; and in the two permanently conquered territories of Sicily and Andalusia the Islamic influence upon the local Western "successor-states" of the Arab Empire was naturally still more wide and deep. Yet this was not the last act in the play; for the attempt made by the mediaeval West to exterminate Islam failed as signally as the Arab empire-builders' attempt to capture the cradle of a nascent Western civilization had failed before; and, once more, a counter-attack was provoked by the unsuccessful offensive.

This time Islam was represented by the Ottoman descendants of the converted Central Asian Nomads, who conquered and reunited the domain of Orthodox Christendom and then attempted to extend this empire into a world state on the Arab and Roman pattern. After the final failure of the Crusades, Western Christendom stood on the defensive against this Ottoman attack during the late mediaeval and early modern ages of Western history—and this not only on the old maritime front in the Mediterranean but on a new continental front in the Danube Basin. These defensive tactics, however, were not so much a confession of weakness as a masterly piece of half-unconscious strategy on the grand scale; for the Westerners managed to bring the Ottoman offensive to a halt without employing more than a small part of their energies; and, while half the energies of Islam were being absorbed in this local border warfare, the Westerners were putting forth their strength to make themselves masters of the ocean and thereby potential masters of the world. Thus they not only anticipated the Muslims in the discovery and occupation of America; they also entered into the Muslims' prospective heritage in Indonesia, India, and tropical Africa; and finally, having encircled the Islamic world and cast their net about it, they proceeded to attack their old adversary in his native lair.

This concentric attack of the modern West upon the Islamic world has inaugurated the present encounter between the two civilizations. It will be seen that this is part of a still larger and more ambitious movement, in which the Western civilization is aiming at nothing less than the incorporation of all mankind in a single great society, and the control of everything in the earth, air, and sea which mankind can turn to account by means of modern Western technique. What the West is doing now to Islam, it is doing simultaneously to the other surviving civilizations —the Orthodox Christian, the Hindu, and the Far Eastern world—and to the surviving primitive societies, which are now at bay even in their last strongholds in tropical Africa. Thus the contemporary encounter between Islam and the West is not only more active and intimate than any phase of their contact in the past; it is also distinctive in being an incident in an attempt by Western man to "Westernize" the world—an enterprise which will possibly rank as the most momentous, and almost certainly as the most interesting, feature in the history even of a generation that has lived through two world wars.

Thus Islam is once more facing the West with her back to the wall; but this time the odds are more heavily against her than they were even at the most critical moment of the Crusades, for the modern West is superior to her not only in arms but also in the technique of economic life, on which military science ultimately depends, and above all in spiritual culture—the inward force which alone creates and sustains the outward manifestations of what is called civilization.

Whenever one civilized society finds itself in this dangerous situation *vis-à-vis* another, there are two alternative ways open to it of responding to the challenge; and we can see obvious examples of both these types of response in the reaction of Islam to Western pressure to-day. It is legitimate as well as convenient to apply to the present situation certain terms which were coined when a similar situation once arose in the encounter between the ancient civilizations of Greece and Syria. Under the impact of Hellenism during the centuries immediately before and after the beginning of the Christian era, the Jews (and, we might add, the Iranians and the Egyptians) split into two parties. Some became "Zealots" and others "Herodians."

The "Zealot" is the man who takes refuge from the unknown in the familiar; and when he joins battle with a stranger who practises superior tactics and employs formidable newfangled weapons, and finds himself getting the worst of the encounter, he responds by practising his own traditional art of war with abnormally scrupulous exactitude. "Zealotism," in fact, may be described as archaism evoked by foreign pressure; and its most conspicuous representatives in the contemporary Islamic world are "puritans" like the North African Sanūsīs and the Central Arabian Wahhābīs.

The first point to notice about these Islamic "Zealots" is that their strongholds lie in sterile and sparsely populated regions which are remote from the main international thoroughfares of the modern world and which have been unattractive to Western enterprise until the recent dawn of the oil age. The exception which proves the rule up to date is the Mahdist Movement which dominated the Eastern Sudan from 1883 to 1898. The Sudanese Mahdi, Muhammad Ahmad, established himself astride the waterway of the Upper Nile after Western enterprise had taken "the opening up of Africa" in hand. In this awkward geographical position the Sudanese Mahdi's Khalīfah collided with a Western power and—pitting archaic weapons against

modern ones—was utterly overthrown. We may compare
the Mahdi's career with the ephemeral triumph of the Maccabees during the brief relaxation of pressure from Hellenism which the Jews enjoyed after the Romans had
overthrown the Seleucid power and before they had taken
its place; and we may infer that, as the Romans overthrew
the Jewish "Zealots" in the first and second centuries of the
Christian era, so some great power of the Western world of
to-day—let us say, the United States—could overthrow the
Wahhābīs now any time it chose if the Wahhābīs' "Zealotism" became a sufficient nuisance to make the trouble of
suppressing it seem worth while. Suppose, for instance, that
the Saʻūdī Arabian government, under pressure from its
fanatical henchmen, were to demand exorbitant terms for
oil concessions, or were to prohibit altogether the exploita-
tion of its oil resources. The recent discovery of this hidden
wealth beneath her arid soil is decidedly a menace to the
independence of Arabia; for the West has now learnt how
to conquer the desert by bringing into play its own technical inventions—railroads and armoured cars, tractors that
can crawl like centipedes over sand-dunes, and aeroplanes
that can skim above them like vultures. Indeed, in the
Moroccan Rīf and Atlas on the north-west frontier of
India during the inter-war years, the West demonstrated
its ability to subdue a type of Islamic "Zealot" who is much
more formidable to deal with than the denizen of the
desert. In these mountain fastnesses the French and British
have encountered and defeated a highlander who has obtained possession of modern Western small arms and has
learnt to a nicety how to use them on his own ground to
the best advantage.

But of course the "Zealot" armed with a smokeless
quick-firing rifle is no longer the "Zealot" pure and unde-
filed, for, in as much as he has adopted the Westerner's
weapon, he has set foot upon unhallowed ground. No
doubt if ever he thinks about it—and that is perhaps seldom, for the "Zealot's" behaviour is essentially irrational
and instinctive—he says in his heart that he will go thus far
and no farther; that, having adopted just enough of the
Westerner's military technique to keep any aggressive Western power at arm's length, he will consecrate the liberty

thus preserved to the "keeping of the law" in every other respect and will thereby continue to win God's blessing for himself and for his offspring.

This state of mind may be illustrated by a conversation which took place in the nineteen-twenties between the Zaydī Imām Yahyā of San'ā and a British envoy whose mission was to persuade the Imām to restore peacefully a portion of the British Aden Protectorate which he had occupied during the general War of 1914-18 and had refused to evacuate thereafter, notwithstanding the defeat of his Ottoman overlords. In a final interview with the Imām, after it had become apparent that the mission would not attain its object, the British envoy, wishing to give the conversation another turn, complimented the Imām upon the soldierly appearance of his new-model army. Seeing that the Imām took the compliment in good part, he went on:

"And I suppose you will be adopting other Western institutions as well?"

"I think not," said the Imām with a smile.

"Oh, really? That interests me. And may I venture to ask your reasons?"

"Well, I don't think I should like other Western institutions," said the Imām.

"Indeed? And what institutions, for example?"

"Well, there are parliaments," said the Imām. "I like to be the Government myself. I might find a parliament tiresome."

"Why, as for that," said the Englishman, "I can assure you that responsible parliamentary representative government is not an indispensable part of the apparatus of Western civilization. Look at Italy. She has given that up, and she is one of the great Western powers."

"Well, then there is alcohol," said the Imām, "I don't want to see that introduced into my country, where at present it is happily almost unknown."

"Very natural," said the Englishman; "but, if it comes to that, I can assure you that alcohol is not an indispensable adjunct of Western civilization either. Look at America. She has given up that, and she too is one of the great Western powers."

"Well, anyhow," said the Imām, with another smile which seemed to intimate that the conversation was at an end, "I don't like parliaments and alcohol *and that kind of thing*."

The Englishman could not make out whether there was any suggestion of humour in the parting smile with which the last five words were uttered; but, however that might be, those words went to the heart of the matter and showed that the inquiry about possible further Western innovations at San'ā had been more pertinent than the Imām might have cared to admit. Those words indicated, in fact, that the Imām, viewing Western civilization from a great way off, saw it, in that distant perspective, as something one and indivisible and recognized certain features of it, which to a Westerner's eye would appear to have nothing whatever to do with one another, as being organically related parts of that indivisible whole. Thus, on his own tacit admission, the Imām, in adopting the rudiments of the Western military technique, had introduced into the life of his people the thin edge of a wedge which in time would inexorably cleave their close-compacted traditional Islamic civilization asunder. He had started a cultural revolution which would leave the Yamanites, in the end, with no alternative but to cover their nakedness with a complete ready-made outfit of Western clothes. If the Imām had met his Hindu contemporary Mr. Ghandi, that is what he would have been told, and such a prophecy would have been supported by what had happened already to other Islamic peoples who had exposed themselves to the insidious process of "Westernization" several generations earlier.

This, again, may be illustrated by a passage from a report on the state of Egypt in 1839 which was prepared for Lord Palmerston by Dr. John Bowring on the eve of one of the perpetual crises in "the Eastern question" of Western diplomacy and towards the close of the career of Mehmed "Alī, an Ottoman statesman who, by that time, had been governing Egypt and systematically "Westernizing" the life of the inhabitants of Egypt, for thirty-five years. In the course of this report, Dr. Bowring records the at first sight extraordinary fact that the only maternity hospital for

Muslim women which then existed in Egypt was to be found within the bounds of Mehmed "Alī's naval arsenal at Alexandria, and he proceeds to unravel the cause. Mehmed "Alī wanted to play an independent part in international affairs. The first requisite for this was an effective army and navy. An effective navy meant a navy built on the Western model of the day. The Western technique of naval architecture could only be practised and imparted by experts imported from Western countries; but such experts were unwilling to take service with the Pasha of Egypt, even on generous financial terms, unless they were assured of adequate provision for the welfare of their families and their subordinates according to the standards to which they were accustomed in their Western homes. One fundamental condition of welfare, as they understood it, was medical attendance by trained Western practitioners. Accordingly, no hospital, no arsenal; and therefore a hospital with a Western staff was attached to the arsenal from the beginning. The Western colony at the arsenal, however, was small in numbers; the hospital staff were consumed by that devouring energy with which the Franks had been cursed by God; the natives of Egypt were legion; and maternity cases are the commonest of all in the ordinary practice of medicine. The process by which a maternity hospital for Egyptian women grew up within the precincts of a naval arsenal managed by Western experts is thus made clear.

This brings us to a consideration of the alternative response to the challenge of pressure from an alien civilization; for, if the Imām Yahyā of San'ā may stand for a representative of "Zealotism" in modern Islam (at least, of a "Zealotism" tempered by a belief in keeping his powder dry), Mehmed 'Alī was a representative of "Herodianism" whose genius entitles him to rank with the eponymous hero of the sect. Mehmed 'Alī was not actually the first "Herodian" to arise in Islam. He was, however, the first to take the "Herodian" course with impunity, after it had been the death of the one Muslim statesman who had anticipated him: the unfortunate Ottoman Sultan Selim III. Mehmed 'Alī was also the first to pursue the "Herodian" course steadily with substantial success—in contrast to the chequered career of his contemporary and suzerain at Constantinople, Sultan Mahmūd II.

The "Herodian" is the man who acts on the principle that the most effective way to guard against the danger of the unknown is to master its secret; and, when he finds himself in the predicament of being confronted by a more highly skilled and better armed opponent, he responds by discarding his traditional art of war and learning to fight his enemy with the enemy's own tactics and own weapons. If "Zealotism" is a form of archaism evoked by foreign pressure, "Herodianism" is a form of cosmopolitanism evoked by the self-same external agency; and it is no accident that, whereas the strongholds of modern Islamic "Zealotism" have lain in the inhospitable steppes and oases of Najd and the Sahara, modern Islamic "Herodianism"—which was generated by the same forces at about the same time, rather more than a century and a half ago—has been focused, since the days of Selim III and Mehmed 'Alī, at Constantinople and Cairo. Geographically, Constantinople and Cairo represent the opposite extreme, in the domain of modern Islam, to the Wahhābīs' capital at Riyādh on the steppes of the Najd and to the Sanūsīs' stronghold at Kufarā. The oases that have been the fastnesses of Islamic "Zealotism" are conspicuously inaccessible; the cities that have been the nurseries of Islamic "Herodianism" lie on, or close to, the great natural international thoroughfares of the Black Sea Straits and the Isthmus of Suez; and for this reason, as well as on account of the strategic importance and economic wealth of the two countries of which they have been the respective capitals, Cairo and Constantinople have exerted the strongest attraction upon Western enterprise of all kinds, ever since the modern West began to draw its net close round the citadel of Islam.

It is self-evident that "Herodianism" is by far the more effective of the two alternative responses which may be evoked in a society that has been thrown on the defensive by the impact of an alien force in superior strength. The "Zealot" tries to take cover in the past, like an ostrich burying its head in the sand to hide from its pursuers; the "Herodian" courageously faces the present and explores the future. The "Zealot" acts on instinct, the "Herodian" by reason. In fact, the "Herodian" has to make a combined effort of intellect and will in order to overcome the "Zealot" impulse, which is the normal first spontaneous reaction of human nature to the challenge confronting "Zealot" and "Herodian" alike. To have turned "Herodian" is in itself a mark of character (though not necessarily of an amiable character); and it is noteworthy that the Japanese, who, of all the non-Western peoples that the modern West has challenged, have been perhaps the least unsuccessful exponents of "Herodianism" in the world so far, were the most effective exponents of "Zealotism" previously, from the sixteen-thirties to the eighteen-sixties. Being people of strong character, the Japanese made the best that could be made out of the "Zealot's" response; and for the same reason, when the hard facts ultimately convinced them that a persistence in this response would lead them into disaster, they deliberately veered about and proceeded to sail their ship on the "Herodian" tack.

Nevertheless, "Herodianism," though it is an incomparably more effective response than "Zealotism" to the inexorable "Western question" that confronts the whole contemporary world, does not really offer a solution. For one thing, it is a dangerous game; for, to vary our metaphor, it is a form of swapping horses while crossing a stream, and the rider who fails to find his seat in the new saddle is swept off by the current to a death as certain as that which awaits the "Zealot" when, with spear and shield, he charges a machine-gun. The crossing is perilous, and many there be that perish by the way. In Egypt and Turkey, for example—the two countries which have served the Islamic pioneers of "Herodianism" as the fields for their experiment—the epigoni proved unequal to the extraordinarily difficult task which the "elder statesmen" had bequeathed to them. The consequence was that in both countries the "Herodian" movement fell on evil days less than a hundred years after its initiation, that is to say, in the earlier years of the last quarter of the nineteenth century; and the stunting and retarding effect of this set-back is still painfully visible, in different forms, in the life of both countries.

Two still more serious, because inherent, weaknesses of "Herodianism" may be discerned if we turn our attention to Turkey as she is to-day, when her leaders, after overcoming the Hamidian set-back by a heroic *tour de force*, have carried "Herodianism" to its logical conclusion in a revolution which, for ruthless thoroughness, puts even the two classical Japanese revolutions of the seventh and the nineteenth centuries into the shade. Here, in Turkey, is a revolution which, instead of confining itself to a single plane, like our successive economic and political and aesthetic and religious revolutions in the West, has taken place on all these planes simultaneously and has thereby convulsed the whole life of the Turkish people from the heights to the depths of social experience and activity.

The Turks have not only changed their constitution (a relatively simple business, at least in respect of constitutional forms), but this unfledged Turkish Republic has deposed the Defender of the Islamic Faith and abolished his office, the Caliphate; disendowed the Islamic Church and dissolved the monasteries; removed the veil from women's faces, with a repudiation of all that the veil implied; compelled the male sex to confound themselves with unbelievers by wearing hats with brims which make it impossible for the wearer to perform the complete traditional Islamic prayer-drill by touching the floor of the mosque with his forehead; made a clean sweep of the Islamic law by translating the Swiss civil code into Turkish verbatim and the Italian criminal code with adaptations, and then bringing both codes into force by a vote of the National Assembly; and exchanged the Arabic script for the Latin: a change which could not be carried through without jettisoning the greater part of the old Ottoman literary heritage. Most noteworthy and most audacious change of all, these "Herodian" revolutionaries in Turkey have placed before their people a new social ideal—inspiring them to set their hearts no longer, as before, on being husbandmen and warriors and rulers of men, but on going into commerce and industry and proving that, when they try, they can hold their own against the Westerner himself, as well as against the Westernized Greek, Armenian, or Jew, in activities in which they have formerly disdained to compete because they have traditionally regarded them as despicable.

This "Herodian" revolution in Turkey has been carried through with such spirit, under such serious handicaps and against such heavy odds, that any generous-minded observer will make allowances for its blunders and even for its crimes and will wish it success in its formidable task. *Tantus labor non sit cassus*—and it would be particularly ungracious in a Western observer to cavil or scoff; for, after all, these Turkish "Herodians" have been trying to turn their people and their country into something which, since Islam and the West first met, we have always denounced them for not being by nature: they have been trying, thus late in the day, to produce replicas, in Turkey, of a Western nation and a Western state. Yet, as soon as we have clearly realized the goal, we cannot help wondering whether all this labour and travail that has been spent on striving to reach it has been really worth while.

Certainly we did not like the outrageous old-fashioned Turkish "Zealot" who flouted us in the posture of the Pharisee thanking God daily that he was not as other men were. So long as he prided himself on being "a peculiar people" we set ourselves to humble his pride by making his peculiarity odious; and so we called him "the Unspeakable Turk" until we pierced his psychological armour and goaded him into that "Herodian" revolution which he has now consummated under our eyes. Yet now that, under the goad of our censure, he has changed his tune and has searched out every means of making himself indistinguishable from the nations around him, we are embarrassed and even inclined to be indignant—as Samuel was when the Israelites confessed the vulgarity of their motive for desiring a king.

In the circumstances, this new complaint of ours against the Turk is ungracious, to say the least. The victim of our censure might retort that, whatever he does, he cannot do right in our eyes, and he might quote against us, from our own Scriptures: "We have piped unto you and ye have not danced; we have mourned to you and ye have not wept." Yet it does not follow that, because our criticism is ungracious, it is also merely captious or altogether beside the mark. For what, after all, will be added to the heritage of civilization if this labour proves to have been not in vain and if the aim of these thoroughgoing Turkish "Herodians" is achieved in the fullest possible measure?

It is at this point that the two inherent weaknesses of "Herodianism" reveal themselves. The first of them is that "Herodianism" is, *ex hypothesi,* mimetic and not creative, so that, even if it succeeds, it is apt simply to enlarge the quantity of the machine-made products of the imitated society instead of releasing new creative energies in human souls. The second weakness is that this uninspiring success, which is the best that "Herodianism" has to offer, can bring salvation—even mere salvation in this world—only to a small minority of any community which takes the "Herodian" path. The majority cannot look forward even to becoming passive members of the imitated civilization's ruling class. Their destiny is to swell the ranks of the imitated civilization's proletariat. Mussolini once acutely remarked that there are proletarian nations as well as proletarian classes and individuals; and this is evidently the category into which the non-Western peoples of the contemporary world are likely to enter, even if, by a *tour de force* of "Herodianism," they succeed outwardly in transforming their countries into sovereign independent national states on the Western pattern and become associated with their Western sisters as nominally free and equal members of an all-embracing international society.

Thus, in considering the subject of this paper—the influence which the present encounter between Islam and the West may be expected to have on the future of mankind—we may ignore both the Islamic "Zealot" and the Islamic "Herodian" in so far as they carry their respective reactions through to such measure of success as is open to them; for their utmost possible success is the negative achievement of material survival. The rare "Zealot" who escapes extermination becomes the fossil of a civilization which is extinct as a living force; the rather less infrequent "Herodian" who escapes submergence becomes a mimic of the living civilization to which he assimilates himself. Neither the one nor the other is in a position to make any creative contribution to this living civilization's further growth.

We may note incidentally that, in the modern encounter of Islam with the West, the "Herodian" and "Zealot" reactions have several times actually collided with each other and to some extent cancelled each other out. The first use which Mehmed 'Alī made of his new "Westernized" army was to attack the Wahhābīs and quell the first outburst of their zeal. Two generations later, it was the uprising of the Mahdī against the Egyptian regime in the Eastern Sudan that gave the *coup de grâce* to the first "Herodian" effort to make Egypt into a power capable of standing politically on her own feet "under the strenuous conditions of the modern world"; for it was this that confirmed the British military occupation of 1882, with all the political consequences which have flowed therefrom since then.

Again, in our time, the decision of the late king of Afghanistan to break with a tradition of "Zealotism" which had previously been the keynote of Afghan policy since the first Anglo-Afghan War of 1838-42 has probably decided the fate of the "Zealot" tribesmen along the northwest frontier of India. For though King Amānallāh's impatience soon cost him his throne and evoked a "Zealot" reaction among his former subjects, it is fairly safe to prophesy that his successors will travel—more surely because more slowly—along the same "Herodian" path. And the progress of Herodianism in Afghanistan spells the tribesmen's doom. So long as these tribesmen had behind them an Afghanistan which cultivated as a policy that reaction towards the pressure of the West which the tribesmen themselves had adopted by instinct, they themselves could continue to take the "Zealot's" course with impunity. Now that they are caught between two fires—on the one side from India as before, and on the other side from an Afghanistan which has taken the first steps along the "Herodian" path—the tribesmen seem likely sooner or later to be confronted with a choice between conformity and extermination. It may be noted, in passing, that the "Herodian," when he does collide with the "Zealot" of his own household, is apt to deal with him much more ruthlessly than the Westerner would have the heart to do. The Westerner chastises the Islamic "Zealot" with whips; the Islamic "Herodian" chastises him with scorpions. The "frightfulness" with which King Amānallāh suppressed his Pathan rebellion in 1924, and President Mustafā Kemāl Atatürk his Kurdish rebellion in 1925, stands out in striking contrast to the more humane methods by which, at that very time, other recalcitrant Kurds were being brought to heel in what was then the British mandated territory of 'Iraq and other Pathans in the north-west frontier province of what was then British India.

To what conclusion does our investigation lead us? Are we to conclude that, because, for our purpose, both the successful Islamic "Herodian" and the successful Islamic "Zealot" are to be ignored, the present encounter between Islam and the West will have on the future of mankind no influence whatsoever? By no means; for, in dismissing from consideration the successful "Herodian" and "Zealot," we have only disposed of a small minority of the members of the Islamic society. The destiny of the majority, it has already been suggested above, is neither to be exterminated nor to be fossilized nor to be assimilated, but to be submerged by being enrolled in that vast, cosmopolitan, ubiquitous proletariat which is one of the most portentous by-products of the "Westernization" of the world.

At first sight it might appear that, in thus envisaging the future of the majority of Muslims in a "Westernized" world, we had completed the answer to our question, and this in the same sense as before. If we convict the "Herodian" Muslim and the "Zealot" Muslim of cultural sterility, must we not convict the "proletarian" Muslim of the same fatal defect à fortiori? Indeed, is there any one who would dissent from that verdict on first thoughts? We can imagine arch-"Herodians" like the late President Mustafā Kemāl Atatürk and arch-"Zealots" like the Grand Sanūsī concurring with enlightened Western colonial administrators like the late Lord Cromer or General Lyautey to exclaim with one accord: "Can any creative contribution to the civilization of the future be expected from the Egyptian fallāh or the Constantinopolitan hammāl?" Just so, in the early years of the Christian era, when Syria was feeling the

pressure of Greece, Herod Antipas and Gamaliel and those
zealous Theudases and Judases who, in Gamaliel's memory,
had perished by the sword, would almost certainly have
concurred with a Greek poet *in partibus Orientalium* like
Meleager of Gadara, or a Roman provincial governor like
Gallio, in asking, in the same satirical tone: "Can any good
thing come out of Nazareth?" Now when the question is
put in that historic form, we have no doubt as to the
answer, because the Greek and Syrian civilizations have
both run their course and the story of their relations is
known to us from beginning to end. The answer is so
familiar now that it requires a certain effort of the imagination for us to realize how surprising and even shocking
this particular verdict of history would have been to intelligent Greeks and Romans and Idumaeans and Jews of
the generation in which the question was originally asked.
For although, from their profoundly different standpoints,
they might have agreed in hardly anything else, they would
almost certainly have agreed in answering that particular
question with an emphatic and contemptuous "No."

In the light of history, we perceive that their answer
would have been ludicrously wrong if we take as our criterion of goodness the manifestation of creative power.
In that pammixia which arose from the intrusion of the
Greek civilization upon the civilizations of Syria and Iran
and Egypt and Babylonia and India, the proverbial sterility
of the hybrid seems to have descended upon the dominant
class of the Hellenic society as well as upon those Orientals
who followed out to the end the alternative "Herodian"
and "Zealot" courses. The one sphere in which this Graeco-
Oriental cosmopolitan society was undoubtedly exempted
from that course was the underworld of the Oriental
proletariat, of which Nazareth was one type and symbol;
and from this underworld, under these apparently adverse
conditions, there came forth some of the mightiest creations
hitherto achieved by the spirit of man: a cluster of higher
religions. Their sound has gone forth into all lands, and it
is still echoing in our ears. Their names are names of
power: Christianity and Mithraism and Manichaeism; the
worship of the Mother and her dying and rising husband-
son under the alternative names of Cybele-Isis and Attis-

Osiris; the worship of the heavenly bodies; and the Mahayana School of Buddhism, which—changing, as it travelled, from a philosophy into a religion under Iranian and Syrian influence—irradiated the Far East with Indian thought embodied in a new art of Greek inspiration. If these precedents have any significance for us—and they are the only beams of light which we can bring to bear upon the darkness that shrouds our own future—they portend that Islam, in entering into the proletarian underworld of our latterday Western civilization, may eventually compete with India and the Far East and Russia for the prize of influencing the future in ways that may pass our understanding.

Indeed, under the impact of the West, the great deeps of Islam are already stirring, and even in these early days we can discern certain spiritual movements which might conceivably become the embryos of new higher religions. The Bahā'ī and Ahmadī movements, which, from Acre and Lahore, have begun to send out their missionaries to Europe and America, will occur to the contemporary Western observer's mind; but at this point of prognostication we have reached our Pillars of Hercules, where the prudent investigator stays his course and refrains from attempting to sail out into an ocean of future time in which he can take no more than the most general bearings. While we can speculate with profit on the general shape of things to come, we can foresee the precise shadows of particular coming events only a very short way ahead; and those historical precedents which we have taken as our guiding lights inform us that the religions which are generated when civilizations clash take many centuries to grow to maturity and that, in a race that is so long drawn out, a dark horse is often the winner.

Six and a half centuries separated the year in which Constantine gave public patronage to Christianity from the year in which the Hellespont had been crossed by Alexander the Great; five and a half centuries separated the age of the first Chinese pilgrims to the Buddhist Holy Land in Bihār from that of Menander, the Greek ruler of Hindustan who put to Indian Buddhist sages the question: "What is truth?" The present impact of the West on Islam, which began to make its pressure felt little more than a hundred and fifty years ago, is evidently unlikely, on these analogies, to produce comparable effects within any time that falls within the range of our powers of precise prevision; and therefore any attempt to forecast such possible effects might be an unprofitable exercise of the fancy.

We can, however, discern certain principles of Islam which, if brought to bear on the social life of the new cosmopolitan proletariat, might have important salutary effects on "the great society" in a nearer future. Two conspicuous sources of danger—one psychological and the other material—in the present relations of this cosmopolitan proletariat with the dominant element in our modern Western society are race consciousness and alcohol; and in the struggle with each of these evils the Islamic spirit has a service to render which might prove, if it were accepted, to be of high moral and social value.

The extinction of race consciousness as between Muslims is one of the outstanding moral achievements of Islam, and in the contemporary world there is, as it happens, a crying need for the propagation of this Islamic virtue; for, although the record of history would seem on the whole to show that race consciousness has been the exception and not the rule in the constant inter-breeding of the human species, it is a fatality of the present situation that this consciousness is felt—and felt strongly—by the very peoples which, in the competition of the last four centuries between several Western powers, have won—at least for the moment—the lion's share of the inheritance of the Earth.

Though in certain other respects the triumph of the English-speaking peoples may be judged, in retrospect, to have been a blessing to mankind, in this perilous matter of race feeling it can hardly be denied that it has been a misfortune. The English-speaking nations that have established themselves in the New World overseas have not, on the whole, been "good mixers." They have mostly swept away their primitive predecessors; and, where they have either allowed a primitive population to survive, as in South Africa, or have imported primitive "man-power" from elsewhere, as in North America, they have developed the rudiments of that paralysing institution which in India—

where in the course of many centuries it has grown to its full stature—we have learnt to deplore under the name of "caste." Moreover, the alternative to extermination or segregation has been exclusion—a policy which averts the danger of internal schism in the life of the community which practises it, but does so at the price of producing a not less dangerous state of international tension between the excluding and the excluded races—especially when this policy is applied to representatives of alien races who are not primitive but civilized, like the Hindus and Chinese and Japanese. In this respect, then, the triumph of the English-speaking peoples has imposed on mankind a "race question" which would hardly have arisen, or at least hardly in such an acute form and over so wide an area, if the French, for example, and not the English, had been victorious in the eighteenth-century struggle for the possession of India and North America.

As things are now, the exponents of racial intolerance are in the ascendent, and, if their attitude towards "the race question" prevails, it may eventually provoke a general catastrophe. Yet the forces of racial toleration, which at present seem to be fighting a losing battle in a spiritual struggle of immense importance to mankind, might still regain the upper hand if any strong influence militating against race consciousness that has hitherto been held in reserve were now to be thrown into the scales. It is conceivable that the spirit of Islam might be the timely reinforcement which would decide this issue in favour of tolerance and peace.

As for the evil of alcohol, it is at its worst among primitive populations in tropical regions which have been "opened up" by Western enterprise; and, though the more enlightened part of Western public opinion has long been conscious of this evil and has exerted itself to combat it, its power of effective action is rather narrowly limited. Western public opinion can only take action in such a matter by bringing its influence to bear upon Western administrators of the tropical dependencies of Western powers; and, while benevolent administrative action in this sphere has been strengthened by international conventions, and these are now being consolidated and extended under the auspices of the United Nations, the fact remains that even the most statesmanlike preventive measures imposed by external authority are incapable of liberating a community from a social vice unless a desire for liberation and a will to carry this desire into voluntary action on its own part are awakened in the hearts of the people concerned. Now Western administrators, at any rate those of "Anglo-Saxon" origin, are spiritually isolated from their "native" wards by the physical "colour bar" which their race-consciousness sets up; the conversion of the native's soul is a task to which their competence can hardly be expected to extend; and it is at this point that Islam may have a part to play.

In these recently and rapidly "opened up" tropical territories, the Western civilization has produced an economic and political plenum and, in the same breath, a social and spiritual void. The frail customary institutions of the primitive societies which were formerly at home in the land have been shattered to pieces by the impact of the ponderous Western machine, and millions of "native" men, women, and children, suddenly deprived of their traditional social environment, have been left spiritually naked and abashed. The more liberal-minded and intelligent of the Western administrators have lately realized the vast extent of the psychological destruction which the process of Western penetration has unintentionally but inevitably caused; and they are now making sympathetic efforts to save what can still be saved from the wreck of the "native" social heritage, and even to reconstruct artificially, on firmer foundations, certain valuable "native" institutions which have been already overthrown. Yet the spiritual void in the "native's" soul has been, and still remains, a great abyss; the proposition that "Nature abhors a vacuum" is as true in the spiritual world as in the material; and the Western civilization, which has failed to fill this spiritual vacuum itself, has placed at the disposal of any other spiritual forces which may choose to take the field an incomparable system of material means of communication.

In two of these tropical regions, Central Africa and Indonesia, Islam is the spiritual force which has taken advantage of the opportunity thus thrown open by the Western pioneers of material civilization to all comers on the spiritual plane; and, if ever the "natives" of these regions succeed in recapturing a spiritual state in which they are able to call their souls their own, it may prove to have been the Islamic spirit that has given fresh form to the void. This spirit may be expected to manifest itself in many practical ways; and one of these manifestations might be a liberation from alcohol which was inspired by religious conviction and which was therefore able to accomplish what could never be enforced by the external sanction of an alien law.

Here, then, in the foreground of the future, we can remark two valuable influences which Islam may exert upon the cosmopolitan proletariat of a Western society that has cast its net round the world and embraced the whole of mankind; while in the more distant future we may speculate on the possible contributions of Islam to some new manifestation of religion. These several possibilities, however, are all alike contingent upon a happy outcome of the situation in which mankind finds itself to-day. They presuppose that the discordant pammixia set up by the Western conquest of the world will gradually and peacefully shape itself into a harmonious synthesis out of which, centuries hence, new creative variations might again gradually and peacefully arise. This presupposition, however, is merely an unverifiable assumption which may or may not be justified by the event. A pammixia may end in a synthesis, but it may equally well end in an explosion; and, in that disaster, Islam might have quite a different part to play as the active ingredient in some violent reaction of the cosmopolitan underworld against its Western masters.

At the moment, it is true, this destructive possibility does not appear to be imminent; for the impressive word "Pan-Islamism"—which has been the bugbear of Western colonial administrators since it was first given currency by the policy of Sultan 'Abd-al-Hamīd—has lately been losing such hold as it may ever have obtained over the minds of Muslims. The inherent difficulties of conducting a "Pan-Islamic" movement are, indeed, plain to see. "Pan-Islamism" is simply a manifestation of that instinct which prompts a herd of buffalo, grazing scattered over the plain, to form a phalanx, heads down and horns outward, as soon as an enemy appears within range. In other words, it is an example of that reversion to traditional tactics in face of a superior and unfamiliar opponent, to which the name of "Zealotism" has been given in this paper. Psychologically, therefore, "Pan-Islamism" should appeal *par excellence* to Islamic "Zealots" in the Wahhābī or Sanūsī vein; but this psychological predisposition is balked by a technical difficulty; for in a society that is dispersed abroad, as Islam is, from Morocco to the Philippines and from the Volga to the Zambesi, the tactics of solidarity are as difficult to execute as they are easy to imagine.

The herd-instinct emerges spontaneously; but it can hardly be translated into effective action without taking advantage of the elaborate system of mechanical communications which modern Western ingenuity has conjured up: steamships, railways, telegraphs, telephones, aeroplanes, motor-cars, newspapers, and the rest. Now the use of these instruments is beyond the compass of the Islamic "Zealot's" ability; and the Islamic "Herodian," who has succeeded in making himself more or less master of them, *ex hypothesi* desires to employ them, not in captaining a "Holy War" against the West, but in reorganizing his own life on a Western pattern. One of the most remarkable signs of the times in the contemporary Islamic world is the emphasis with which the Turkish Republic has repudiated the tradition of Islamic solidarity. "We are determined to work out our own salvation," the Turks seem to say, "and this salvation, as we see it, lies in learning how to stand on our own feet in the posture of an economically self-sufficient and politically independent sovereign state on the Western model. It is for other Muslims to work out their salvation for themselves as may seem good to them. We neither ask their help any longer nor offer them ours. Every people for itself, and the Devil take the hindermost, *alla franca!*"

Now though, since 1922, the Turks have done almost everything conceivable to flout Islamic sentiment, they have gained rather than lost prestige among other Muslims —even among some Muslims who have publicly denounced the Turks' audacious course—in virtue of the very success with which their audacities have so far been attended.

And this makes it probable that the path of nationalism which the Turks are taking so decidely to-day will be taken by other Muslim peoples with equal conviction to-morrow. The Arabs and the Persians are already on the move. Even the remote and hitherto "Zealot" Afghans have set their feet on this course, and they will not be the last. In fact, nationalism, and not Pan-Islamism, is the formation into which the Islamic peoples are falling; and for the majority of Muslims the inevitable, though undesired, out-come of nationalism will be submergence in the cosmo-politan proletariat of the Western world.

This view of the present prospects of "Pan-Islamism" is borne out by the failure of the attempt to resuscitate the Caliphate. During the last quarter of the nineteenth century the Ottoman Sultan 'Abd-al-Hamīd, discovering the title of Caliph in the lumber-room of the Seraglio, began to make play with it as a means of rallying "Pan-Islamic" feeling round his own person. After 1922, however, Mus-tafā Kemāl Atatürk and his companions, finding this re-suscitated Caliphate incompatible with their own radically "Herodian" political ideas, first committed the historical solecism of equating the Caliphate with "spiritual" as op-posed to "temporal" power and finally abolished the office altogether. This action on the part of the Turks stimu-lated other Muslims, who were distressed by such high-handed treatment of a historic Muslim institution, to hold a Caliphate Conference at Cairo in 1926 in order to see if anything could be done to adapt a historic Muslim insti-tution to the needs of a newfangled age. Anyone who examines the records of this conference will carry away the conviction that the Caliphate is dead, and that this is so because Pan-Islamism is dormant.

Pan-Islamism is dormant—yet we have to reckon with the possibility that the sleeper may awake if ever the cos-mopolitan proletariat of a "Westernized" world revolts against Western domination and cries out for anti-Western leadership. That call might have incalculable psychological effects in evoking the militant spirit of Islam—even if it had slumbered as long as the Seven Sleepers—because it might awaken echoes of a heroic age. On two historic occasions in the past, Islam has been the sign in which an

Oriental society has risen up victoriously against an Occidental intruder. Under the first successors of the Prophet, Islam liberated Syria and Egypt from a Hellenic domination which had weighed on them for nearly a thousand years. Under Zangī and Nūr-ad-Dīn and Saladin and the Mamlūks, Islam held the fort against the assaults of Crusaders and Mongols. If the present situation of mankind were to precipitate a "race war," Islam might be moved to play her historic role once again. *Absit omen.*

11

ENCOUNTERS BETWEEN CIVILIZATIONS

I

What will be singled out as the salient event of our time by future historians, centuries hence, looking back on the first half of the twentieth century and trying to see its activities and experiences in that just proportion which the time-perspective sometimes reveals? Not, I fancy, any of those sensational or tragic or catastrophic political and economic events which occupy the headlines of our newspapers and the foregrounds of our minds; not wars, revolutions, massacres, deportations, famines, gluts, slumps, or booms, but something of which we are only half-conscious, and out of which it would be difficult to make a headline. The things that make good headlines attract our attention because they are on the surface of the stream of life, and they distract our attention from the slower, impalpable, imponderable movements that work below the surface and penetrate to the depths. But of course it is really these deeper, slower movements that, in the end, make history, and it is they that stand out huge in retrospect, when the sensational passing events have dwindled, in perspective, to their true proportions.

Mental perspective, like optical perspective, comes into focus only when the observer has put a certain distance between himself and his object. When, for example, you are travelling by air from Salt Lake City to Denver, the nearest view of the Rockies is not the best one. While you are actually over the mountains, you see nothing but a maze of peakes, ridges, gullies, and crags. It is not until you have left the mountains behind you and are looking back at them as you fly over the plains that they rise up before you in their magnificent order, range behind range. It is only then that you have a vision of the Rockies themselves.

With this vision in my mind, I believe that future historians will be able to see our age in better proportion than we can. What are they likely to say about it?

Future historians will say, I think, that the great event of the twentieth century was the impact of the Western civilization upon all the other living societies of the world of that day. They will say of this impact that it was so powerful and so pervasive that it turned the lives of all its victims upside down and inside out—affecting the behaviour, outlook, feelings, and beliefs of individual men, women, and children in an intimate way, touching chords in human souls that are not touched by mere external material forces—however ponderous and terrifying. This will be said, I feel sure, by historians looking back on our times even from as short a time hence as A.D. 2047.

What will the historians of A.D. 3047 say? If we had been living a century ago, I should have had to apologize for the fantastic conceit of pretending to speculate about anything that might be said or done at so immensely remote a date. Eleven hundred years was a very long time for people who believed that the world had been created in 4004 B.C. But I need not apologize to-day; for, since our great-grandfathers' time, there has been so great a revolution in our time-scale that, if I were to try to plot out to scale, on one of these pages, a chart of the history of this planet since its birth, I should not be able to make so short a period as eleven hundred years visible to the naked eye.

The historians of A.D. 3047, then, may have something far more interesting than those of A.D. 2047 to say, because they, by their time, may know much more of the story of which we, to-day, are perhaps in a rather early chapter. The historians of A.D. 3047 will, I believe, be chiefly interested in the tremendous counter-effects which, by that time, the victims will have produced in the life of the aggressor. By A.D. 3047, our Western civilization, as we and our Western predecessors have known it, say, for the last twelve or thirteen hundred years, since its emergence out of the Dark Ages, may have been transformed, almost out of all recognition, by a counter-radiation of influences from the foreign worlds which we, in our day, are in the act of engulfing in ours—influences from Orthodox Christendom, from Islam, from Hinduism, from the Far East.

By A.D. 4047 the distinction—which looms large to-day —between the Western civilization, as an aggressor, and the other civilizations, as its victims, will probably seem unimportant. When radiation has been followed by counter-radiation of influences, what will stand out will be a single great experience, common to the whole of mankind: the experience of having one's parochial social heritage battered to bits by collision with the parochial heritages of other civilizations, and then finding a new life—a new common life—springing up out of the wreckage. The historians of A.D. 4047 will say that the impact of the Western civilization on its contemporaries, in the second half of the second millennium of the Christian era, was the epoch-making event of that age because it was the first step towards the unification of mankind into one single society. By their time, the unity of mankind will perhaps have come to seem one of the fundamental conditions of human life—just part of the order of nature— and it may need quite an effort of imagination on their part to recall the parochial outlook of the pioneers of civilization during the first six thousand years or so of its existence. Those Athenians, whose capital city was no more than a day's walk from the farthest frontiers of their country, and those American contemporaries—or virtual contemporaries—of theirs, whose country you could fly across from sea to sea in sixteen hours—how could they behave (as we know they did behave) as if their own little country were the universe?

And the historians of A.D. 5047? The historians of A.D. 5047 will say, I fancy, that the importance of this social unification of mankind was not to be found in the field of technics and economics, and not in the field of war and politics, but in the field of religion.

II

Why do I venture on these prophecies about how the history of our own time will appear to people looking back at it several thousand years hence? Because we have about six thousand years of past history to judge by, since the first emergence of human societies of the species we call "civilizations."

Six thousand years is an almost infinitesimally short time compared to the age of the human race, of mammals, of life on earth, of the planetary system round our sun, of the sun itself, and of the star-cluster of which our sun is a not particularly conspicuous member. Still, for our present purpose, these last six thousand years—brief though they are—do provide us with other examples of the phenomenon we are studying—examples of encounters between different civilizations. In relation to some of these cases, we ourselves, in our day, are already enjoying the advantage—which the historians living in A.D. 3047 or 4047 are going to have in looking back at us—of knowing the whole story. It is with some of these past encounters in mind that I have been speculating on how our own encounter with our own contemporaries is likely to turn out.

Take the history of one of our predecessors, the Graeco-Roman civilization, and consider how this looks to us in the fairly distant perspective in which we are now able to see it:

As a result of the conquests of Alexander the Great and of the Romans, the Graeco-Roman civilization radiated over most of the Old World—into India, into the British Isles, and even as far as China and Scandinavia. The only civilizations of that day which remained untouched by its influence were those of Central America and Peru, so that its expansion was not incomparable to our own in extent and vigour. When we look back on the history of the Graeco-Roman world during the last four centuries B.C., it is this great movement of expansion and penetration that stands out now. The wars, revolutions, and economic crises that ruffled the surface of Graeco-Roman history during those centuries, and occupied so much of the attention of the men and women who were struggling to live through them, do not mean much to us now compared with that great tide of Greek cultural influence invading Asia Minor, Syria, Egypt, Babylonia, Persia, India, China.

But why does the Graeco-Roman impact on these other civilizations matter to us now? Because of the counter-attack of these other civilizations on the Graeco-Roman world.

This counter-attack was partly delivered in the same style as the original Graeco-Roman attack: that is, by force of arms. But we are not much interested to-day in the forlorn hope of Jewish armed resistance to Greek and Roman imperialism in Palestine; or in the successful counter-attack of the Parthians and their Persian successors under the Sasanian Dynasty east of the Euphrates; or in the sensational victories of the early Muslim Arabs, who in the seventh century of the Christian era liberated the Middle East from Graeco-Roman rule in as short a number of years as it had taken Alexander the Great to conquer it a thousand years earlier.

But there was another counter-attack, a non-violent one, a spiritual one, which attacked and conquered, not fortresses and provinces, but hearts and minds. This attack was delivered by the missionaries of new religions which had arisen in the worlds which the Graeco-Roman civilization had attacked by force and submerged. The prince of these missionaries was Saint Paul, who, starting from Antioch, made the audacious march on Macedonia, Greece, and Rome which King Antiochus the Great had once attempted unsuccessfully. These religions were different in kind from the native religion of the Graeco-Roman world. The gods of Graeco-Roman paganism had been rooted in the soil of particular communities; they had been parochial and political: Athene Polias, Fortuna Praenestina, Dea Roma. The gods of the new religions that were making this non-violent counter-attack on Greek and Roman hearts and minds had risen above their original local origins. They had become universal gods, with a message of salvation for all mankind, Jew and Gentile, Scythian and Greek. Or, to put this great historical event in religious terms, one might say that the One True God had taken this opportunity of the opening of men's minds through the collision and collapse of their old local traditions; He had taken advantage of this excruciating experience in order to illuminate these momentarily open minds with a fuller and truer vision of His nature and purpose than they had been capable of receiving before.

Take the two words "Jesus Christ," which are so very important for us, and which, we may venture to prophesy, will still be important for mankind two or three thousand years hence. These very words are witnesses to the encounter between a Graeco-Roman civilization and a Syrian civilization out of, which Christianity came to birth. "Jesus" is the third person singular of a Semitic verb; "Christ" is the passive participle of a Greek verb. The double name testifies that Christianity was born into this world from a marriage between those two cultures.

Consider the four higher religions, with a world-wide mission, which exist in the world to-day: Christianity, Islam, Hinduism, and the Mahayana form of Buddhism which prevails in the Far East. All four are, historically, products of the encounter between the Graeco-Roman civilization and its contemporaries. Christianity and Islam arose as alternative responses of the Syrian world to Graeco-Roman penetration: Christianity a non-violent response, Islam a violent one. Mahayanian Buddhism and Hinduism are the gentle and the violent responses of the Hindu world to the same Graeco-Roman challenge.

Looking back on Graeco-Roman history to-day, about thirteen hundred years after the date when the Graeco-Roman civilization became extinct, we can see that, in this perspective, the most important thing in the history of the Graeco-Roman world is its meeting with other civilizations; and these encounters are important, not for their immediate political and economic consequences, but for their long-term religious consequences. This Graeco-Roman illustration, of which we know the whole story, also gives us some idea of the time-span of encounters between civilizations. The Graeco-Roman world's impact upon other contemporary civilizations, which corresponds to the modern Western world's impact on its own contemporaries since the turn of the fifteenth and sixteenth centuries, started with the conquests of Alexander the Great in the fourth century B.C.; and the Middle Eastern world was still translating the classical works of Greek philosophy and science some five or six centuries after the liberation of the Middle East from Graeco-Roman rule by the early Muslim Arabs in the seventh century of the Christian era. From the fourth century B.C. to the thirteenth century of the Christian era, it took the best part of sixteen hundred years for the encounter between the Graeco-Roman civilization and its contemporaries to work itself out.

Now measure against that span of sixteen hundred years the duration, to date, of the encounter between our modern Western civilization and its contemporaries. One may say that this encounter began with the Ottoman attack on the homelands of the Western civilization and with the great Western voyages of discovery at the turn of the fifteenth and sixteenth centuries of our era. That makes only four-and-a-half centuries to the present.

Let us assume, if you like, that people's hearts and minds move rather faster nowadays (though I know of no evidence that the unconscious part of the human psyche ever greatly varies its pace)—even so, it looks as if we were still only in an early chapter of the story of our encounter with the civilizations of Mexico and Peru and Orthodox Christendom and Islam and the Hindu world and the Far East. We are just beginning to see some of the effects of our action on them, but we have hardly begun to see the effects—which will certainly be tremendous —of their coming counter-action upon us.

It is only in our generation that we have seen one of the first moves in this counter-offensive, and we have found it very disturbing; whether we have liked it or not, we have felt it to be momentous. I mean, of course, the move made by the offshoot of Orthodox Christendom in Russia. It is momentous and disturbing not because of the material power behind it. The Russians, after all, do not yet possess the atom bomb; but they have already shown (and this is the point) the power to convert Western souls to a non-Western "ideology."

The Russians have taken up a Western secular social philosophy, Marxism; you might equally well call Marxism a Christian heresy, a leaf torn out of the book of Christianity and treated as if it were the whole gospel. The Russians have taken up this Western heretical religion, transformed it into something of their own, and are now shooting it back at us. This is the first shot in the anti-Western counter-offensive; but this Russian counter-discharge in the form of Communism may come to seem a small affair when the probably far more potent civilizations of India and China respond in their turn to our Western challenge. In the long run India and China seem likely to produce much deeper effects on our Western life than Russia can ever hope to produce with her Communism. But even the comparatively feeble native civilization of Mexico is beginning to react. The revolution through which Mexico has been passing since A.D. 1910 may be interpreted as a first move to shake off the top-dressing of Western civilization which we imposed on Mexico in the sixteenth century; and what is happening to-day in Mexico may happen tomorrow in the seats of the native civilization of South America: in Peru, Bolivia, Ecuador, and Colombia.

III

Before leaving off, I must say a word about one question which I have begged up to this point, and that is: what do we mean by a "civilization"? Clearly, we do mean something, for even before we have tried to define what our meaning is, this classification of human societies—the Western civilization, the Islamic, the Far Eastern, the Hindu, and so on—does seem to make sense. These names do call up distinct pictures in our minds in terms of religion, architecture, painting, manners, and customs. Still, it is better to try to get closer to what we mean by a term which we have already been working so hard. I believe I do know what I mean by a civilization; at least, I am sure I know how I have arrived at my own idea of it.

I mean, by a civilization, the smallest unit of historical study at which one arrives when one tries to understand the history of one's own country: the United States, say, or the United Kingdom. If you were to try to understand the history of the United States by itself, it would be unintelligible: you could not understand the part played in

American life by federal government, representative government, democracy, industrialism, monogamy, Christianity, unless you looked beyond the bounds of the United States—out beyond her frontiers to Western Europe and to the other overseas countries founded by West Europeans, and back beyond her local origins to the history of Western Europe in centuries before Columbus or Cabot had crossed the Atlantic. But, to make American history and institutions intelligible for practical purposes, you need not look beyond Western Europe into Eastern Europe or the Islamic world, nor behind the origins of our Western European civilization to the decline and fall of the Graeco-Roman civilization. These limits of time and space give us the intelligible unit of social life of which the United States or Great Britain or France or Holland is a part: call it Western Christendom, Western civilization, Western society, the Western world. Similarly, if you start from Greece or Serbia or Russia, and try to understand their histories, you arrive at an Orthodox Christendom or Byzantine world. If you start from Morocco or Afghanistan, and try to understand their histories, you arrive at an Islamic world. Start from Bengal or Mysore or Rajputana, and you find a Hindu world. Start from China or Japan and you find a Far Eastern world.

While the state of which we happen to be citizens makes more concrete and more imperious claims on our allegiance, especially in the present age, the civilization of which we are members really counts for more in our lives. And this civilization of which we are members includes—at most stages in its history—the citizens of other states besides our own. It is older than our own state: the Western civilization is about thirteen hundred years old, whereas the Kingdom of England is only one thousand years old, the United Kingdom of England and Scotland less than two hundred and fifty, the United States not much more than one hundred and fifty. States are apt to have short lives and sudden deaths: the Western civilization of which you and I are members may be alive centuries after the United Kingdom and the United States have disappeared from the political map of the world like their late contemporaries, the Republic of Venice and the

Dual Monarchy of Austria-Hungary. This is one of the reasons why I have been asking you to look at history in terms of civilizations, and not in terms of states, and to think of states as rather subordinate and ephemeral political phenomena in the lives of the civilizations in whose bosoms they appear and disappear.

12

CHRISTIANITY AND CIVILIZATION

As I was re-reading my notes for this essay during the last few days, there floated into my mind the picture of a scene which was transacted in the capital of a great empire about fourteen hundred years ago, when that capital was full of war—not a war on a front but a war in the rear, a war of turmoil and street fighting. The emperor of that empire was holding council to decide whether he should carry on the struggle or whether he should take ship and sail away to safety. At the crown council his wife, the empress, was present and spoke, and she said: "You, Justinian, can sail away if you like; the ship is at the quay and the sea is still open; but I am going to stay and see it out, because καλὸν ἐντάφιον ἡ βασιλεία: 'Empire is a fine winding sheet.'" I thought of this passage and my colleague, Professor Baynes, found it for me; and, as I thought of it, and also thought of the day and the circumstances in which I was writing, I decided to emend it; and I emended it to κάλλιον ἐντάψιον ἡ βασιλεία τοῦ Θεοῦ: "a finer winding-sheet is the Kingdom of God"—a finer because that is a winding-sheet from which there is a resurrection. Now that paraphrase of a famous phrase of Greek comes, I venture to think, rather near to the three Latin words which are the motto of the University of Oxford; and, if we believe in these three words *Dominus Illuminatio Mea* and can live up to them, we can look forward without dismay to any future that may be coming to us. The material future is very little in our power. Storms might come which might lay low that noble and beloved building and leave not one stone upon another. But, if the truth about this university and about ourselves is told in those three Latin words, than we know for certain that, though the stones may fall, the light by which we live will not go out.

Now let me come by a very easy transition to what is my subject in this essay—the relation between Christianity and civilization. This is a question which has always been at issue since the foundation of the Christian Church, and of course there have been a number of alternative views on it.

One of the oldest and most persistent views is that Christianity was the destroyer of the civilization within whose framework it grew up. That was, I suppose, the view of the Emperor Marcus, as far as he was aware of the presence of Christianity in his world. It was most emphatically and violently the view of his successor the Emperor Julian, and it was also the view of the English historian Gibbon, who recorded the decline and fall of the Roman Empire long after the event. In the last chapter of Gibbon's history there is one sentence in which he sums up the theme of the whole work. Looking back, he says: "I have described the triumph of barbarism and religion." And, to understand his meaning, you have to turn from the middle of Chapter LXXI to the opening passage of Chapter I, that extraordinarily majestic description of the Roman Empire at peace in the age of the Antonines, in the second century after Christ. He starts you there, and at the end of the long story he says "I have described the triumph of barbarism and religion," meaning that it was Christianity as well as barbarism which overthrew the civilization for which the Antonines stood.

One hesitates to question Gibbon's authority, but I believe there is a fallacy in this view which vitiates the whole of it. Gibbon assumes that the Graeco-Roman civilization stood at its height in the age of the Antonines and that in tracing its decline from that moment he is tracing that decline from the beginning. Evidently, if you take that view, Christianity rises as the empire sinks, and the rise of

Christianity is the fall of civilization. I think Gibbon's initial error lies in supposing that the ancient civilization of the Graeco-Roman world began to decline in the second century after Christ and that the age of the Antonines was that civilization's highest point. I think it really began to decline in the fifth century before Christ. It died not by murder, but by suicide; and that act of suicide was committed before the fifth century B.C. was out. It was not even the philosophies which preceded Christianity that were responsible for the death of the ancient Graeco-Roman civilization. The philosophies arose because the civic life of that civilization had already destroyed itself by turning itself into an idol to which men paid an exorbitant worship. And the rise of the philosophies, and the subsequent rise of the religions out of which Christianity emerged as the final successor of them all, was something that happened after the Graeco-Roman civilization had already put itself to death. The rise of the philosophies, and *a fortiori* that of the religions, was not a cause; it was a consequence.

When Gibbon in that opening passage of his work looks at the Roman Empire in the age of the Antonines, he does not say explicitly—but I am sure this was in his mind —that he is also thinking of himself as standing on another peak of civilization and looking back towards that distant peak in the past across a broad trough of barbarism in between. Gibbon thought to himself: "On the morrow of the death of the Emperor Marcus the Roman Empire went into decline. All the values that I, Gibbon, and my kind care for began then to be degraded. Religion and barbarism began to triumph. This lamentable state of affairs continued to prevail for hundreds and hundreds of years; and then, a few generations before my time, no longer ago than the close of the seventeenth century, a rational civilization began to emerge again." From his peak in the eighteenth century Gibbon looks back to the Antonine peak in the second century, and that view—which is, I think, implicit in Gibbon's work—has been put very clearly and sharply by a writer of the twentieth century, from whom I propose to quote a passage somewhat at length because it is, so to speak, the formal antithesis of the thesis which I want to maintain.

Greek and Roman society was built on the conception of the subordination of the individual to the community, of the citizen to the state; it set the safety of the commonwealth, as the supreme aim of conduct, above the safety of the individual whether in this world or in a world to come. Trained from infancy in this unselfish ideal, the citizens devoted their lives to the public service and were ready to lay them down for the common good; or, if they shrank from the supreme sacrifice, it never occurred to them that they acted otherwise than basely in preferring their personal existence to the interests of their country. All this was changed by the spread of Oriental religions which inculcated the communion of the soul with God and its eternal salvation as the only objects worth living for, objects in comparison with which the prosperity and even the existence of the state sank into insignificance. The inevitable result of this selfish and immoral doctrine was to withdraw the devotee more and more from the public service, to concentrate his thoughts on his own spiritual emotions, and to breed in him a contempt for the present life, which he regarded merely as a probation for a better and an eternal. The saint and the recluse, disdainful of earth and rapt in ecstatic contemplation of heaven, became in popular opinion the highest ideal of humanity, displacing the old ideal of the patriot and hero who, forgetful of self, lives and is ready to die for the good of his country. The earthly city seemed poor and contemptible to men whose eyes beheld the City of God coming in the clouds of heaven. Thus the centre of gravity, so to say, was shifted from the present to a future life, and, however much the other world may have gained, there can be little doubt that this one lost heavily by the change. A general disintegration of the body politic set in. The ties of the state and the family were loosened: the structure of society tended to resolve itself into its individual elements and thereby to relapse into barbarism; for civilization is only possible through the active co-operation of the citizens and their willingness to subordinate their private interests to the common good. Men refused to defend their country and even to continue their kind. In their anxiety to save their own souls and the souls of others, they were content to leave the material world, which they identified with the principle of evil, to perish around them. This obsession lasted for a thousand years. The revival of

Roman law, of the Aristotelian philosophy, of ancient art and literature at the close of the Middle Ages, marked the return of Europe to native ideals of life and conduct, to saner, manlier views of the world. The long halt in the march of civilization was over. The tide of Oriental invasion had turned at last. It is ebbing still.

It is ebbing indeed! And one might speculate about what the author of this passage, which was first published in 1906, would now write if he were revising his work for a fourth edition to-day. Many reading this article are, of course, familiar with the passage. I have not yet mentioned the author's name; but, for those who do not know it already, I would say that it is not Alfred Rosenberg; it is Sir James Frazer.[1] I wonder what that gentle scholar thinks of the latest form in which Europe's return "to native ideals of life and conduct" is manifesting itself.

Now you will have seen that the most interesting thesis in that passage of Frazer's is the contention that trying to save one's soul is something contrary to, and incompatible with, trying to do one's duty to one's neighbour. I am going, in the course of this essay, to challenge that thesis; at the moment I merely want to point out that Frazer is at the same time putting Gibbon's thesis and stating it in explicit terms; and on this point I would give Frazer the answer that I have already ventured to give to Gibbon: that Christianity was not the destroyer of the ancient Greek civilization, because that civilization had decayed from inherent defects of its own before Christianity arose. But I would agree with Frazer, and would ask you to agree with me, that the tide of Christianity has been ebbing and that our post-Christian Western secular civilization that has emerged is a civilization of the same order as the pre-Christian Graeco-Roman civilization. This observation opens up a second possible view of the relation between Christianity and civilization—not the same view as that held in common by Gibbon and Frazer, not the view that Christianity has been the destroyer of civilization, but an

[1] Frazer, Sir J. G.: *The Golden Bough,* Part IV: "Adonis, Attis, Osiris," vol. 1, pp. 300-301 (third edition, London 1914, Macmillan, preface dated January, 1914).

alternative view in which Christianity appears in the role of civilization's humble servant.

According to this second possible view, Christianity is, as it were, the egg, grub, and chrysalis between butterfly and butterfly. Christianity is a transitional thing which bridges the gap between one civilization and another, and I confess that I myself held this rather patronizing view for many years. On this view you look at the historical function of the Christian Church in terms of the process of the reproduction of civilizations. Civilization is a species of being which seeks to reproduce itself, and Christianity has had a useful but a subordinate role in bringing two new secular civilizations to birth after the death of their predecessor. You find the ancient Graeco-Roman civilization in decline from the close of the second century after Christ onwards. And then after an interval you find—perhaps as early as the ninth century in Byzantium, and as early as the thirteenth century in the West in the person of the *Stupor Mundi* Frederick II—a new secular civilization arising out of the ruins of its Graeco-Roman predecessor. And you look at the role of Christianity in the interval and conclude that Christianity is a kind of chrysalis which has held and preserved the hidden germs of life until these have been able to break out again into a new growth of secular civilization. That is an alternative view to the theory of Christianity being the destroyer of the ancient Graeco-Roman civilization; and, if one looks abroad through the history of civilizations, one can see other cases which seem to conform to the same pattern.

Take the other higher religions which are still living on in the world of to-day side by side with Christianity: Islam, Hinduism, and the Mahayana form of Buddhism which now prevails in the Far East. You can see the role of Islam as a chrysalis between the ancient civilization of Israel and Iran and the modern Islamic civilization of the Near and Middle East. Hinduism, again, seems to bridge a gap in the history of civilization in India between the modern Hindu culture and the ancient culture of the Aryas; and Buddhism, likewise, seems to play the same part as a mediator between the modern history of the Far East and the history of ancient China. In that picture the

Christian Church would be simply one of a series of churches whose function is to serve as chrysalises to provide for the reproduction of civilizations and thus to preserve that secular species of society.

Now I think there is perhaps a chrysalis-like element in the constitution of the Christian Church—an institutional element that I am going to deal with later—which may have quite a different purpose from that of assisting in the reproduction of civilizations. But, before we accept at all an account of the place and role of Christianity and of the other living higher religions in social history which represents these religions as being mere instruments for assisting in the process of the reproduction of civilizations, let us go on testing the hypothesis by examining whether, in every instance of the parent-and-child relation between civilizations, we find a chrysalis-church intervening between the parent civilization and the daughter civilization. If you look at the histories of the ancient civilizations of South-Western Asia and Egypt, you find there a rudimentary higher religion in the form of the worship of a god and a related goddess. I call it rudimentary because, in the worship of Tammuz and Ishtar, of Adonis and Astarte, of Attis and Cybele, of Osiris and Isis, you are very close to the nature-worship of the Earth and her fruits; and I think that, here again, you can see that this rudimentary higher religion, in each of its different variants, has in every case played the historical role of filling a gap where there was a break in the continuity of secular civilization.

If, however, we complete our survey, we shall find that this apparent "law" does not always hold good. Christianity intervenes in this way between our own civilization and the Graeco-Roman one. Go back behind the Graeco-Roman one and you find a Minoan civilization behind that. But between the Minoan and the Graeco-Roman you do not find any higher religion corresponding to Christianity. Again, if you go back behind the ancient civilization of Aryan India, you find vestiges of a still more ancient pre-Aryan civilization in the Indus Valley which have only been excavated within the last twenty years, but here again you do not seem to find any higher religion intervening between the two. And, if you pass from the Old World to the New and look at the civilization of the Mayas in Central America, which, again, has had daughter civilizations born from it, you do not find, here either, in the intervening period, any trace at all of any higher religion or church of the same species as Christianity or Islam or Hinduism or Mahayanian Buddhism; nor again is there any evidence of any such chrysalis bridging the transition from primitive societies to the earliest known civilizations—to what we might call the first generation of civilizations; and so, when we complete our view of the whole field of civilizations, as we have now done in a very summary way, we find that the relation between higher religions and civilizations seems to differ according to the generation of the civilization with which we are dealing. We seem to find no higher religion at all between primitive societies and civilizations of the first generation, and between civilizations of the first and those of the second generation either none or only rudiments. It is between civilizations of the second and those of the third generation that the intervention of a higher religion seems to be the rule, and here only.

If there is anything in this analysis of the relation between civilizations and higher religions, this suggests a third possible view of that relation which would be the exact inverse of the second view which I have just put before you. On that second view, religion is subsidiary to the reproduction of secular civilizations, and the inverse of that would be that the successive rises and falls of civilizations may be subsidiary to the growth of religion.

The breakdowns and disintegrations of civilizations might be stepping-stones to higher things on the religious plane. After all, one of the deepest spiritual laws that we know is the law that is proclaimed by Aeschylus in the two words πάθει μάθος—"it is through suffering that learning comes"—and in the New Testament in the verse "whom the Lord loveth, He chasteneth; and scourgeth every son whom He receiveth." If you apply that to the rise of the higher religions which has culminated in the flowering of Christianity, you might say that in the mythical passions of Tammuz and Adonis and Attis and Osiris the Passion of Christ was foreshadowed, and that the Passion of Christ was the culminating and crowning experience of the sufferings of human souls in successive failures in the enterprise of secular civilization. The Christian Church itself arose out of the spiritual travail which was a consequence of the breakdown of the Graeco-Roman civilization. Again, the Christian Church has Jewish and Zoroastrian roots, and those roots sprang from an earlier breakdown, the breakdown of a Syrian civilization which was a sister to the Graeco-Roman. The kingdoms of Israel and Judah were two of the many states of this ancient Syrian world; and it was the premature and permanent overthrow of these worldly commonwealths and the extinction of all the political hopes which had been bound up with their existence as independent polities that brought the religion of Judaism to birth and evoked the highest expression of its spirit in the elegy of the Suffering Servant, which is appended in the Bible to the book of the prophet Isaiah. Judaism, likewise, has a Mosaic root which in its turn sprang from the withering of the second crop of the ancient Egyptian civilization. I do not know whether Moses and Abraham are historical characters, but I think it can be taken as certain that they represent historical stages of religious experience, and Moses' forefather and forerunner Abraham received his enlightenment and his promise at the dissolution, in the nineteenth or eighteenth century before Christ, of the ancient civilization of Sumer and Akkad—the earliest case, known to us, of a civilization going to ruin. These men of sorrows were precursors of Christ; and the sufferings through which they won their enlightenment were Stations of the Cross in anticipation of the Crucifixion. That is, no doubt, a very old idea, but it is also an ever new one.

If religion is a chariot, it looks as if the wheels on which it mounts towards Heaven may be the periodic downfalls of civilizations on Earth. It looks as if the movement of civilizations may be cyclic and recurrent, while the movement of religion may be on a single continuous upward line. The continuous upward movement of religion may be served and promoted by the cyclic movement of civilizations round the cycle of birth, death, birth.

If we accept this conclusion, it opens up what may seem a rather startling view of history. If civilizations are the handmaids of religion and if the Graeco-Roman civilization served as a good handmaid to Christianity by bringing it to birth before that civilization finally went to pieces, then the civilizations of the third generation may be vain repetitions of the Gentiles. If, so far from its being the historical function of higher religions to minister, as chrysalises, to the cyclic process of the reproduction of civilizations, it is the historical function of civilizations to serve, by their downfalls, as stepping-stones to a progressive process of the revelation of always deeper religious insight, and the gift of ever more grace to act on this insight, then the societies of the species called civilizations will have fulfilled their function when once they have brought a mature higher religion to birth; and, on this showing, our own Western post-Christian secular civilization might at best be a superfluous repetition of the pre-Christian Graeco-Roman one, and at worst a pernicious back-sliding from the path of spiritual progress. In our Western world of to-day, the worship of Leviathan— the self-worship of the tribe—is a religion to which all of us pay some measure of allegiance; and this tribal religion is, of course, sheer idolatry. Communism, which is another of our latter-day religions, is, I think, a leaf taken from the book of Christianity—a leaf torn out and misread. Democracy is another leaf from the book of Christianity, which has also, I fear, been torn out and, while perhaps not misread, has certainly been half emptied of meaning by being divorced from its Christian context and secularized; and we have obviously, for a number of generations past, been living on spiritual capital, I mean clinging to Christian practice without possessing the Christian belief—and practice unsupported by belief is a wasting asset, as we have suddenly discovered, to our dismay, in this generation.

If this self-criticism is just, then we must revise the whole of our present conception of modern history; and if we can make the effort of will and imagination to think this ingrained and familiar conception away, we shall arrive at a very different picture of the historical retrospect. Our present view of modern history focuses attention on the rise of our modern Western secular civilization as the latest great new event in the world. As we follow that rise, from the first premonition of it in the genius of Frederick II Hohenstaufen, through the Renaissance to the eruption of democracy and science and modern scientific technique, we think of all this as being the great new event in the world which demands our attention and commands our admiration. If we can bring ourselves to think of it, instead, as one of the vain repetitions of the Gentiles —an almost meaningless repetition of something that the Greeks and Romans did before us and did supremely well —then the greatest new event in the history of mankind will be seen to be a very different one. The greatest new event will then not be the monotonous rise of yet another secular civilization out of the bosom of the Christian Church in the course of these latter centuries; it will still be the Crucifixion and its spiritual consequences. There is one curious result of our immense modern scientific discoveries which is, I think, often overlooked. On the vastly changed time-scale which our astronomers and geologists have opened up to us, the beginning of the Christian era is an extremely recent date; on a time-scale in which nineteen hundred years are no more than the twinkling of an eye, the beginning of the Christian era is only yesterday. It is only on the old-fashioned time-scale, on which the creation of the world and the beginning of life on the planet were reckoned to have taken place not more than six thousand years ago, that a span of nineteen hundred years seems a long period of time and the beginning of the Christian era therefore seems a far-off event. In fact it is a very recent event—perhaps the most recent significant event in history—and that brings us to a consideration of the prospects of Christianity in the future history of mankind on Earth.

On this view of the history of religion and of the civilizations, it has not been the historical function of the

Christian Church just to serve as a chrysalis between the Graeco-Roman civilization and its daughter civilizations in Byzantium and the West; and, supposing that these two civilizations, which are descended from the ancient Graeco-Roman one, turn out to be no more than vain repetitions of their parent, then there will be no reason to suppose that Christianity itself will be superseded by some distinct, separate, and different higher religion which will serve as a chrysalis between the death of the present Western civilization and the birth of its children. On the theory that religion is subservient to civilization, you would expect some new higher religion to come into existence on each occasion, in order to serve the purpose of tiding over the gap between one civilization and another. If the truth is the other way round—if it is civilization that is the means and religion that is the end—then, once again, a civilization may break down and break up, but the replacement of one higher religion by another will not be a necessary consequence. So far from that, if our secular Western civilization perishes, Christianity may be expected not only to endure but to grow in wisdom and stature as the result of a fresh experience of secular catastrophe.

There is one unprecedented feature of our own post-Christian secular civilization which, in spite of being a rather superficial feature, has a certain importance in this connection. In the course of its expansion our modern Western secular civilization has become literally world-wide and has drawn into its net all other surviving civilizations as well as primitive societies. At its first appearance, Christianity was provided by the Graeco-Roman civilization with a universal state, in the shape of the Roman Empire with its policed roads and shipping routes, as an aid to the spread of Christianity round the shores of the Mediterranean. Our modern Western secular civilization in its turn may serve its historical purpose by providing Christianity with a completely world-wide repetition of the Roman Empire to spread over. We have not quite arrived at our Roman Empire yet, though the victor in this war may be the founder of it. But, long before a world is unified politically, it is unified economically and in other material ways; and the unification of our present world has long since opened the way for St. Paul, who once travelled from the Orontes to the Tiber under the aegis of the *Pax Romana,* to travel on from the Tiber to the Mississippi and from the Mississippi to the Yangtse; while Clement's and Origen's work of infusing Greek philosophy into Christianity at Alexandria might be emulated in some city of the Far East by the infusion of Chinese philosophy into Christianity. This intellectual feat has indeed been partly performed already. One of the greatest of modern missionaries and modern scholars, Matteo Ricci, who was both a Jesuit father and a Chinese literatus, set his hand to that task before the end of the sixteenth century of the Christian era. It is even possible that as, under the Roman Empire, Christianity drew out of and inherited from the other Oriental religions the heart of what was best in them, so the present religions of India and the form of Buddhism that is practised to-day in the Far East may contribute new elements to be grafted onto Christianity in days to come. And then one may look forward to what may happen when Caesar's empire decays—for Caesar's empire always does decay after a run of a few hundred years. What may happen is that Christianity may be left as the spiritual heir of all the other higher religions, from the post-Sumerian rudiment of one in the worship of Tammuz and Ishtar down to those that in A.D. 1948 are still living separate lives side by side with Christianity, and of all the philosophies from Ikhnaton's to Hegel's; while the Christian Church as an institution may be left as the social heir of all the other churches and all the civilizations.

That side of the picture brings one to another question which is both always old and always new—the question of the relation of the Christian Church to the Kingdom of Heaven. We seem to see a series of different kinds of society succeeding one another in this world. As the primitive species of societies has given place to a second species known as the civilizations within the brief period of the last six thousand years, so this second species of local and ephemeral societies may perhaps give place in its turn to a third species embodied in a single world-wide and enduring representative in the shape of the Christian Church. If we can look forward to that, we shall have to ask ourselves this question: Supposing that this were to happen, would it mean that the Kingdom of Heaven would then have been established on Earth?

I think this question is a very pertinent one in our day, because some kind of earthly paradise is the goal of most of the current secular ideologies. To my mind the answer is emphatically "No," for several reasons which I shall now do my best to put before you.

One very obvious and well-known reason lies in the nature of society and in the nature of man. Society is, after all, only the common ground between the fields of action of a number of personalities, and human personality, at any rate as we know it in this world, has an innate capacity for evil as well as for good. If these two statements are true, as I believe them to be, then in any society on Earth, unless and until human nature itself undergoes a moral mutation which would make an essential change in its character, the possibility of evil, as well as of good, will be born into the world afresh with every child and will never be wholly ruled out as long as that child remains alive. This is as much as to say that the replacement of a multiplicity of civilizations by a universal church would not have purged human nature of original sin; and this leads to another consideration: so long as original sin remains an element in human nature, Caesar will always have work to do, and there will still be Caesar's things to be rendered to Caesar, as well as God's to God, in this world. Human society on Earth will not be able wholly to dispense with institutions of which the sanction is not purely the individual's active will to make them work, but is partly habit and partly even force. These imperfect institutions will have to be administered by a secular power which might be subordinated to religious authority but would not thereby be eliminated. And even if Caesar were not merely subordinated but were wholly eliminated by the Church, something of him would still survive in the constitution of his supplanter; for the institutional element has historically, up to date, been dominant in the life of the Church herself in her traditional Catholic form, which, on the long historical view, is the form in which one has to look at her.

In this Catholic form of the Church, I see two funda-mental institutions, the Sacrifice of the Mass and the Hier-archy, which are indissolubly welded together by the fact that the priest, by definition, is the person with the power to perform the rite. If, in speaking of the Mass, one may speak, without offence, with the tongues of the historian and the anthropologist, then, using this language, one may describe the Sacrifice of the Mass as the mature form of a most ancient religious rite of which the rudiments can be traced back to the worship of the ferility of the Earth and her fruits by the earliest tillers of the soil. (I am speak-ing here merely of the mundane origin of the rite.) As for the hierarchy of the Church in its traditional form, this, as one knows, is modelled on a more recent and less awe-inspiring yet nevertheless most potent institution, the im-perial civil service of the Roman Empire. The Church in its traditional form thus stands forth armed with the spear of the Mass, the shield of the Hierarchy, and the helmet of the Papacy; and perhaps the subconscious purpose—or the divine intention, if you prefer that language—of this heavy panoply of institutions in which the Church has clad herself is the very practical one of outlasting the toughest of the secular institutions of this world, includ-ing all the civilizations. If we survey all the institutions of which we have knowledge in the present and in the past, I think that the institutions created, or adopted and adapted, by Christianity are the toughest and the most en-during of any that we know and are therefore the most likely to last—and outlast all the rest. The history of Protestantism would seem to indicate that the Protestant act of casting off this armour four hundred years ago was premature; but that would not necessarily mean that this step would always be a mistake; and, however that may be, the institutional element in the traditional Catholic form of the Church Militant on Earth, even if it proves to be an invaluable and indispensable means of survival, is all the same a mundane feature which makes the Church Militant's life different from that of the Kingdom of

Heaven, in which they neither marry nor are given in marriage but are as the angels of God, and in which each individual soul catches the spirit of God from direct communion with Him—"like light caught from a leaping flame," as Plato puts it in his Seventh Letter. Thus, even if the Church had won a fully world-wide allegiance and had entered into the inheritance of the last of the civilizations and of all the other higher religions, the Church on Earth would not be a perfect embodiment here on Earth of the Kingdom of Heaven. The Church on Earth would still have sin and sorrow to contend with as well as to profit by as a means of grace on the principle of πάθει μάθος, and she would still have to wear for a long time to come a panoply of institutions to give her the massive social solidity that she needs in the mundane struggle for survival, but this at the inevitable price of spiritually weighing her down. On this showing, the victorious Church Militant on Earth will be a province of the Kingdom of God, but a province in which the citizens of the heavenly commonwealth have to live and breathe and labour in an atmosphere that is not their native element.

The position in which the Church would then find herself is well conveyed in Plato's conceit, in the *Phaedo,* of the true surface of the Earth. We live, Plato suggests, in a large but local hollow, and what we take to be the air is really a sediment of fog. If one day we could make our way to the upper levels of the surface of the Earth, we should there breathe the pure ether and should see the light of the Sun and stars direct; and then we should realize how dim and blurred had been our vision down in the hollow, where we see the heavenly bodies, through the murky atmosphere in which we breathe, as imperfectly as the fishes see them through the water in which they swim. This Platonic conceit is a good simile for the life of the Church Militant on Earth; but the truth cannot be put better than it has been by Saint Augustine.

It is written of Cain that he founded a commonwealth; but Abel—true to the type of the pilgrim and sojourner that he was—did not do the like. For the Commonwealth of the Saints is not of this world, though it does give birth to citizens here in whose persons it performs its pilgrimage until the time of its kingdom shall come—the time when it will gather them all together.[2]

This brings me in conclusion to the last of the topics on which I am going to touch, that of the relation between Christianity and progress.

If it is true, as I think it is, that the Church on Earth will never be a perfect embodiment of the Kingdom of Heaven, in what sense can we say the words of the Lord's Prayer: "Thy Kingdom come, Thy will be done in Earth as it is in Heaven"? Have we been right, after all, in coming to the conclusion that—in contrast to the cyclic movement of the rises and falls of civilizations—the history of religion on Earth is a movement in a single continuous upward line? What are the matters in which there has been, in historical times, a continuous religious advance? And have we any reason to think that this advance will continue without end? Even if the species of societies called civilizations does give way to a historically younger and perhaps spiritually higher species embodied in a single world-wide and enduring representative in the shape of the Christian Church, may there not come a time when the tug of war between Christianity and original sin will settle down to a static balance of spiritual forces?

Let me put forward one or two considerations in reply to these questions.

In the first place, religious progress means spiritual progress, and spirit means personality. Therefore religious progress must take place in the spiritual lives of personalities—it must show itself in their rising to a spiritually higher state and achieving a spiritually finer activity.

Now, in assuming that this individual progress is what spiritual progress means, are we after all admitting Frazer's thesis that the higher religions are essentially and incurably anti-social? Does a shift of human interest and energy from trying to create the values aimed at in the civilizations to trying to create the values aimed at in the higher religions mean that the values for which the civilizations stand are bound to suffer? Are spiritual and social values antithetical and inimical to each other? Is it true that the fabric of

[2] Saint Augustine: *De Civitate Dei,* Book xv, chap. i.

civilization is undermined if the salvation of the individual soul is taken as being the supreme aim of life?

Frazer answers these questions in the affirmative. If his answer were right it would mean that human life was a tragedy without a catharsis. But I personally believe that Frazer's answer is not right, because I think it is based on a fundamental misconception of what the nature of souls or personalities is. Personalities are inconceivable except as agents of spiritual activity; and the only conceivable scope for spiritual activity lies in relations between spirit and spirit. It is because spirit implies spiritual relations that Christian theology has completed the Jewish doctrine of the Unity of God with the Christian doctrine of the Trinity. The doctrine of the Trinity is the theological way of expressing the revelation that God is a spirit; the doctrine of the Redemption is the theological way of expressing the revelation that God is Love. If man has been created in the likeness of God, and if the true end of man is to make this likeness ever more and more like, then Aristotle's saying that "man is a social animal" applies to man's highest potentiality and aim—that of trying to get into ever closer communion with God. Seeking God is itself a social act. And if God's love has gone into action in this world in the Redemption of mankind by Christ, then man's efforts to make himself liker to God must include efforts to follow Christ's example in sacrificing himself for the redemption of his fellow men. Seeking and following God in this way, that is God's way, is the only true way for a human soul on Earth to seek salvation. The antithesis between trying to save one's own soul by seeking and following God and trying to do one's duty to one's neighbour is therefore wholly false. The two activities are indissoluble. The human soul that is truly seeking to save itself is as fully social a being as the ant-like Spartan or the bee-like Communist. Only, the Christian soul on Earth is a member of a very different society from Sparta or Leviathan. He is a citizen of the Kingdom of God, and therefore his paramount and all-embracing aim is to attain the highest degree of communion with, and likeness to, God Himself; his relations with his fellow men are consequences of, and corollaries to, his relations with

God; and his way of loving his neighbour as himself will be to try to help his neighbour to win what he is seeking for himself—that is, to come into closer communion with God and to become more godlike.

If this is a soul's recognized aim for itself and for its fellow souls in the Christian Church Militant on Earth, then it is obvious that under a Christian dispensation God's will *will* be done in Earth as it is in Heaven to an immeasurably greater degree than in a secular mundane society. It is also evident that, in the Church Militant on Earth, the good social aims of the mundane societies will incidentally be achieved very much more successfully than they ever have been or can be achieved in a mundane society which aims at these objects direct, and at nothing higher. In other words, the spiritual progress of individual souls in this life will in fact bring with it much more social progress than could be attained in any other way. It is a paradoxical but profoundly true and important principle of life that the most likely way to reach a goal is to be aiming not at that goal itself but at some more ambitious goal beyond it. This is the meaning of the fable in the Old Testament of Solomon's Choice and of the saying in the New Testament about losing one's life and saving it.

Therefore, while the replacement of the mundane civilizations by the world-wide and enduring reign of the Church Militant on Earth would certainly produce what to-day would seem a miraculous improvement in those mundane social conditions which the civilizations have been seeking to improve during the last six thousand years, the aim, and test, of progress under a truly Christian dispensation on Earth would not lie in the field of mundane social life; the field would be the spiritual life of individual souls in their passages through this earthly life from birth into this world to death out of it.

But if spiritual progress in time in this world means progress achieved by individual human souls during their passages through this world to the other world, in what sense can there be any spiritual progress over a time-span far longer than that of individual lives on Earth, and running into thousands of years, such as that of the historical development of the higher religions from the rise of Tammuz-worship and the generation of Abraham to the Christian era?

I have already confessed my own adherence to the traditional Christian view that there is no reason to expect any change in unredeemed human nature while human life on Earth goes on. Till this Earth ceases to be physically habitable by man, we may expect that the endowments of individual human beings with original sin and with natural goodness will be about the same, on the average, as they always have been as far as our knowledge goes. The most primitive societies known to us in the life or by report provide examples of as great natural goodness as, and no lesser wickedness than, the highest civilizations or religious societies that have yet come into existence. There has been no perceptible variation in the average sample of human nature in the past; there is no ground, in the evidence afforded by History, to expect any great variation in the future either for better or for worse.

The matter in which there might be spiritual progress in time on a time-span extending over many successive generations of life on Earth is not the unregenerate nature of man, but the opportunity open to souls, by way of the learning that comes through suffering, for getting into closer communion with God, and becoming less unlike Him, during their passage through this world.

What Christ, with the Prophets before Him and the Saints after Him, has bequeathed to the Church, and what the Church, by virtue of having been fashioned into an incomparably effective institution, succeeds in accumulating, preserving, and communicating to successive generations of Christians, is a growing fund of illumination and of grace—meaning by "illumination" the discovery or revelation or revealed discovery of the true nature of God and the true end of man here and hereafter, and by "grace," the will or inspiration or inspired will to aim at getting into closer communion with God and becoming less unlike Him. In this matter of increasing spiritual opportunity for souls in their passages through life on Earth, there is assuredly an inexhaustible possibility of progress in this world.

Is the spiritual opportunity given by Christianity, or by

one or other of the higher religions that have been forerunners of Christianity and have partially anticipated Christianity's gifts of illumination and grace to men on Earth,
an indispensable condition for salvation—meaning by "salvation" the spiritual effect on a soul of feeling after God
and finding Him in its passage through life on Earth?

If this were so, then the innumerable generations of men
who never had the chance of receiving the illumination
and grace conveyed by Christianity and the other higher
religions would have been born and have died without a
chance of the salvation which is the true end of man and
the true purpose of life on Earth. This might be conceivable, though still repugnant, if we believed that the true
purpose of life on Earth was not the preparation of souls
for another life, but the establishment of the best possible
human society in this world, which in the Christian belief
is not the true purpose, though it is an almost certain by-
product of a pursuit of the true purpose. If progress is
taken as being the social progress of Leviathan and not the
spiritual progress of individual souls, then it would perhaps
be conceivable that, for the gain and glory of the body
social, innumerable earlier generations should have been
doomed to live a lower social life in order that a higher
social life might eventually be lived by successors who had
entered into their labours. This would be conceivable on
the hypothesis that individual human souls existed for the
sake of society, and not for their own sakes or for God's.
But this belief is not only repugnant but is also inconceivable when we are dealing with the history of religion,
where the progress of individual souls through this world
towards God, and not the progress of society in this world,
is the end on which the supreme value is set. We cannot
believe that the historically incontestable fact that illumination and grace have been imparted to men on Earth
in successive instalments, beginning quite recently in the
history of the human race on Earth, and even then coming
gradually in the course of generations, can have entailed
the consequence that the vast majority of souls born into
the world up to date, who have had no share in this
spiritual opportunity, have, as a result, been spiritually

lost. We must believe that the possibilities, provided by God, of learning through suffering in this world have always afforded a sufficient means of salvation to every soul that has made the best of the spiritual opportunity offered to it here, however small that opportunity may have been.

But, if men on Earth have not had to wait for the advent of the higher religions, culminating in Christianity, in order to qualify, in their life on Earth, for eventually attaining, after death, the state of eternal felicity in the other world, then what difference has the advent on Earth of the higher religions, and of Christianity itself, really made? The difference, I should say, is this, that, under the Christian dispensation, a soul which does make the best of its spiritual opportunities will, in qualifying for salvation, be advancing farther towards communion with God and towards likeness to God under the conditions of life on Earth, before death, than has been possible for souls that have not been illuminated, during their pilgrimage on Earth, by the light of the higher religions. A pagan soul, no less than a Christian soul, has ultimate salvation with its reach; but a soul which has been offered, and has opened itself to, the illumination and the grace that Christianity conveys, will, while still in this world, be more brightly irradiated with the light of the other world than a pagan soul that has won salvation by making the best, in this world, of the narrower opportunity here to open to it. The Christian soul can attain, while still on Earth, a greater measure of man's greatest good than can be attained by any pagan soul in this earthly stage of its existence.

Thus the historical progress of religion in this world, as represented by the rise of the higher religions and by their culmination in Christianity, may, and almost certainly will, bring with it, incidentally, an immeasurable improvement in the conditions of human social life on Earth; but its direct effect and its deliberate aim and its true test is the opportunity which it brings to individual souls for spiritual progress in this world during the passage from birth to death. It is this individual spiritual progress in this world for which we pray when we say "Thy will be done in Earth as it is in Heaven." It is for the salvation that is open to all men of good will—pagan as well as Christian, primitive as well as civilized—who make the most of their spiritual opportunities on Earth, however narrow these opportunities may be, that we pray when we say "Thy Kingdom come."

13

THE MEANING OF HISTORY FOR THE SOUL

Theologia Historici

The questions discussed in this essay have been debated acutely, for centuries past, by theologians and philosophers. In taking them up, the present writer is therefore likely to fall into errors that will seem elementary to his readers. He will certainly be treading on ground that is familiar and well-worn to them. He ventures, nevertheless, on this inquiry in the hope that it may be of some interest to theologians to see how these old theological questions are approached by a historian. In any case, theologians may perhaps find some amusement in watching an unwary historian floundering in well-known and minutely charted theological morasses.

Let us start our inquiry by examining successively two point of view which lie at opposite extremes of the historico-theological gamut, but which, if respectively tenable, would each solve the problem of the meaning of history for the soul in fairly simple terms. In the writer's opinion (he may as well declare in advance) both points of view are in truth untenable, though each does contain an element of truth which it invalidates through the exaggeration of pushing it to extremes.

A Purely This-Worldly View

The first of these two extreme views is that, for the soul, the whole meaning of its existence is contained in history.

On this view, the individual human being is nothing but a part of the society of which he is a member. The individual exists for society, not society for the individual. Therefore the significant and important thing in human life is not the spiritual development of souls but the social development of communities. In the writer's opinion, this thesis is not true, and, when it has been taken as true and has been put into action, it has produced moral enormities.

The proposition that the individual is a mere part of a social whole may be the truth about social insects—bees, ants, and termites—but it is not the truth about any human beings of whom we have any knowledge. An early twentieth-century school of anthropologists, of which Durkheim was the leading representative, drew a picture of primitive man which portrayed him as being almost of a different mental and spiritual breed from our allegedly rational selves. Drawing its evidence from descriptions of surviving primitive societies, this school represented primitive man as being governed not by the rational operation of the individual intellect, but by the collective emotion of the human herd. This sharp distinction between an "uncivilized" and a "civilized" breed of man has, however, to be radically revised and toned down in the light of the illuminating psychological discoveries that have been made since Durkheim's day. Psychological research has shown us that the so-called savage has no monopoly of the emotionally governed life of the collective unconscious. Though it happens to have been first laid bare in the soul of primitive man by anthropological observation, psychological research has made it clear that, in our comparatively sophisticated souls too, the collective unconscious underlies a consciousness that rides on it like a cockleshell floating precariously on a bottomless and shoreless ocean. Whatever the constitution of the human psyche may prove to be, we can already be more or less certain that it is substantially the same in human beings like ourselves, who are in the act of attempting to climb from the level of primitive human life to the ledge of civilization, and in ex-primitives, like the Papuans of New Guinea and the Negritos of Central Africa, who have been played upon, within the last few thousand years, by the radiation of societies that have been in process of civilization within that period. The psychic make-up of all extant human beings, in all extant types of society, appears to be substantially identical, and we have no ground for believing it to have been different in the earliest representatives of the species *sapiens* of the genus *homo* that are known to us, not from the anthropologist's personal intercourse with living people, but from the archaeologist's and the physiologist's deciphering of the revealing evidence of artifacts and skeletons. In the most primitive as well as in the least primitive state in which *homo sapiens* is in any way known to us, we may conclude that the individual human being possesses some measure of self-conscious personality that raises his soul above the level of the water of the collective unconscious, and this means that the individual soul does have a genuine life of its own which is distinct from the life of society. We may also conclude that individuality is a pearl of great moral price, when we observe the moral enormities that occur when this pearl is trampled in the mire.

These enormities are most conspicuous in extreme examples: the Spartan way of life in the society of classical Greece, the Ottoman Sultan's slave household in the early modern Islamic world, the totalitarian regimes that have been established by force in a number of Western or partially Westernized countries in our own day. But when once we have grasped, from such extreme cases, what the nature of these moral enormities is, it is more instructive to detect the Spartan tincture in the patriotism of the ordinary classical Greek city-state, and the totalitarian tincture in our ordinary modern Western nationalism. In religious terms, this treatment of the individual as a mere part of the community is a denial of the personal relation between the soul and God and is a substitution, for the worship of God, of a worship of the human community— Leviathan, the abomination of desolation, standing in the place where it ought not. The German National-Socialist youth leader, Baldur von Schirach, once declared that his task was "to build a great altar to Germany in every German heart." It must be wrong to worship a man-made institution which is ephemeral, imperfect, and often utterly evil in its operation, and it is worth recalling that a particularly noble—perhaps the noblest conceivable—form of this Leviathan-worship was intransigently rejected by early Christianity. If any human community were ever worthy of worship, it would be a universal state, like the Roman Empire, that has brought the blessings of unity and peace to a world long racked by war and revolution. Yet the early Christians challenged the apparently irresistible might of the Roman Imperial Government rather than compromise with a Leviathan-worship that was persuasively commended to them as being nothing more sinister than an amiable formality.

Leviathan-worship is a moral enormity, even at its noblest and mildest; yet there is an element of truth underlying this mistaken belief that society is the end of man and that the individual is merely a means to that end. This underlying truth is that man is a social creature. He cannot achieve the potentialities of his nature except by going outside himself and entering into relations with other spiritual beings. The Christian would say that the most important of the soul's relations is its communion with God, but that it also needs to have relations with its fellow creatures, who are God's other children.

A Solely Other-Worldly View

Let us now take a flying leap to the opposite pole and examine the antithetical view that, for the soul, the whole meaning of its existence lies outside history.

On this view, this world is wholly meaningless and evil. The task of the soul in this world is to endure it, to detach itself from it, to get out of it. This is the view of the Buddhist, Stoic and Epicurean schools of philosophy (whatever the Buddha's own personal outlook may have been). There is a strong vein of it in Platonism. And it has been one of the historic interpretations (in the writer's belief, a mistaken one) of Christianity.

According to the extreme Buddhist view, the soul itself is part and parcel of the phenomenal world, so that, in order to get rid of the phenomenal world, the soul has to extinguish itself. At any rate, it has to extinguish elements in itself which, to the Christian mind, are essential for the soul's existence: for example, above all, the feelings of love and pity. This is unmistakably evident in the Hinayana interpretation of Buddhism, but it is also implicit in the Mahayana, however reluctant the followers of the Mahayana school may be to dwell on the ultimate implications of their own tenets. The Mahayanian Bodhisattva may be moved, by his love and pity for his fellow sentient beings, to postpone his own entry into Nirvana for aeons upon aeons for the sake of helping his fellows to follow the path that he has found for himself. Yet this path is, after all, the orthodox one that leads to salvation through self-extinction, and the Bodhisattva's sacrifice, though immense, is not irrevocable or everlasting. At long last, he is going to take that final step into the Nirvana on whose threshold he already stands, and, in the act, he will extinguish, with himself, the love and pity that have won for him the answering love and gratitude of mankind.

The Stoic might be described (perhaps too unkindly) as a would-be Buddhist who has not had quite the full courage of his convictions. As for the Epicurean, he regards this world as an accidental, meaningless, and evil product of the mechanical interplay of atoms, and—since the probable duration of the particular ephemeral world in which he happens to find himself may be drearily long by comparison with a human being's expectation of life—he must look forward to, or expedite, his own dissolution as the only way out for himself.

The Christian of the extreme other-worldly school does, of course, believe that God exists and that this world has been created by Him for a purpose, but this purpose, as he sees it, is the negative one of training the soul, by suffering, for life in another world with which this world has nothing positive in common.

This view that the whole meaning of the soul's existence lies outside history seems to the writer to present difficulties, even in its attenuated Christian version, that are insurmountable from the Christian standpoint.

In the first place, any such view is surely incompatible with the distinctive belief of Christianity about the nature of God: the belief that God loves His creatures and so loved the world that He became incarnate in order to bring redemption to human souls during their life on Earth. It is hard to conceive of a loving God as creating this, or any, world of sentient creatures not for its own sake but merely as a means to some end in another world for whose blissful denizens this world is a waste land beyond the pale. It is even harder to conceive of Him as deliberately charging this forlorn waste land of his alleged creation with sin and suffering, in the cold-blooded spirit of a military commander who creates an exercise ground for his troops by taking, or making, a wilderness and sowing it with live mines, strewing it with unexploded shells and hand grenades, and drenching it with poison gas in order to train his soldiers to cope with these infernal machines at grievous cost to them in life and limb.

Moreover, whatever may or may not be possible for God, we can declare with assurance that it is not possible for the soul to treat its relations in this world with other souls as being of no importance in themselves, but as being merely a means to its own salvation. So, far from being a good training in this world for Christian perfection in another world, such odious inhumanity in man's attitude towards his fellow men would be an education in hardening his heart against the promptings of Christian love. In other words, it would be the worst conceivable mis-education from the Christian point of view.

Finally, if we believe that all souls are objects of absolute value to God, we cannot but believe that they must also be of absolute value to one another whenever and wherever they meet: of absolute value in this world in anticipation of the next.

The view that, for the soul, the whole meaning of its existence lies outside history thus proves to be no less repellent than the antithetical view which we examined first; yet, in this case, as in that, there is an element of truth underlying the mistaken belief. While it is not true that man's social life and human relations in this world are merely a means towards a personal spiritual end, the underlying truths are that in this world we do learn by suffering; that life in this world is not an end in itself and by itself; that it is only a fragment (even if an authentic one) of some larger whole; and that, in this larger whole, the central and dominant (though not the only) feature in the soul's spiritual landscape is its relation to God.

A Third View: the World a Province of the Kingdom of God

We have now rejected two views, both of which offer an answer to our question: What is the meaning of history for the soul? We have refused to admit that, for the soul, the meaning of its existence lies either wholly in history or wholly outside history. And this pair of negative conclusions confronts us with a dilemma.

In rejecting the view that the meaning of the soul's existence lies wholly in history, we have vindicated the primacy—as a fact, as a right, and as a duty—of each individual soul's relation to God. But if every soul, at any time or place, and in any social or historical situation in this world, is in a position to know and love God—or, in traditional theological terms, in a position to find salvation —this truth might seem to empty history of significance. If the most primitive people, in the most rudimentary conditions of social and spiritual life in this world, can achieve the true end of man in man's relation to God, then why should we strive to make this world a better place? Indeed, what intelligible meaning could be attached to those words? On the other hand, in rejecting the view that the meaning of the soul's existence lies wholly outside history, we have vindicated the primacy of God's love in His relation to His creatures. But, if this world has the positive value that it must have if God loves it and has become incarnate in it, then His attempts, and our attempts under His inspiration and on His behalf, to make this world a better place must be right and significant in some sense.

Can we resolve this apparent contradiction? We might perhaps resolve it for practical purposes if we could find an answer to the question: In what sense can there be progress in this world?

The progress with which we are here concerned is a progressive improvement, continuous and cumulative from generation to generation, in our social heritage. By progress, we must mean this; for there is no warrant for supposing that, within "historical times," there has been any progress in the evolution of human nature itself, either physical or spiritual. Even if we push our historical horizon back to the date of the first emergence of *homo sapiens,* the period is infinitesimally short on the time scale of the evolution of life on this planet. Western man, at the present high level of his intellectual powers and technological aptitudes, has not sloughed off Adam's heirloom of original sin, and, to the best of our knowledge, *homo aurignacius,* a hundred thousand years ago, must have been endowed, for good or evil, with the self-same spiritual, as well as physical, characteristics that we find in ourselves. Progress then, if discernible within "historical times," must have been progress in the improvement of our social heritage and not progress in the improvement of our breed, and the evidence for social progress is, of course, impressive in the field of scientific knowledge and its application to technology: in everything, that is to say, which has to do with man's command over non-human nature. This, however, is a side issue; for the impressiveness of the evidence for progress in this particular field is matched by the obviousness of the fact that man is relatively good at dealing with non-human nature. What he is bad at is his dealing with human nature in himself and in his fellow human beings. *A fortiori,* he has proved to be very bad indeed at getting into the right relation with God. Man has been a dazzling success in the field of intellect and "know-how" and a dismal failure in the things of the spirit, and it has been the great tragedy of human life on Earth that this sensational inequality of man's respective achievements in the non-human and in the spiritual sphere should, so far at any rate, have been this way round; for the spiritual side of man's life is of vastly greater importance for man's well-being (even for his material well-being, in the last resort) than is his command over non-human nature.

What is the position, then, in terms of this spiritual side of life which matters so much to man and in which he has so far been so backward? Can there be cumulative progress in the improvement of our social heritage in terms of the spiritual life of mankind—which means the spiritual life of individual souls, since man's relation to God is personal and not collective? A conceivable kind of progress in these spiritual terms—a kind that would give significance to history and would, so to speak, justify God's love for this world and His incarnation in it—would be a cumulative increase in the means of Grace at the disposal of each soul in this world. There are, of course, elements, and very important elements, in man's spiritual situation in this world which would not be affected by such an increase in the means of Grace available. It would not affect either man's innate tendency to original sin or his capacity for obtaining salvation in this world. Every child would be born in the bondage of original sin under the new and the old spiritual dispensation alike, though the child born under the new dispensation might be far better armed and aided than his predecessors were for obtaining his liberation. Again, under the old and the new dispensation alike, the opportunity for obtaining salvation in this world would be open to every soul, since every soul always and everywhere has within its reach the possibility of knowing and loving God. The actual—and momentous—effect of a cumulative increase in the means of Grace at man's disposal in this world would be to make it possible for human souls, while still in this world, to come to know God better and come to love Him more nearly in his own way.

On such a view, this world would not be a spiritual exercise ground beyond the pale of the Kingdom of God; it would be a province of the Kingdom—one province only, and not the most important one, yet one which had the same absolute value as the rest, and therefore one in which spiritual action could, and would, be fully significant and worth while; the one thing of manifest and abiding value in a world in which all other things are vanity.

THE WORLD AND THE WEST

PREFACE

The encounter between the World and the West may well prove, in retrospect, to be the most important event in modern history. It is an outstanding instance of an historical phenomenon of which there are other famous instances in the past, and the comparative study of the course and consequences of these encounters between civilizations that are one another's contemporaries is one of the keys to an understanding of the history of mankind.

The present book reproduces, for a reader's eye, the Reith Lectures that were delivered by the author in the year 1952 on the invitation of the B.B.C. When the B.B.C. asked me to be their Reith Lecturer for that year, they suggested that I might offer for my subject one of the topics dealt with in the last four volumes of my book *A Study of History* which are now in the press and which are to be published in 1954. My choice was *The World and the West*; and, now that the Reith Lectures on this subject have been broadcast and been printed in current issues of *The Listener*, they have been collected for publication here in advance of the appearance of the remaining volumes of *A Study of History*.

The purpose of this book is to introduce, in a short and simple presentation, a subject that is dealt with on a so much larger scale in the forthcoming Volume VIII of *A Study of History* that the present treatment of it will not duplicate either the corresponding part of the *Study* (Volume VIII, Part IX) or, indeed, the corresponding passages of the single-volume abridgement of Volumes VII-X of the *Study* which Mr. D. C. Somervell is intending to make on the lines of his masterly abridgement of Volumes I-VI.

A.J.T.

December 1952

1

RUSSIA AND THE WEST

Perhaps the best way for the author to introduce a reader to the subject of this book will be to explain why he has given it the title that it bears. "Why," the reader may be wondering, "has the book been called 'The World and the West'? Isn't the West just another name for as much of the world as has any importance for practical purposes today? And, if the author feels that he must say something about the non-Western rest of the world, why must he put the two words in this order? Why could he not write 'The West and the World' instead of writing 'The World and the West'? He might at least have put the West first."

This title, as it stands, was chosen deliberately, in order to make two points that seem essential for an understanding of the subject. The first point is that the West has never been all of the world that matters. The West has not been the only actor on the stage of modern history even at the peak of the West's power (and this peak has perhaps now already been passed). The second point is this. In the encounter between the world and the West that has been going on by now for four or five hundred years, the world, not the West, is the party that, up to now, has had the significant experience. It has not been the West that has been hit by the world; it is the world that has been hit—and hit hard—by the West; and that is why, in the title of this book, the world has been put first.

A Westerner who wants to grapple with this subject,

must try, for a few minutes, to slip out of his native Western skin and look at the encounter between the world and the West through the eyes of the great non-Western majority of mankind. Different though the non-Western peoples of the world may be from one another in race, language, civilization, and religion, if any Western inquirer asks them their opinion of the West, he will hear them all giving him the same answer: Russians, Muslims, Hindus, Chinese, Japanese, and all the rest. The West, they will tell him, has been the arch-aggressor of modern times, and each will have their own experience of Western aggression to bring up against him. The Russians will remind him that their country has been invaded by Western armies overland in 1941, 1915, 1812, 1709, and 1610; the peoples of Africa and Asia will remind him that Western missionaries, traders, and soldiers from across the sea have been pushing into their countries from the coasts since the fifteenth century. The Asians will also remind him that, within the same period, the Westerners have occupied the lion's share of the world's last vacant lands in the Americas, Australia, New Zealand, and South and East Africa. The Africans will remind him that they were enslaved and deported across the Atlantic in order to serve the European colonizers of the Americas as living tools to minister to their Western masters' greed for wealth. The descendants of the aboriginal population of North America will remind him that their ancestors were swept aside to make room for the West European intruders and for their African slaves.

This indictment will surprise, shock, grieve, and perhaps even outrage most Westerners today. Dutch Westerners are conscious of having evacuated Indonesia, and British Westerners of having evacuated India, Pakistan, Burma, and Ceylon, since 1945. British Westerners have no aggressive war on their consciences since the South African War of 1899-1902, and American Westerners none since the Spanish-American War of 1898. We forget all too easily that the Germans, who attacked their neighbours, including Russia, in the First World War and again in the Second World War, are Westerners too, and that the Russians, Asians, and Africans do not draw fine distinctions between different hordes of "Franks"—which is the world's common name for Westerners in the mass. "When the world passes judgement, it can be sure of having the last word," according to a well-known Latin proverb. And certainly the world's judgement on the West does seem to be justified over a period of about four and a half centuries ending in 1945. In the world's experience of the West during all that time, the West has been the aggressor on the whole; and, if the tables are being turned on the West by Russia and China today, this is a new chapter of the story which did not begin until after the end of the Second World War. The West's alarm and anger at recent acts of Russian and Chinese aggression at the West's expense are evidence that, for us Westerners, it is today still a strange experience to be suffering at the hands of the world what the world has been suffering at Western hands for a number of centuries past.

What, then, has been the world's experience of the West? Let us begin with Russia's experience, for Russia is part of the world's great non-Western majority. Though the Russians have been Christians and are, many of them, Christians still, they have never been Western Christians. Russia was converted not from Rome, as England was, but from Constantinople; and, in spite of their common Christian origins, Eastern and Western Christendom have always been foreign to one another, and have often been mutually antipathetic and hostile, as Russia and the West unhappily still are today, when each of them is in what one might call a "post-Christian" phase of its history.

This on the whole unhappy story of Russia's relations with the West did, though, have a happier first chapter; for, in spite of the difference between the Russian and the Western way of life, Russia and the West got on fairly well with one another in the early Middle Ages. The peoples traded, and the royal families intermarried. An English King Harold's daughter, for instance, married a Russian prince. The estrangement began in the thirteenth century, after the subjugation of Russia by the Tatars. The Tatars' domination over Russia was temporary, because the Tatars were Nomads from the Steppes who could not ever make themselves at home in Russia's fields and forests. Russia's lasting losses as a result of this temporary Tatar conquest were, not to her Tatar conquerors, but to her Western neighbours; for these took advantage of Russia's prostration in order to lop off, and annex to Western Christendom, the western fringes of the Russian world in White Russia and in the western half of the Ukraine. It was not till 1945 that Russia recaptured the last piece of these huge Russian territories that were taken from her by Western Powers in the thirteenth and fourteenth centuries.

These Western conquests at Russia's expense in the late Middle Ages had an effect on Russia's life at home, as well as on her relations with her Western assailants. The pressure on Russia from the West did not merely estrange Russia from the West; it was one of the hard facts of Russian life that moved the Russians to submit to the yoke of a new native Russian Power at Moscow which, at the price of autocracy, imposed on Russia the political unity that she now had to have if she was to survive. It was no accident that this new-fangled autocratic centralizing government of Russia should have arisen at Moscow; for Moscow stood in the fairway of the easiest line for the invasion of what was left of Russia by a Western aggressor. The Poles in 1610, the French in 1812, the Germans in 1941, all marched this way. Since an early date in the fourteenth century, autocracy and centralization have been the dominant notes of all successive Russian régimes. This Muscovite Russian political tradition has perhaps always been as disagreeable for the Russians themselves as it has certainly been distasteful and alarming to their neighbours; but unfortunately the Russians have learnt to put up with it, partly perhaps out of sheer habit, but also, no doubt, because they have felt it to be a lesser evil than the alternative fate of being conquered by aggressive neighbours.

This Russian attitude of resignation towards an autocratic régime that has become traditional in Russia is, of course, one of the main difficulties, as we Westerners see it, in the relations between Russia and the West today.

The great majority of people in the West feel that tyranny is an intolerable social evil. At a fearful cost we have put down tyranny when it has raised its head among our Western selves in the forms of Fascism and National Socialism. We feel the same detestation and distrust of it in its Russian form, whether this calls itself Czarism or calls itself Communism. We do not want to see this Russian brand of tyranny spread; and we are particularly concerned about this danger to Western ideals of liberty now that we Franks find ourselves thrown upon the defensive for the first time in our history since the second Turkish siege of Vienna in 1682-3. Our present anxiety about what seems to us to be post-war threat to the West from Russia is a well-justified anxiety in our belief. At the same time, we must take care not to allow the reversal in the relation between Russia and the West since 1945 to mislead us into forgetting the past in our natural pre-occupation with the present. When we look at the encounter between Russia and the West in the historian's instead of the journalist's perspective, we shall see that, over a period of several centuries ending in 1945, the Russians have had the same reason for looking askance at the West that we Westerners feel that we have for looking askance at Russia today.

During the last few centuries, this threat to Russia from the West, which has been a constant threat from the thirteenth century till 1945, has been made more serious for Russia by the outbreak, in the West, of a technological revolution which has become chronic and which does not yet show any signs of abating.

When the West adopted fire-arms, Russia followed suit, and in the sixteenth century she used these new weapons from the West to conquer the Tatars in the Volga valley and more primitive peoples in the Urals and in Siberia. But in 1610 the superiority of the Western armaments of the day enabled the Poles to occupy Moscow and to hold it for two years, while at about the same time the Swedes were also able to deprive Russia of her outlet on the Baltic Sea at the head of the Gulf of Finland. The Russian retort to these seventeenth-century Western acts of aggression was to adopt the technology of the West wholesale, together with as much of the Western way of life as was inseparable from Western technology.

It was characteristic of the autocratic centralizing Muscovite régime that this technological and accompanying social revolution in Russia at the turn of the seventeenth and eighteenth centuries should have been imposed upon Russia from above downwards, by the fiat of one man of genius, Peter the Great. Peter is a key figure for an understanding of the world's relations with the West not only in Russia but everywhere; for Peter is the arche-type of the autocratic Westernizing reformer who, during the last two and a half centuries, has saved the world from falling entirely under Western domination by forcing the world to train itself to resist Western aggression with Western weapons. Sultans Selīm III and Mahmūd II and President Mustafā Kemāl Atatürk in Turkey, Mehmed 'Ali Pasha in Egypt, and "the Elder Statesmen," who made the Westernizing revolution in Japan in the eighteen-sixties, were, all of them, following in Peter the Great's footsteps consciously or unconsciously.

Peter launched Russia on a technological race with the West which Russia is still running. Russia has never yet been able to afford to rest, because the West has continually been making fresh spurts. For example, Peter and his eighteenth-century successors brought Russia close enough abreast of the Western world of the day to make Russia just able to defeat her Swedish Western invaders in 1709 and her French Western invaders in 1812; but, in the nineteenth-century Western industrial revolution, the West once more left Russia behind, so that in the First World War Russia was defeated by her German Western invaders as she had been defeated, two hundred years earlier, by the Poles and the Swedes. The present Communist autocratic government was able to supplant the Czardom in Russia in consequence of Russia's defeat by an industrial Western technology in 1914-17; and the Communist régime then set out, from 1928 to 1941, to do for Russia, all over again, what the Czar Peter had done for her about 230 years earlier.

For the second time in the modern chapter of her history Russia was now put, by an autocratic ruler, through a forced march to catch up with a Western technology that had once more shot ahead of hers; and Stalin's tyrannical course of technological Westernization was eventually justified, like Peter's, through an ordeal by battle. The Communist technological revolution in Russia defeated the German invaders in the Second World War, as Peter's technological revolution had defeated the Swedish invaders in 1709 and the French invaders in 1812. And then, a few months after the completion of the liberation of Russian soil from German Western occupation in 1945, Russia's American Western allies dropped in Japan an atom bomb that announced the outbreak of a third Western technological revolution. So today, for the third time, Russia is having to make a forced march in an effort to catch up with a Western technology that, for the third time, has left her behind by shooting ahead. The result of this third event in the perpetual competition between Russia and the West still lies hidden in the future; but it is already clear that this renewal of the technological race is another of the very serious difficulties now besetting the relations between these two ex-Christian societies.

Technology is, of course, only a long Greek name for a bag of tools; and we have to ask ourselves: What are the tools that count in this competition in the use of tools as means to power? A power-loom or a locomotive is obviously a tool for this purpose, as well as a gun, an aeroplane, or a bomb. But all tools are not of the material kind; there are spiritual tools as well, and these are the most potent that Man has made. A creed, for instance, can be a tool; and, in the new round in the competition between Russia and the West that began in 1917, the Russians this time threw into their scale of the balances a creed that weighed as heavily against their Western competitors' material tools as, in the Roman story of the ransoming of Rome from the Gauls, the sword thrown in by Brennus weighed against the Roman gold.

Communism, then, is a weapon; and, like bombs, aeroplanes, and guns, this is a weapon of Western origin.

If it had not been invented by a couple of nineteenth-century Westerners, Karl Marx and Friedrich Engels, who were brought up in the Rhineland and spent the best part of their working lives in London and in Manchester respectively, Communism could never have become Russia's official ideology. There was nothing in the Russian tradition that could have led the Russians to invent Communism for themselves; and it is certain that they would never have dreamed of it if it had not been lying, ready-made, there in the West, for a revolutionary Russian régime to apply in Russia in 1917.

In borrowing from the West a Western ideology, besides a Western industrial revolution, to serve as an anti-Western weapon, the Bolsheviki in 1917 were making a great new departure in Russian history; for this was the first time that Russia had ever borrowed a creed from the West. We have already noticed that Christianity had come to Russia, not from the West, but from Byzantium, where Christianity had a distinctive, non-Western form and spirit; and a fifteenth-century Western attempt to impose Western Christianity on Russia had been a failure. In A.D. 1439, at an ecclesiastical council held at Florence, representatives of the Eastern Orthodox Church in what then still remained of the Byzantine Empire had unwillingly recognized the ecclesiastical supremacy of the Roman See in the hope that, in return, the Western world would save Constantinople from conquest by the Turks. The metropolitan arch-bishop of Moscow, who was a suffragan of the Greek Patriarch of Constantinople, had been attending the council, and he had voted the same way as his brethren who were representing the Greek Orthodox Church; but, when he came home to Moscow, his recognition of the Pope's supremacy was repudiated there and he himself was deposed.

Two hundred and fifty years later, when Peter the Great went to the West to learn the "know-how" of Western technology, there was no longer any question of Russia's being required to adopt a Western form of Christianity as the price of being initiated into the secrets of Western technological efficiency. Before the end of the seventeenth century there had been a revulsion in the West, not merely against religious fanaticism, but against religion itself, in consequence of the West's weariness of its own domestic wars of religion. The Western world, whose apprentice Russia became in Peter's day, was thus an irreligious world, and the sophisticated minority of Russians who became the agents of the Westernization of Russia followed the example of their sophisticated Western contemporaries by turning lukewarm towards the Russian form of Christianity without adopting any Western form of Christianity instead. So, in adopting Communism in 1917, Russia was making a breach with her traditions by taking up a Western creed for the first time in her history.

The reader will also have noticed that this Western creed, which Russia did take up in 1917, was one that was particularly well suited to serve Russia as a Western weapon for waging an anti-Western spiritual warfare. In the West, where Communism had arisen, this new creed was a heresy. It was a Western criticism of the West's failure to live up to her own Christian principles in the economic and social life of this professedly Christian society; and a creed of Western origin which was at the same time an indictment of Western practice was, of course, just the spiritual weapon that an adversary of the West would like to pick up and turn against its makers. With this Western spiritual weapon in her hands, Russia could carry her war with the West into the enemy's country on the spiritual plane. Since Communism had originated as a product of uneasy Western consciences, it could appeal to other uneasy Western consciences when it was radiated back into the Western world by a Russian propaganda. And so now, for the first time in the modern Western world's history since the close of the seventeenth century, when the flow of Western converts to Islam almost ceased, the West has again found itself threatened with spiritual disintegration from inside, as well as with an assault from outside. In thus threatening to undermine the Western civilization's foundations on the West's own home ground, Communism has already proved itself a more effective anti-Western weapon in Russian hands than any material weapon could ever be.

Communism has also served Russia as a weapon for bringing into the Russian camp the Chinese quarter of the human race, as well as other sections of that majority of mankind that is neither Russian nor Western. We know that the outcome of the struggle to win the allegiance of these neutrals may be decisive for the outcome of the Russo-Western conflict as a whole, because this non-Western and non-Russian majority of mankind may prove to hold the casting vote in a competition between Russia and the West for world power. Now Communism can make a twofold appeal to a depressed Asian, African, and Latin American peasantry when it is the voice of Russia that is commending Communism to them. The Russian spokesman can say to the Asian peasantry first: "If you follow the Russian example, Communism will give you the strength to stand up against the West, as a Communist Russia can already stand up against the West today." The second appeal of Communism to the Asian peasantry is Communism's claim that it can, and that private enterprise neither can nor would if it could, get rid of the extreme inequality between a rich minority and a poverty-stricken majority in Asian countries. Discontented Asians, however, are not the only public for whom Communism has an appeal. Communism also has an appeal for all men, since it can claim to offer mankind the unity which is our only alternative to self-destruction in an atomic age.

It looks as if, in the encounter between Russia and the West, the spiritual initiative, though not the technological lead, has now passed, at any rate for the moment, from the Western to the Russian side. We Westerners cannot afford to resign ourselves to this, because this Western heresy—Communism—which the Russians have taken up, seems to the great majority of people in the West to be a perverse, misguided, and disastrous doctrine and way of life. A theologian might put it that our great modern Western heresiarch Karl Marx has made what is a heretic's characteristic intellectual mistake and moral aberration. In putting his finger on one point in orthodox practice in which there has been a crying need for reform, he had lost sight of all other considerations and therefore has produced a remedy that is worse than the disease.

The Russian's recent success in capturing the initiative from us Westerners by taking up this Western heresy called Communism and radiating it out into the world in a cloud of anti-Western poison-gas does not, of course, mean that Communism is destined to prevail. Marx's version seems, in non-Marxian eyes, far too narrow and too badly warped to be likely to prove permanently satisfying to human hearts and minds. All the same, Communism's success, so far as it has gone, looks like a portent of things to come. What it does tell us is that the present encounter between the world and the West is now moving off the technological plane on to the spiritual plane. Some light on this next chapter of the story, which for us still lies in the future, may be found in the history of the world's earlier encounter with Greece and Rome. But, before looking at that, we have to see how Islam, India, and the Far East have been faring in their present encounters with both the West and Russia.

2

ISLAM AND THE WEST

In the first chapter, two points have been made about Russia's encounter with the West: the first is that Russia has managed to hold her own against the West by adopting Western weapons; the second point is that one of these Western weapons adopted by Russia has been a creed, and that, through her adoption of this Western creed of Communism, Russia has been able to pass over from the defensive into the counter-offensive that is causing so much concern to us in the West today. This story of Russia's relations with our Western Society within our own lifetime is in some points a repetition of an older story, in which the modern Western civilization's part was played by its predecessor the Graeco-Roman civilization, and Russia's part was played by Islam.

Communism has been called a Christian heresy, and the same description applies to Islam as well. Islam, like Communism, won its way as a programme of reform for dealing with abuses in the contemporary practice of Christianity. And the success of Islam in its early days shows how powerful the appeal of a reforming heresy can be when the orthodoxy that this heresy is attacking is reluctant to mend its ways. In the seventh century of the Christian Era the Muslim Arabs liberated from a Christian Graeco-Roman ascendancy a string of Oriental countries—from Syria right across North Africa to Spain —which had been under Greek or Roman rule for nearly a thousand years—ever since Alexander the Great had

conquered the Persian Empire and the Romans had overthrown Carthage. After that, between the eleventh century
and the sixteenth, the Muslims went on to conquer, by
stages, almost the whole of India, and their religion spread
peacefully still farther afield: into Indonesia and China
on the east and into Tropical Africa on the south-west.
Russia too, as we have seen, was temporarily subject, in
the Later Middle Ages, to Tatars who became converts
to Islam, and all the rest of Eastern Orthodox Christendom, in Asia Minor and in South-Eastern Europe, was
conquered in the fourteenth and fifteenth centuries by
the Muslim Ottoman Turks. Vienna was besieged by the
Turks for the second time no longer ago than 1682-83;
and, though the failure of that siege marked the beginning
of a turn of the tide in favour of the West in the West's
encounter with an aggressive Ottoman Empire, the cres-
cent flag could be seen still flying over the east coast of
the Adriatic, opposite the heel of Italy, no longer ago than
1912.

Those tremendous military and political successes in
the earlier chapters of the history of Islam explain why
it was that the Turks and other Muslim peoples were so
slow in following Pete the Great's policy of holding one's
own against the West by adopting Western weapons, tools,
institutions, and ideas. The technological Westernization
of Russia by Peter the Great started less than a hundred
years after Russia had had the experience of seeing Moscow occupied by Polish Western invaders in 1610-12.
On the other hand, more than a hundred years passed
after the Turkish disaster at Vienna in 1683 before a
Turkish Sultan took the first step towards training Turkish
infantry on a Western model, and 236 years passed before
a Turkish statesman fired his countrymen to adopt the
Western way of life whole-heartedly and without any
reservations.

The military reforms initiated by Sultan Selīm III, who
came to the throne in 1789, were prompted by the shock
of Turkey's defeat by Russia in the Great Russo-Turkish
War of 1768-74. Till then, the Turks had thought of the
Russians as country cousins of the Turks' own despised
Eastern Orthodox Christian Greek and Bulgarian subjects;

and now the Turks had suffered a crushing defeat at these rustic Russians' hands because the Russians had mastered the Western military technique. As for the out-and-out Westernizing movement, which was launched by Mustafā Kemāl Atatürk in 1919, we may doubt whether even Atatürk's imaginative insight and demonic driving-power would have succeded in jolting the Turks out of an age-old conservatism if, after the First World War, the Turks had not found themselves confronted with a stark and inescapable choice between whole-hearted Westernization and outright extinction.

The fact is that the Western counter-attack on the Islamic world, which, after the Turk's failure at Vienna in 1683, was bound to come sooner or later, was delayed by long Western memories of the Turks' and other Muslim peoples' historic military prowess. The Western world's retort to the Turks' conquest of Eastern Orthodox Christendom in the fourteenth and fifteenth centuries had been, not to make a fresh frontal attack on the Islamic world on the lines of the disastrously unsuccessful crusades, but to encircle Islam by conquering the Ocean. The circumnavigation of Africa had brought Portuguese Western seafarers to the west coast of India some years before the Mughals, who were the last wave of the Muslim invaders of India, came in by land from central Asia. The transit of the Atlantic Ocean and the Pacific Ocean, via Mexico, by the Spaniards, opened up in the Philippine Islands a new East Asian frontier between a Western Christendom and an Islam who had been neighbours, hitherto, only on the opposite side of the globe: in the Danube valley and in the western Mediterranean. Indeed, before the end of the sixteenth century, the West, thanks to its conquest of the Ocean, had succeeded in throwing a lasso round Islam's neck; but it was not till the nineteenth century that the West ventured to pull the rope tight. Till as late as that, enduring memories, on both sides, of past Muslim military prowess kept the Westerners cautious and the Muslims self-complacent.

The experience that did slowly break the spell of this Muslim self-complacency was the repeated military defeat of the Ottoman Empire and other Muslim Powers by adversaries equipped with Western weapons and with the technology and the science that are the sinews of the modern Western art of war; and the Muslims' reaction to this experience was the same as the Russians'.

In Turkey from 1789 to 1919, as in Russia from 1699 to 1825, the typical revolutionary Westernizer was a young military or naval officer; and to Western minds this is surprising, because, in a Western country, the corps of professional officers in the fighting services is apt to be, not a hot-bed of revolution, but a stronghold of conservatism. Yet the facts are indisputable. In Russia, the Westernizing Czar Peter the Great's most effective agents for the execution of his revolutionary programme were his young guards officers; and, more than a hundred years after Peter's day, the planners of the unsuccessful revolution of 1825 against the conservative Czar Nicholas I were, once again, military officers who had been infected with the Western political ideas of the day in 1814, when they had been serving in the international army of occupation in France. In the nineteenth century one of the typical careers of a Russian revolutionary prophet or leader was to be born the son of a well-to-do landowner, to enter the military of civil service, to publish philosophizing articles in a literary magazine, to retire at an early age from the imperial service, and to spend the rest of his life living as a rentier and serving the cause of political and social reform in Russia on Westernizing lines. In Turkey it was in essence the same story. The unsuccessful pioneer Westernizer Sultan Selīm III, and his more effective successor Mahmūd II, both started by building up Western-trained military units; and in the Turkish revolution of 1908, which was a successful counterpart of the unsuccessful Russian revolution of 1825, young military officers were the moving spirits.

In the Turkish case, the reason for the prominence of young officers in the Westernizing movement is obvious. The purpose of the Turkish revolution of 1908 was to re-establish the Westernizing parliamentary Turkish constitution of 1876, which had been almost immediately set on one side by the reactionary Sultan 'Abd-al-Hamīd II. 'Abd-al-Hamīd's political strategy, during his thirty years of absolute government, for making sure that Western Liberalism should never raise its head again in Turkey, had been to suppress all forms of "dangerous thought." Under his régime there was a severe censorship of books and control of education; but the one exception to 'Abd-al-Hamīd's systematically obscurantist rule was the education of the cadets for the professional fighting services. 'Abd-al-Hamīd's was morbidly afraid of revolution, but at the same time he had the wit to realize that he would lose his empire in another way—through conquest by some militarily efficient foreign power—if he were to make it impossible for Turkish military cadets to keep abreast of the progress of Western military science. He tried, of course, to keep these Turkish cadets' Western education within the narrowest possible professional limits; but, when once these young Turks had been allowed to learn Western languages in order to study Western military textbooks, it proved impossible to keep their minds insulated from Western political ideas. The military cadets were thus the one class in Hamidian Turkey that was able to keep a mental window open to influences from the West; and this is why in 1908, after thirty years of an obscurantist despotic régime, the spearhead of a fresh attack of Western Liberalism in Turkey was the younger generation in the corps of military officers.

The necessity for Westernizing the Turkish army, which was thus admitted even by so extreme a reactionary as Sultan 'Abd-al-Hamīd II, had been recognized, as has been mentioned, a hundred years before this tyrant's time, by his unfortunate liberal-minded predecessor Selīm III. But, in this first chapter of the story, even the convinced Westernizers in Turkey had, at heart, no love for the alien Western civilization that they were deliberately introducing. Their intention was to take just the mimimum dose of Western culture that was calculated to keep "the sick man of Europe" alive; and this grudging spirit caused one instalment of Westernizing reforms in Turkey after another to miscarry. The verdict of history on this old school of Turkish Westernizers is "Every time too little and too late." They hoped to make Turkey able to hold her own in wars with Western Powers like Austria or Westernizing Powers like Russia just by putting Western uniforms on Turkish soldiers' bodies and Western weapons in their hands, and by giving Turkish officers a Western professional training. They wanted to keep all the rest of Turkish life on its traditional Islamic basis. The reason why this policy of a minimum dose of Westernization failed, and was bound to fail, was because it flew in the face of a truth to which these early Turkish military reformers were blind—though Peter the Great had shown his genius by perceiving it. This truth was that any civilization, any way of life, is an indivisible whole in which all the parts hang together and are interdependent.

For example, the secret of the West's superiority to the rest of the world in the art of war from the seventeenth century onwards is not to be found just in Western weapons, drill, and military training. It is not even to be found just in the civilian technology that supplies the military equipment. It cannot be understood without also taking into account the whole mind and soul of the Western Society of the day; and the truth is that the Western art of war has always been one facet of the Western way of life. Hence, an alien society that tried to acquire the art without attempting to live the life was bound to fail to master the art; while, conversely, a Russian, Turkish, or other non-Western military officer who did succeed in his profession up to the normal Western standard could achieve this only by acquiring much more of the Western civilization than was to be found in the textbook or on the parade-ground. In fact, the long-sought minimum solution of Turkey's ever more insistent "Western Question" was no solution at all, and there were two practical alternative endings to the story: in the end, the Turks would either pay for their mistake of taking minimum doses of the Western civilization by going under, or else save themselves from extinction by Westernizing with all their heart and mind and soul and strength. After they had brought themselves to the verge of destruction by taking the former of these two courses, they did just save themselves by plunging, before it was too late, into a course of unlimited Westernization under the leadership of Mustafā Kemāl Atatürk.

Mustafā Kemāl was one of those young officers who had imbibed Western ideas in the process of receiving a Western professional military education in the last days of the Hamidian régime; and he had then taken an active part in the Revolution of 1908. Mustafā Kemāl's chance came when Turkey was down and out in consequence of having shared her ally Germany's defeat in the First World War. Kemāl had the wit to see that half-measures of Westernization, which had always been disastrous for Turkey, would be fatal for her now; and he also had the character to move his countrymen to follow his lead. Mustafā Kemāl's policy was to aim at nothing short of an out-and-out conversion of Turkey to the Western way of life; and in the nineteen-twenties he put through in Turkey what was perhaps as revolutionary a programme as has ever been carried out in any country deliberately and systematically in so short a span of time. It was as if, in our Western world, the Renaissance, the Reformation, the secularist scientific mental revolution at the end of the seventeenth century, the French Revolution, and the Industrial Revolution had all been telescoped into a single lifetime and been made compulsory by law. In Turkey the emancipation of women, the disestablishment of the Islamic religion, and the substitution of the Latin alphabet for the Arabic alphabet as the script for conveying the Turkish language were all enacted between 1922 and 1928.

This revolution was carried out by a dictator working through a single party enjoying a monopoly of power, and probably so much could not have been done so quickly by any less high-handed method. In the nineteen-twenties Turkey had either to turn her life inside out or else to perish, and the Turkish people chose to survive at all costs. One of the costs was a period of submission to a régime of the Facist-Nazi-Communist type—though, in Turkey, the dictatorial institution of single-party government was never carried to totalitarian extremes. The sequel, though, is impressive and promising. In the Turkish general election of 1950, Turkey moved from a one-party to a two-party régime by consent, without violence or bloodshed. The party that had for so long held a monopoly of office now accepted the will of the electors, first by letting them vote freely, and secondly by taking the adverse vote as a signal for the hitherto dominant party to retire from office and let the Opposition take the Government over; and the Opposition, on their side, showed the same constitutional spirit. When they found themselves in power, they did not abuse their power by taking any vindictive measures against opponents who had respected the results of a free election by voluntarily making way for the victors at the polls.

It looks as if in Turkey, whose statesmen had tried for so many generations to "make do" with the Western art of war alone, the Western institution of parliamentary constitutional government, which is so much nearer than our art of war is to the heart of our Western civilization, had now genuinely taken root. If so, this is a notable triumph for a sense of fair play and moderation in politics which, we Westerners believe, is one of the good gifts that the West is able to give to the world. Since 1917 we have seen many partially or nominally democratic peoples lapsing into divers forms of tyrannical government, and some of these peoples—for instance the Italians and the Germans—have been, not recent proselytes to our Western civilization, but native-born members of our Western family. The victory of the Western constitutional spirit in the Turkish elections of 1950 is thus a landmark which may perhaps even signify a turn of the political tide in the world as a whole.

There are, of course, other Western ideas and institutions which are doubtful blessings; and one of these is our Western Nationalism. The Turks, and many other Islamic peoples with them, have become as strongly infected with Nationalism as with other Western notions, salutary or pernicious. And we have to ask ourselves what is going to be the consequence of the intrusion of this narrow-hearted Western political ideal into an Islamic world whose own ancestral tradition is that all Muslims are brothers in virtue of their common religion, in spite of differences of race, language, and habitat. Now, in a world in which distance has been "annihilated" by the progress of Western technology, and in which the Western way of life is having to compete with the Russian way of life for the allegiance of all mankind, the Islamic tradition of the brotherhood of Man would seem to be a better ideal for meeting the social need of the times than the Western tradition of sovereign independence for dozens of separate nationalities. In the new situation in which the Western community finds itself since the Second World War, its internal partition into about forty sovereign independent national states is threatening to bring about the fall of a house divided against itself. And yet the prestige of the West in the world is still high enough to make the Western virus of Nationalism still infectious. It is to be hoped that, in the Islamic world at any rate, the spread of this Western political malady may be arrested by the strength of a traditional Islamic feeling for unity. A world-wide political and social unity is necessary for us men and for our salvation today, in an atomic age, far more urgently than it has been in the past.

The Turkish people, under Atatürk's inspiration, have certainly done a service to the whole Islamic world in trying to solve a common "Western Question" by adopting the modern Western way of life without reservations— Western Nationalism and all. But the other Islamic countries need not necessarily follow precisely the trail that these Turkish pioneers have blazed.

There are the Arabic-speaking Muslim countries, for instance, in which a common language is spoken in different dialects, but is written in one single standard literary language, from the Atlantic coast of Morocco to the western borders of Persia, and from Aleppo and Mosul on the north to Khartum and Aden and Maskat and Zanzibar on the south. Books and newspapers published in Cairo and Damascus and Beyrout circulate all over this huge Arabic-reading area and beyond it—for Arabic is the language of religion even in Islamic countries where it is not the language of everyday life. Is it really necessary that the Arabic-speaking world should break up—as the former Spanish Empire in the Americas has so unfortunately broken up—into about twenty mutually independent national states living in so many water-tight compartments on the Western pattern? This is a seamy side of our Western civilization which it would surely be a pity for the Arabic-speaking peoples to copy exactly.

And then, on all the fringes of the Islamic world—in Tropical Africa, India, China, and the Soviet Union— there are Muslim minorities—scattered abroad among non-Muslim majorities—who will never be able to gather all their members together into geographically compact blocks capable of forming so many sovereign independent states. These scattered Muslim communities—which amount to many millions of people all told—are not, as we shall see, the only communities of the kind; and, for all scattered communities like these, the gospel of Western Nationalism spells, as we shall find, not a call to a new life but a condemnation to death. Take the case of the great Muslim community that is scattered over the face of the sub-continent of India. In 1947, when Great Britain withdrew from India, the Western spirit of Nationalism unfortunately did not follow the good example set by the human representatives of the particular Western nation that had introduced this Western ideology into India. Our Western Nationalism stayed on in India, after the former British administrators' departure, to split a previously united sub-continent into two bickering successor-states—a Hindu Indian Union and a Muslim Pakistan—and for both of them this split has surely been a misfortune. The Indian Union is something less than a united India; Pakistan is a country composed of two fragments divided from one another by the whole breadth of the Indian Union; and, even after this jigsaw work, millions of Hindus and Indian Muslims have found themselves living on the wrong side of the new frontiers and have been faced with the cruel choice of leaving their homes or else falling under the rule of a government that is not going to love them.

The Pakistanis do now possess a national state of their own, and it is a large and a populous one. But these Indian Muslims have had to pay a higher price for this than the Turks, and a much higher price than the Egyptians.

They have discovered, from experience, both the cost of our Western Nationalism and its drawbacks. So the Pakistanis, as well as the Turks, have been learning political lessons that are going to be valuable, not only for other Islamic peoples, but also for the world as a whole.

3

INDIA AND THE WEST

In India's encounter with the West there has been one experience that has not been shared with India by any other society in the world. India is a whole world in herself; she is a society of the same magnitude as our Western society; and she is the one great non-Western society that has been, not merely attacked and hit, but overrun and conquered outright by Western arms, and not merely conquered by Western arms but ruled, after that, by Western administrators. In Bengal this Western rule lasted for nearly two hundred years, and in the Panjab for more than a hundred. India's experience of the West has thus been more painful and more humiliating than China's or Turkey's, and much more so than Russia's or Japan's; but, just for this reason, it has been also much more intimate. Personal contacts between Indians and Westerners have been more numerous, and our Western iron has probably entered deeper into India's soul.

Perhaps India would not have been conquered by Western arms if she had not been conquered by Muslim arms first. The reader has already been reminded that the Mughal last wave of Muslim conquerors of India overland arrived in India not many years after the first landing in India, in 1498, of the Portuguese first wave of Western mariners. These Mughal Muslims forestalled the British Westerners in bringing almost the whole of India under a single government. The Mughal peace in India may not have been so effective as the subsequent British peace was to be at its zenith; but the Mughal peace lasted as long as the British peace was to last, and, when, in the eighteenth century, it fell to pieces, it left legacies that made it not so difficult for the Mughals' British successors to reassemble the fragments of the Mughal Empire. One legacy was an imperial land-revenue organization which ran on by its own momentum during the eighteenth-century bout of anarchy in India. It ran on because it had become an Indian habit, and the conditioning of Indian hearts and minds to acquiesce, by force of habit, in an empire imposed on India by alien conquerors was the second of the Mughal legacies from which the Mughals' British successors profited.

The British successors of the Mughal rulers of India condemned their own revival of the Mughal rāj to come to an end when, in the eighteen-thirities, they deliberately set out to change the habits that their Mughal predecessors had implanted in Indian minds. In the eighteen-thirties the British rulers of India opened a window to the West for Indian minds by substituting a Western for an Islamic and a Hindu higher education in India and thereby introducing the Indians to their British rulers' own Western ideas of liberty, parliamentary constitutional government, and Nationalism. The Indians took this Western political education to heart. It moved them to demand for India, and eventually moved the British to concede to India, the self-government that Great Britain enjoys; and today the Hindu successors of the British rāj in the Indian Union, and the Muslim successors of the British rāj in Pakistan, are dedicated to the enterprise of ruling their shares of the sub-continent on the lines on which their British predecessors in the government of India have been conducting the government of Great Britian since 1688.

It is perhaps particularly noteworthy that the present Hindu rulers of the greater part of the Indian sub-continent should have chosen, as they have, to carry on the Government on Western lines originally laid down by alien conquerors. In the territories included in the Indian Union, the Hindus are now masters in their own house for the first time since the beginning of the Muslim conquest of India eight or nine hundred years ago. In the eighteenth century, when the Mughal Muslim rāj was breaking up, there were moments when it looked as if it was going to be followed immediately by the establishment of Hindu successor-states. In the eighteenth-century scramble for the Mughals' heritage, a Marāthā Hindu Power seemed for a time to be well on the way to winning the lion's share of the spoils. This eighteenth-century attempt to transform the Mughal rāj into a Marāthā Hindu rāj was foiled by the intervention of a more powerful Western hand. But the establishment of a British rāj instead of a Marāthā rāj did not bring to a halt the resurgence of the Hindus in their homeland. When the military line taken by the Hindu renaissance in the eighteenth century ended in a military failure, the gathering stream of Hindu energy was merely diverted into a different channel. Under the British rāj in the nineteenth and twentieth centuries, as during the interregnum in the eighteenth century, the Hindus continued steadily to gain power in India, but under the British régime they gained it, not by force of arms, but by force of mastering a Western system of education, administration and law which were so many keys to power in a Westernizing world.

The Hindus were quicker than the Indian Muslims to see and seize the opportunity that, in a Western age of Indian history, was open to Indians who effectively cultivated the Western arts of peace. Unlike the Indian Muslims, the Hindus had no enervating memories of recently lost power and glory to keep them brooding ineffectively over a dead past instead of reaching out into the future; and so a balance of power which had begun to incline against the Muslims in an anarchic eighteenth century continued to go against them in the nineteenth and twentieth centuries under a British peace which set a premium on intellectual ability, in place of military prowess, as the qualification for advancement in the continuing competition between Hindus and Indian Muslims who were now alike subjects of a Western Crown. The Indian Muslims did, of course, eventually follow their Hindu fellow Indians' example. They, too, set themselves to master the arts of our Western civilization. Yet, when the voluntary liquidation of the British rāj in India came within sight, the Indian Muslims insisted that the retransfer of the Government of India from British to Indian hands must be accompanied by a partition of India between a Hindu and a Muslim successor state; and this insistence on separation was, in effect, a recognition of the truth that, since the days of "the Great Moguls," there had been a reversal of the balance of power between Muslims and Hindus in India to the Muslims' disadvantage. In a joint Hindu-Muslim state including the whole sub-continent, the Indian Muslims feared that they would now be swamped by the Hindu majority of the population.

Though in 1947 a predominantly Muslim Pakistan thus parted company with a predominantly Hindu Indian Union, the objective of the British Indian Empire's two successor-states has so far been the same. In this first chapter of their histories, the power in both states has been in the hands of the element in their population that has had a Western education and that has been inspired by this with Western ideals. If this element remains in power in India and Pakistan, as well as in Ceylon, we may look forward to seeing the statesmen of these Asian countries use their influence over their countrymen to persuade them to remain members of our "free world." No doubt these same Asian statesmen will continue to demand that, in a "free world" that is to be the common home of Western and Asian peoples, there shall be no unfair and invidious discrimination against the Asian members of the family, and we Western members are bound to give satisfaction to our Asian fellow members on this point if, in calling our world "free," we are sincere. Unless we Western members of "the free world" grievously fail to live up to our professed liberal principles, we may hope to see the present Western-trained and Western-minded rulers of India, Pakistan, and Ceylon continue in partnership with us.

It is one of the vital interests of the Western peoples that this partnership of ours with the peoples of the Indian sub-continent should be preserved; for these Indian peoples together constitute one of the two Asian quarters of the human race; and, only two years after Great Britain had made a move for the reconciliation of Asia with the West by completing the liquidation of British rule in Ceylon, Pakistan, the Indian Union, and Burma, the Chinese, who constitute the second of the two Asian quarters of the human race, went over from the Western camp to the Russian. If after thus losing the friendship of the Chinese sub-continent, our Western world were to lose the friendship of the Indian sub-continent as well, the West would have lost to Russia most of the Old World except for a pair of bridgeheads in Western Europe and Africa; and this might well be a decisive event in the struggle for power between "the free world" and Communism. The Indian Union—the successor-state of the British Empire which covers most of the Indian sub-continent, and the state in which the Hindus are predominant—occupies a commanding position in the divided world of today, in which the United States and her associates are competing for world power with the Soviet Union and her associates. In which direction is the Hindu fifth of the human race going to incline? Let us look at some of the considerations telling for and against the likelihood of the Hindus continuing to go our Western way.

Let us take a promising point first. It looks as if, today, personal relations between Indians and Westerners are more friendly than they have ever been. Many citizens of the United Kingdom will certainly have had the experience—which the writer has had a number of times since 1947—of being surprised and touched by the friendliness that Indians have been going out of their way to show to British people. This has happened to the writer several times in foreign countries, where local observers were on the lookout to see what the relations between the Indians and the British really were now; and he has found Indians in conspicuous positions abroad going out of their way to show that the former unhappy estrangement between them and the British was now dead and buried as far as they were concerned. When Great Britain did completely fulfil her promise to liquidate her rule in India, the Indians were, it seems, taken aback. They had perhaps never fully

believed that the British intended ever to fulfil their prom-
ises to India; and so, when the British did keep their word,
there was a revulsion of feeling on the Indian side from
hostility to friendliness. It is handsome of the Indians to
make their new friendliness towards the British apparent;
and this happy change in the relations of the Indians and
the British with one another is assuredly something gained
for our "free world" as a whole.

The estrangement between India and a Western world
which, for India, has been represented by Great Britain
goes back behind the beginning of the Indian movement
for independence in the eighteen-nineties, and behind the
tragic conflict in 1857. It goes back to the reforms in the
British administration in India that were started in the
seventeen-eighties. This birth of estrangement from reform
in the relations between Indians and British people is one
of the ironies of history; and yet there is a genuine inner
connexion between the two events. In the eighteenth century the then newly installed British rulers of India were
free and easy with their newly acquired Indian subjects in
two senses. They were unscrupulous in using their political
power to fleece and oppress them, and at the same time
they were uninhibited in their social relations with them.
They hob-nobbed with their Indian subjects off duty, besides meeting them at work on less agreeable terms. The
more intellectual British residents in India in the eighteenth century enjoyed the game of capping Persian verses
with Indian colleagues; the more lively Indians enjoyed
being initiated into English sports. Look at Zoffany's picture "Colonel Mordaunt's Cock Match at Lucknow"
painted in 1786. It tells one at a glance that, at that date,
Indians and Englishmen could be hail-fellow-well-met with
one another. The British rulers of India in the first generation behaved, in fact, very much as their Hindu and
Muslim predecessors had behaved. They were humanly
corrupt and therefore not inhumanly aloof; and the
British reformers of British rule, who were rightly determined to stamp out the corruption and who were
notably successful in this difficult undertaking, deliberately
stamped out the familiarity as well, because they held that
the British could not be induced to be superhumanly

upright and just in their dealings with their Indian subjects without being made to feel and behave as if they were tin gods set on pedestals high and dry above those Indian human beings down below.

Today, when the Indians are once more governing themselves, so that Lord Cornwallis's problem of finding how to make Western administrators in India behave decently no longer arises, there is nothing to prevent the relations between Indians and Westerners from being intimate and decent at the same time, and this is a promising change for the better as far as it goes. But just how far does it go? After all, so few thousands out of India's 450 millions ever did or do meet a Westerner—or even meet a member of that Western-minded minority of the Indian people that is now governing India in the former Western rulers' place. And what is the future of this new Indian governing class? Will it be able to maintain its present leadership? And will the Western outlook and ideals, that have been implanted in the souls of this minority by their education, be able to hold their own, even here, against the Hindu tradition?

It is remarkable that even a minority in the great Hindu world should have gone so far as this now ruling minority has gone in assimilating Western ideas and ideals, considering how alien the Western and Hindu outlooks on life are from one another. In the two first chapters, in which we were concerned with Russia's and Islam's relations with the West, we were dealing with two cases in which the non-Western party with whom the West had collided had something in common with the West which Hinduism does not possess. Though our Russian contemporaries are not the children of Western Christians, they are the children of Eastern Orthodox Christians; and so both the Christian religion and also the Graeco-Roman civilization—which the Christian Church has taken over and preserved and handed down—are parts of the Russians' spiritual background, as they are parts of ours in the West. Our Muslim contemporaries, again, are adherents of a religion which, like Communism, can be described as being a Christian heresy; and the philosophy and science of the Greeks are parts of the Muslims' spiritual background, as they are of ours. In fact, if, looking at the contemporary world as a whole, one were to try to make the broadest and simplest analysis of the main cultural divisions in it, one would find oneself grouping the Muslims, the ex-Eastern Orthodox Christians and the ex-Western Christians together as members of a single great society which one could distinguish from both the Indian world and the Far Eastern world by giving this society, like each of those, an overall label of its own. Since the spiritual possession that all we Christians and Muslims have in common with one another is a pair of common heritages—one from the Jews and another from the Greeks—we could label our Christian-Muslim society the Graeco-Judaic, to distinguish it both from a Hindu Society in India and from a Confucian-Buddhist Society in the Far East.

From this bird's-eye view that takes in the whole of mankind, the divers Muslim and Christian variations on a common Graeco-Judaic way of life fade almost out of view. They look quite insignificant by comparison with the characteristics that are common to all of us Muslim and Christian members of our Graeco-Judaic cultural family. When we contrast our Muslim-Christian way of life as a whole with the Hindu way or with the Far Eastern, the differences, inside our Muslim-Christian family, between Eastern Orthodox Christendom and Western Christendom, or between either of these Christendoms and Islam, almost cease to be visible. And yet we know that these relatively small cultural differences can produce violent spiritual disturbances in the souls of the children of one of these Graeco-Judaic sister-civilizations of ours when these souls are played upon by the spiritual radiation of one of the other civilizations in our family.

A notable example is the effect produced on Russian souls by the impact on them of the Western civilization since the time of Peter the Great. The two parties to this encounter were, both of them, members of the same Graeco-Judaic family; yet the disturbance produced in Russian Graeco-Judaic souls by the strangeness of the intruding Western variety of the same Graeco-Judaic spirit has been very great. We can measure the severity of this disturbance psychologically by the tormented and tormenting vein in a nineteenth-century Russian literature which expresses, and gives vent to, the distress suffered by a soul when it is required to live in two different spiritual universes at once—even when these two claimants on the same soul's spiritual allegiance are rather closely akin to one another. We can also measure the severity of the Western stress and strain upon Russian souls politically by the explosiveness of the revolution in which this spiritual tension discharged itself in 1917.

Now the disturbance, produced by the impact of the West on Russian souls, which has come to the surface in these sensational manifestations, is presumably a good deal milder than the latent disturbance produced in Indian souls by the same alien Western spiritual force; for the disturbance in Russian souls, violent though it has been, must have been mitigated by the presence, in Russia's cultural heritage, of Jewish and Greek elements that were also present in the heritage of the intruding Western civilization, whereas in the Indian heritage there have been no Greek or Jewish elements, or at any rate none to speak of, to break the force of the shock administered by the impact of the West here. What, then, in India, is going to be the resolution of this presumably far sharper tension between a native and an alien spiritual force? On the surface, those Hindus who have adopted our, to them, extremely alien Western culture on the planes of technology and science, language and literature, administration and law, appear to have been more successful than the Russians in harmonizing with their native way of life a Western way that is intrinsically more alien to them than it is to the Russians. Yet the tension in Hindu souls must be extreme, and sooner or later it must find some means of discharging itself.

Whatever may be the relief that Hindu souls are going to find for themselves eventually, it seems clear that, for them, there can be no relief from the impact of our Western civilization by opening themselves to the influence of Communism; for Communism—a Western heresy adopted by an ex-Orthodox Christian Russia—is just as much part and parcel of the Graeco-Judaic heritage as the Western way of life is, and the whole of this cultural tradition is alien to the Hindu spirit.

There is, however, one factor in the economic and social situation in India today which might give Communism an opening—exotic though Communism may be in a Hindu environment—and this subversive factor is the rising pressure of population in India on the means of subsistence. This is an important point, because the same factor is at work today in China, Japan, Indo-China, Indonesia, and Egypt. In all these non-Western countries the impact of the West has brought with it a progressive increase in the food supply through irrigation, through the introduction of new crops, and through the improvement in methods of agriculture under Western inspiration; and in all of them, at every stage so far, this increase in the food supply has been spent, not on raising the standard of living of a stationary or gradually growing population, but on maintaining the largest possible population on the old level, which was and is only just above starvation point. Since progressive improvements in productivity must sooner or later bring in diminishing returns, the standard of this swollen population seems bound to decline, and there is no margin between the present standard and sheer disaster on the grand scale.

In some such economically desperate situation as this, Communism might win a foothold in India and in other Asian countries in which Communism is just as foreign as our Western way of life. For Communism has a programme of wholesale compulsory collectivization and mechanization to offer as a specious remedy for the plight of a depressed Asian peasantry, whereas, to people in this plight, it would be a mockery to advise them to solve their problem in the American way. This population problem, and its bearing on the competition between Russia and the West, will confront us again when we come to the Far East, which is the subject of the next chapter.

4

THE FAR EAST AND THE WEST

In the last chapter it was suggested that our Western way of life was more foreign to the Hindus than it was to the Russians and the Muslims, because the Hindu way had in it not more than a minute dose of the Greek and Jewish ingredients that are the common heritage of Islam, Russia, and the West. The Far East has still less in common with the West than the Hindu world has in its cultural background. It is true that in Far Eastern art the influence of Greek art is noticeable; but this Greek influence reached the Far East through an Indian channel; it came in the train of an Indian religion—Buddhism—which captured the Far Eastern world as the Graeco-Roman world was captured by a Judaic religion, Christianity. It is also true that another Judaic religion—Islam—which spread over the greater part of India by conquest, also spread over the western fringes of China by peaceful penetration. Thus the Far East, like India, had already been played upon by influences from our Graeco-Judaic world before it was assaulted by our modern Western civilization in the sixteenth century; but in the Far East these pre-Western Graeco-Judaic influences had been even slighter than they had been in India. They had been too slight to pave the way for the kindred Western civilization's advent. And so, when in the sixteenth century the Portuguese pioneers of the Western civilization made their first landfalls on the coasts of China and Japan, they descended there like uncanny visitants from some other planet.

The effect of this first modern Western visitation on the Far Eastern peoples' feelings was mixed. It was an unstable mixture of fascination and repulsion, and, at this first encounter, the feeling of repulsion finally prevailed. This sixteenth-century wave of Western intruders was thrown back into the Ocean out of which it had broken so unexpectedly upon Far Eastern shores; and, after that, Japan, Korea, and China each closed her doors and set herself, as long as she could, to live as "a hermit kingdom." This, however, was not the end of the story. After the modern Western intruders had been expelled from Japan in the seventeenth century and from China in the eighteenth century, they returned to the charge in the nineteenth century; and, at this second attempt, the succeeded in introducing the Western way of life into the Far East, as by then they had already introduced it into Russia and India and were beginning to introduce it into the Islamic world.

What differences in the situation can we see that will account for the difference in the result of these two successive Western attempts to captivate the Far East?

One obvious difference is a technological one. In the sixteenth and seventeenth centuries, Western ships and weapons were not so decisively superior to Far Eastern ships and weapons as to give the Western intruders the whip hand. In this first round in the encounter between the two civilizations, the Far Easterners remained masters of the situation; and, when they decided that they wanted to break the relation off, their Western visitants were powerless to resist. But, when the Westerners reappeared off the coasts of China and Japan in the nineteenth century, the weight was in the Western scale of the balance of power; for, while Chinese and Japanese armaments were then still what they had been two hundred years back, the Westerners had made the industrial revolution in the meantime; they now came back armed with new-fangled weapons which the Far Eastern Powers could not match; and, in these new circumstances, the Far East was bound to be opened to Western influences in one or the other of two ways. A Far Eastern hermit kingdom that tried to meet the new technological challenge from the

West by ignoring it would soon see its closed doors battered in by Western heavy guns. The only alternative was
to keep the Western intruders at arm's length by learning
the "know-how" of nineteenth-century Western armaments; and this could only be done by voluntarily opening
Far Eastern doors to the new Western technology before
an entry was forced by Western conquerors. The Japanese
were prompter than the Chinese in opting for, and acting
on, this alternative policy of holding their own against
the West by learning how to use and make the latest
types of Western weapons; but the Chinese, too, in the
end, acted just in time to save themselves from India's
fate of being subjugated by a Western Power.

This, though, is not the whole story. For, while the
technological ascendancy gained by the West over the
Far East through a Western industrial revolution may explain why the Far Eastern peoples found themselves
compelled to open their doors to the Western civilization
in the nineteenth century, we have still to explain why
they had been moved to expel their Western visitants and
to break off relations with the Western world in the
seventeenth and eighteenth centuries. This denouement
of the first encounter between the Far East and the
modern West is at first sight surprising; for, when the
Westerners had made their first appearance above the
Far Easterners' horizon in the sixteenth century, the Far
Eastern peoples had shown themselves readier to welcome
these then quite unknown strangers and to adopt their
way of life than they showed themselves three hundred
years later, when the Westerners came again with the bad
reputation that they had acquired on their first visit. Yet
this second encounter, in which the Far Eastern peoples
were decidedly reluctant to engage, ended in the reception
of the Western way of life in the Far East, whereas the
first encounter, which had begun with a welcome, had
ended in a rebuff. What is the key to this remarkable difference between these two acts in the drama of the Far
East's encounter with the West?

The difference in the Far Eastern peoples' reaction to
the Western civilization on these two occasions was not
arbitrary or capricious. They reacted differently because

the challenges with which they were confronted on the two occasions were not the same. In the nineteenth century the Western civilization presented itself primarily as a strange technology; in the sixteenth century it had presented itself primarily as a strange religion. This difference in the aspect displayed by the intrusive Western civilization explains the difference in the reaction that it aroused in Far Eastern hearts and minds at its first and at its second coming; for a strange technology is not so difficult to accept as a strange religion is.

Technology operates on the surface of life, and therefore it seems practicable to adopt a foreign technology without putting oneself in danger of ceasing to be able to call one's soul one's own. This notion that, in adopting a foreign technology, one is incurring only a limited liability may, of course, be a miscalculation. The truth seems to be that all the different elements in a culture-pattern have an inner connexion with each other, so that, if one abandon's one's own traditional technology and adopts a foreign technology instead, the effect of this change on the technological surface of life will not remain confined to the surface, but will gradually work its way down to the depths till the whole of one's traditional culture has been undermined and the whole of the foreign culture has been given entry, bit by bit, through the gap made in the outer ring of one's cultural defences by the foreign technology's entering wedge.

In China and Korea and Japan today, a century or more after the date at which our modern Western technology first began to penetrate these countries, we can see these revolutionary ulterior effects upon the whole of their culture taking place before our eyes. Time, however, is of the essence of this process; and a revolutionary result that is so clearly manifest to all eyes today was not foreseen by Far Eastern statesmen a hundred years ago, when they were reluctantly taking their decision to admit this foreign technology within their walls. Like their Turkish contemporaries, they intended to take the West's technology in the minimum dose required for their own military security, and not to go beyond that. Yet, even if they had had some suspicion of the hidden forces that this mechanically propelled Trojan Horse held in ambush within its iron frame, probably they would still have stood by their decision to wheel it in. For they saw clearly that, if they hesitated to adopt this alien Western technology now, they would immediately become a prey to Western conquerors armed with weapons to which they would then have no retort. The external danger of conquest by some Western Power was the immediate menace with which those nineteenth-century Far Eastern statesmen had to cope. By comparison, the internal danger of being eventually captivated, body and soul, by the Western way of life as a result of adopting the Western technology was a more distant menace which must be left to take care of itself. Sufficient unto the day is the evil thereof.

Thus, in the nineteenth century, the adoption of a now overwhelmingly superior Western technology appeared to Far Eastern statesmen to be a legitimate risk as well as an imperative necessity. And this explains why, this time, they took something from the West which was so little to their taste. It seemed to be at any rate a lesser evil than the alternative of being conquered and subjugated by the Westerners whose weapons they were deciding to adopt as a policy of military and political insurance. On the other hand, the "Western Question" with which these nineteenth-century Far Eastern statesman's seventeenth-century predecessors had had to deal had presented itself in quite a different form.

In this first encounter with the West the immediate danger which Japanese statesmen had to parry was not the danger of seeing their country conquered by Western soldiers armed with irresistibly superior new-fangled weapons; it was the danger of seeing their people converted by Western missionaries preaching an irresistibly attractive foreign religion. Possibly these seventeenth-century Japanese statesmen had no great objection to Western Christianity in itself; for, unlike their seventeenth-century Western Christian visitants, seventeenth-century Far Easterners were not infected with the religious fanaticism which their Western contemporaries had inherited from Christianity's Jewish past and were displaying, in this age, in domestic religious wars in their

European homeland. The Chinese and Japanese statesmen of the day had been brought up in the more tolerant philosophical traditions of Confucianism and Buddhism, and they might not have objected to giving a free field to another religion if they had not suspected the Western Christian missionaries' religious activities of having an ulterior political motive.

What the Japanese statesmen feared was that their countrymen whom these foreign missionaries were converting to Western Christianity would imbibe their adopted religion's fanatical spirit, and that, under this demoralizing influence, they would allow themselves to be used as what, in the West today, we should call "a fifth column." If this suspected design were to succeed, then Portuguese or Spaniards, who in themselves were not a serious menace to Japan's independence, might eventually contrive to conquer Japan through the arms of Japanese traitors. In fact, the Japanese Government in the seventeenth century outlawed and repressed Christianity from the same motive that today is moving twentieth-century Western governments to outlaw and repress Communism; and it has been an element that is common to these two Western faiths—the fanaticism inherited by both of them from Judaism—that has been the stumbling-block in any Asian country in which Christianity has been propagated.

An aggressive foreign religion will, in fact, manifestly be a more serious immediate menace than an aggressive foreign technology will be to a society that it is assailing; and there is a deeper reason for this than the danger of the converts being used as "a fifth column." The deeper reason is that, while technology plays only upon the surface of life in the first instance, religion goes straight down to the roots; and, though a foreign technology, too, may eventually have a deeply disintegrating effect on the spiritual life of a society in which it has once gained a footing, this effect will take some time to make itself apparent. For this reason, an aggressive civilization that presents itself as a religion is likely to arouse stronger and swifter opposition than one that presents itself as a technology; and we can now see why in the Far East, as well as in Russia, our Western civilization was first rejected and was then accepted at the second time of asking. In Russia in the fifteenth century and in the Far East in the seventeenth century, the Western civilization was rejected when what it was demanding was conversion to the Western form of Christianity; and it was no accident that its fortunes in the mission field should have veered right round from conspicuous failures to sensational successes as soon as its attitude towards its own ancestral religion had veered round from a warm devotion to a cool scepticism.

This great spiritual revolution overtook the Western world towards the close of the seventeenth century, when a hundred years' trial of waging savage and inconclusive civil wars under the colours of rival religious sects had at last disgusted the Western peoples, not only with wars of religion, but with religion itself. The Western world reacted to this disillusioning self-inflicted experience of the evils of religious fanaticism by withdrawing its treasure from religion and reinvesting it in technology; and it is this utilitarian technological excerpt from the bible of our Western civilization, with the fanatical religious page torn out, that has run like wildfire round the world during the last two and a half centuries, from the generation of Peter the Great to the generation of Mustafā Kemāl Atatürk.

Perhaps, in looking for some explanation of the striking difference between the results of the West's two successive assaults upon the Far East, we have stumbled upon a "law" (if one may call it that) which applies, not just to this single case, but to all encounters between any civilizations. This "law" is to the effect that a fragment of a culture, split off from the whole and radiated abroad by itself, is likely to meet with less resistance, and therefore likely to travel faster and farther, than the culture as a whole when this is radiated *en bloc*. Our Western technology, divorced from our Western Christianity, has been accepted, not only in China and Japan, but also in Russia and in many other non-Western countries where it was rejected so long as it was offered as part and parcel of a one and indivisible way of life including Western Christianity as well.

The almost world-wide dissemination of a technological splinter flaked off from our Western civilization since the close of the seventeenth century is impressive at first sight if we compare it with the virtual failure to convert non-Western peoples to the Western way of life in an Early Modern Age when our Western civilization was being offered for acceptance or rejection as a whole— technology, religion and all. Today, however, when the West's bid to win the world has been challenged by Russia, we can see that our Western civilization's apparent triumph on the technological plane is precarious for the very reason that has made it easy; and the reason is that this triumph has been superficial. The West has sent its technology racing round the world by the trick of freeing it from the handicap of being coupled with our Western Christianity; but, in the next chapter of the story, this unattached Western technology has been picked up by the Russians and been coupled with Communism; and this new and potent combination of a Western technology with a Western religious heresy is now being offered to the Far Eastern peoples and to the rest of mankind as a rival way of life to ours.

In the nineteenth-century chapter of the story, we Westerners were gratified when we saw the Japanese and the Chinese, who had rejected our Western civilization in its religious version, accepting it in a secularized version in which technology instead of religion had been given the place of honour. The Meiji Revolution in Japan in the eighteen-sixties and the Kuomintang Revolution in China in the nineteen-twenties both seemed, at the time, to be triumphs for the secularized Western civilization of the Late Modern Age. But we have lived to see this secular Western dispensation disappoint us in both countries. In Japan it bred a disastrous militarism; in China it bred a disastrous political corruption; in both countries the disaster brought the régime to a violent end; and in China this failure of the attempt to acclimatize there a secular form of our Western civilization has been followed

by a victory for Communism. What is it that has made
Communism's fortune in China? Not, so far as one
can make out, any great positive enthusiasm for Communism so much as a complete disillusionment with the
Kuomintang's performance in its attempt to govern
China on latter-day secular Western lines. And we may
suspect that the Japanese too, if they were free to go
their own way, might succumb to Communism for the
same negative reason.

In both Japan and China today there are two factors
telling in Communism's favour: first, this disillusionment
with past experiments in trying to lead a secularized
Western way of life, and, second, the pressure of a rapidly
growing population on the means of subsistence—a pressure which, as has been noticed in the preceding chapter,
is also a menace to the present Westernizing régime in
India. The truth is that, in offering the Chinese and Japanese a secularized version of our Western civilization,
we have been offering them a stone instead of bread, while
the Russians, in offering them Communism as well as
technology, have been offering them bread of a sort—
gritty black bread, if you like to call it so; but that is
still an edible substance that contains in it some grain
of nutriment for the spiritual life without which Man
cannot live.

But, if China and Japan could not stomach a sixteenth-
century version of our Western civilization with the
religion left in, and cannot sustain life on a nineteenth-
century version of it with the religion left out, is Communism the only alternative? The answer to this question
is that, in China, and also in India, in the sixteenth and
seventeenth centuries, long before Communism was ever
dreamed of, a different alternative *was* found and tried by
the Jesuit Western Christian missionaries. It is true that
this experiment came to grief, but it was wrecked, not
by any intrinsic faults of its own, but by unfortunate
rivalries and dissensions between the Jesuits and other
Roman Catholic Christian missionary orders.

In China, and India the Jesuits did not make the mistake, that they had made in Japan, of letting their preaching of Christianity fall under suspicion of being conducted

in the political interests of aggressive Western Powers. The Jesuits' approach to their enterprise of propagating Christianity in China was so different and so promising in itself, and is so much to the point today, that our discussion of the Asian peoples' encounter with the West would be incomplete if we did not take into consideration the line which the Jesuits in China and India opened out. Instead of trying, as we have been trying since their day, to disengage a secular version of the Western civilization from Christianity, the Jesuits tried to disengage Christianity from the non-Christian ingredients in the Western civilization and to present Christianity to the Hindus and to the Chinese, not as the local religion of the West, but as a universal religion with a message for all mankind. The Jesuits stripped Christianity of its accidental and irrelevant Western accessories, and offered the essence of it to China in a Chinese, and to India in a Hindu, intellectual and literary dress in which there was no incongruous Western embroidery to jar on Asian sensibilities. This experiment miscarried at the first attempt through the fault of domestic feuds within the bosom of the Roman Catholic Church of the day, which had nothing to do with either Christianity or China or India; but, considering that India and China and Christianity are all still on the map, we may expect—and hope—to see the experiment tried again. The recent victory of Communism in China over a Western civilization divorced from Christianity is no evidence that, in China, Christianity has no future in a coming chapter of history which today is still below our historical horizon.

5

THE PSYCHOLOGY
OF ENCOUNTERS

In the first four chapters of this book we have been
surveying four episodes in which our Western civilization
has been encountered by some contemporary non-Western
society. Russia's, Islam's, India's, and the Far East's experiences of the West have come under view. Our survey has shown that these four different experiences of
being hit by a foreign civilization have had a number of
features in common; and the purpose of the present
chapter is to pick out, for further examination, several
features that appear to be characteristic, not only of the
contemporary world's encounters with the West, but of
all such collisions between one civilization and another.
There seems to be something like a common psychology
of encounters; and this is a subject of practical interest
and importance today, when the sudden "annihilation of
distance," through the achievements of our Western
technology, has brought face to face, at point-blank range,
half a dozen societies, each of which, until yesterday, was
living its own life in its own way almost as independently
of its neighbours as if each society had been marooned
on a planet of its own instead of living in the same world
with the other representatives of its kind.

We may begin by reminding ourselves of a general
phenomenon which came to our notice in the last chapter
when we were taking a comparative view of our Western
civilization's two successive assaults upon China and

Japan. We saw that, on the first occasion, the West tried to induce the Far Eastern peoples to adopt the Western way of life in its entirety, including its religion as well as its technology, and that this attempt did not succeed. And then we saw that, in the second act of the play, the West offered to the same Far Eastern peoples a secularized excerpt from the Western civilization in which religion had been left out and technology, instead of religion, had been made the central feature; and we observed that this technological splinter, which had been flaked off from the religious core of our civilization towards the end of the seventeenth century, did succeed in pushing its way into the life of a Far Eastern Society that had previously repulsed an attempt to introduce the Western way of life *en bloc*—technology and all, including religion.

Here we have an example of something that seems often to happen when the culture-ray of a radioactive civilization hits a foreign body social. The assaulted foreign body's resistance diffracts the culture-ray into its component strands, just as a light-ray is diffracted into the spectrum by the resistance of a prism. In optics we also know that some of the light-strands in the spectrum have a greater penetrative power than others, and we have already seen that it is the same with the component strands of a culture-ray. In the West's impact on the Far East, the technological strand in the radiation of the Western civilization has overcome a resistance by which the religious strand has been repelled; and this difference in the penetrative power of a religious and a technological culture-strand is not a phenomenon that is peculiar to the history of the relations between these two particular civilizations. We have stumbled here upon an instance of one of the "laws" of cultural radiation.

When a travelling culture-ray is diffracted into its component stands—technology, religion, politics, art, and so on—by the resistance of a foreign body social upon which it has impinged, its technological strand is apt to penetrate faster and farther than its religious strand; and this law can be formulated in more general terms. We can say that the penetrative power of a strand of cultural radiation is usually in inverse ratio to this strand's cultural value. A trivial strand arouses less resistance in the assaulted body social than is aroused by a crucial strand, because the trivial strand does not threaten to cause so violent or so painful a disturbance of the assaulted body's traditional way of life. This automatic selection of the most trival elements in a radioactive culture for the widest dissemination abroad is obviously an unfortunate rule of the game of cultural intercourse; but this premium on triviality is not the game's worst point. The very process of diffraction, which is of the essence of the game, threatens to poison the life of the society whose body social is being penetrated by the divers strands of a diffracted culture-ray.

Analogies taken from physics and medicine may be used to illustrate this point. Since our discovery of the trick of splitting the atom, we have learnt to our cost that the particles composing an atom of some inoffensive element cease to be innocuous and become dangerously corrosive so soon as they have been split off from the orderly society of particles of which an atom is constituted, and have been sent flying by themselves on independent careers of their own. We have learnt, too—not to our own cost in this case, but to the cost of the once secluded surviving representatives of Primitive Man—that a disease which is a mild one for us, because it has been rife among us so long that we have developed an effective resistance to it, may prove deadly to South Sea Islanders who have been exempt from it before being suddenly exposed to it by the arrival among them of its European carriers.

A loose strand of cultural radiation, like a loose electron or a loose contagious disease, may prove deadly when it is disengaged from the system within which it has been functioning hitherto and is set free to range abroad by itself in a different milieu. In its original setting, this culture-strand or bacillus or electron was restrained from working havoc because it was kept in order by its association with other components of a pattern in which the divers participants were in equilibrium. In escaping from its original setting, the liberated particle, bacillus, or culture-strand will not have changed its nature; but the same nature will produce a deadly effect, instead of a harmless one, now that the creature has broken loose from its original associations. In these circumstances, "one man's meat" can become "another man's poison."

In the set of encounters between the world and the West which is the subject of this book, there is a classical example of the mischief that an institution can do when it is prised loose from its original social setting and is sent out into the world, conquering and to conquer, all by itself. During the last century and a half we have seen our Late Modern Western political institution of "national states" burst the bounds of its birthplace in Western Europe and blaze a trail of persecution, eviction, and massacre as it has spread abroad into Eastern Europe, South-West Asia, and India—all of them regions where "national states" were not part and parcel of an indigenous social system but were an exotic institution which was deliberately imported from the West, not because it had been found by experimentation to be suitable to the local conditions of these non-Western worlds, but simply because the West's political power had given the West's political institutions an irrational yet irresistible prestige in non-Western eyes.

The havoc which the application of this Western institution of "national states" has worked in these regions where it is an exotic import is incomparably greater than the damage that the same institution has done in Britain, France, and the other West European countries in which it has been, not an artificially introduced innovation, but a spontaneous native growth.

We can see why the same institution has had strikingly different effects in these two different social environments. The institution of "national states" has been comparatively harmless in Western Europe for the same reason that accounts for its having originated there; and that is because, in Western Europe, it corresponds to the local relation between the distribution of languages and the alinement of political frontiers. In Western Europe, people speaking the same language happen, in most cases, to be huddled together in a single continuous and compact block of territory with a fairly well defined linguistic boundary separating it from the similarly compact domains of other languages; and, in a region where, as here, the languages are thus distributed in the pattern of a patchwork quilt, the linguistic map provides a convenient basis for the political map, and "national states" are therefore natural products of the social milieu. Most of the domains of the historic states of Western Europe do, in fact, coincide approximately with homogeneous patches of the linguistic map; and this coincidence has come about, for the most part, undesignedly. The West European peoples have not been acutely conscious of the process by which their political containers have been moulded on linguistic lasts; and, accordingly, the spirit of nationalism has been, on the whole, easy-going in its West European homeland. In West European national states, linguistic minorities who have found themselves on the wrong side of a political frontier have in most cases shown loyalty, and been treated with consideration, because their coexistence with the majority speaking "the national language" as fellow citizens of the same commonwealth has been an historical fact which has not been deliberately brought about by anyone and which has therefore been taken for granted by everyone.

But now let us consider what has happened when this West European institution of "national states," which in its birthplace has been a natural product of the local linguistic map, has been radiated abroad into regions in which the local linguistic map is on a quite different pattern. When we look at a linguistic map, not just of Western Europe, but of the world, we see that the local West European pattern, in which the languages are distributed in fairly clear-cut, compact, and homogeneous blocks, is something rather peculiar and exceptional. In the vastly larger area stretching south-eastward from Danzig and Trieste to Calcutta and Singapore, the pattern of the linguistic map is not like a patchwork quilt; it is like a shot-silk robe. In Eastern Europe, South-West Asia, India, and Malaya the speakers of different languages are not neatly sorted out from one another, as they are in Western

Europe; they are geographically intermingled in alternate houses on the same streets of the same towns and villages; and, in this different, and more normal, social setting, the linguistic map—in which the threads of different colours are interwoven with each other—provides a convenient basis, not for the drawing of frontiers between states, but for the allocation of occupations and trades among individuals.

In the Ottoman Empire, a hundred and fifty years ago, before the Western institution of clear-cut, compact, homogeneous national states made its disastrous entry into this foreign arena, the Turks were peasants and administrators, the Lazes were sailors, the Greeks were sailors and shopkeepers, the Armenians were bankers and shopkeepers, the Bulgars were grooms and market-gardeners, the Albanians were masons and mercenary soldiers, the Kurds were shepherds and porters, the Vlachs were shepherds and pedlars. The nationalities were not only intermingled as a matter of geographical fact; they were also economically and socially interdependent; and this correspondence between nationalities and occupations was the order of nature in a world in which the linguistic map was, not a patchwork, but a macédoine. In this Ottoman world the only way of carving out national states on the Western pattern was to transform the native macédoine into a patchwork on the linguistic pattern of Western Europe; and this could be done only by the methods of barbarism which, for a hundred and fifty years past, have in fact been employed with devastating results in one section after another of an area extending all the way from the Sudetenland to Eastern Bengal. So great can be the havoc worked by an idea or institution or technique when it is cut loose from its original setting and is radiated abroad, by itself, into a social environment in which it conflicts with the historic local pattern of social life.

The truth is that every historic culture-pattern is an organic whole in which all the parts are interdependent, so that, if any part is prised out of its setting, both the isolated part and the mutilated whole behave differently from their behaviour when the pattern is intact. This is why "one man's meat" can be "another man's poison"; and another consequence is that "one thing leads to another." If a splinter is flaked off from one culture and is introduced into a foreign body social, this isolated splinter will tend to draw in after it, into the foreign body in which it has lodged, the other component elements of the social system in which this splinter is at home and from which it has been forcibly and unnaturally detached. The broken pattern tends to reconstitute itself in a foreign environment into which one of its components has once found its way.

If we want to see how, in the game of cultural intercourse, this process of one thing leading to another works in practice, let us look at one or two concrete examples.

In a United Kingdom blue book surveying the social and economic state of Egypt in 1839, it is mentioned that, in the city of Alexandria at this date, the principal maternity hospital is located within the precincts of the naval arsenal. This sounds odd, but we shall see that it was inevitable as soon as we retrace the sequence of events that led to this at first sight surprising result.

By the year 1839 the Ottoman governor-general of Egypt, the celebrated Mehmed 'Alī Pasha, had been working for thirty-two years to equip himself with effective armaments in the Western style of his generation. The failure of Napoleon's expedition to Egypt had opened Mehmed 'Ali's eyes to the importance of sea-power. He was determined to have a navy composed of warships on the contemporary Western model; he realized that he would not be navally self-sufficient till he was in a position to have Egyptian warships built in an Egyptian naval dockyard by Egyptian hands; and he also realized that he could not provide himself with an Egyptian personnel of naval technicians without hiring Western naval architects and other experts to train his Egyptian apprentices. So Mehmed 'Ali advertised for Western experts; and suitable Western candidates were tempted to apply for these jobs in Egypt by the handsome scale of pay that the Pasha was offering. All the same, these Western applicants were unwilling to sign their contracts without being sure of being able to bring their families to Egypt with them;

and they were unwilling to bring their families without
being sure of there being suitable provision for the care
of their health up to contemporary Western standards
of medical service. So Mehmed 'Ali found that he could
not hire his urgently required Western naval experts
without also hiring Western doctors of medicine to at-
tend on the naval experts' wives and children; and, as
his heart was set on his ambition to create an Egyptian
navy, he did hire the doctors as well. Doctors and experts and their families all arrived from the West together; the experts duly installed the arsenal and the
doctors duly attended on the women and children in the
new Western community at Alexandria; but, when the
doctors had done all their duty by their Western patients,
they found that they still had some working time on their
hands; and, being the energetic and public-spirited medical practitioners that they were, they resolved to do
something for the local Egyptian population as well. With
what should they begin? Maternity work was obviously
the first call. So a maternity hospital arose within the
precincts of the naval arsenal by a train of events which,
as you will now recognize, was inevitable.

The moral of this story is the speed with which, in
cultural intercourse, one thing can lead to another, and
the revolutionary length to which the process may go.
Within the lifetime of all concerned, the traditional se-
clusion of Muslim women from contact with men outside
their own household had still been so strictly enforced
that in eighteenth-century Turkey, even when one of the
Sultan's most dearly beloved wives was so ill that her
life was in danger, the most that the Islamic code of
manners would allow a Western doctor to do for this
precious imperial patient was just to feel the pulse of a
hand held out timidly between the tightly drawn curtains
of the invisible lady's bed. This was the nearest that a
Western physician had been permitted to approach a
patient whose life was one of the principal treasures of
a ruler who was deemed to be an autocrat. In those day's
the Sultan's autocracy had been impotent to override a
traditional Islamic social convention, even in a matter of
life and death which was next to the so-called autocrat's

heart. And now, within the same lifetime, Muslim women were boldly venturing inside the precincts of an outlandish arsenal to avail themselves of the services of infidel Western obstetricians. This dire breach with the traditional Islamic conceptions of decency in the social relations between the sexes had been a consequence of the Pasha of Egypt's decision to equip himself with a navy in the Western style; and this undesigned and, at first sight, remote social effect had followed its technological cause within the span of less than half a lifetime.

This piece of social history, which is piquant but not unrepresentative, gives the measure of the degree to which those nineteenth-century Ottoman statesmen were deluding themselves when they imagined that they would be able to fit their country out with adequate Western armaments and then to arrest the process of Westernization at that point. It was not till the time of Mustafā Kemāl Atatürk, in our own day, that the 'Osmanlis admitted to themselves the truth that, in the game of cultural intercourse, one thing is bound to go on leading to another until the adoption of Western weapons, drill, and uniforms will inevitably bring in its train not only the emancipation of Muslim women but the replacement of the Arabic by the Latin alphabet and the disestablishment of an Islamic Church which, in Muslim countries in the past, has reigned unchallenged over the whole field of life.

In our own day in India, President Atatürk's great Hindu contemporary the Mahatma Gandhi did realize that in cultural intercourse one thing insidiously leads to another. Gandhi saw that a myriad threads of cotton—grown in India, perhaps, but spun in Lancashire and woven there into clothes for India's people—were threatening to entangle India with the Western world in gossamer meshes that might soon be as hard to break as if they had been steel fetters. Gandhi saw that, if Hindus went on wearing clothes made by Western machinery in the West, they would soon take to using the same Western machinery in India for the same purpose. First they would import jennies and power-looms from England; then they would learn how to build these implements for themselves; next they would be leaving their fields in order to

work in their new Indian cotton-mills and Indian found-
ries; and, when they had become used to spending their
working-time doing Western jobs, they would take to
spending their leisure on Western amusements—movies,
talkies, greyhound racing, and the rest—till they would
find themselves growing Western souls and forgetting how
to be Hindus. With a prophet's vision the Mahatma saw
this grain of cotton-seed waxing into a great tree whose
spreading branches would over-shadow a continent; and
this Hindu prophet called upon his Hindu countrymen
to save their Hindu souls by laying an axe to this rank
Western tree's roots. He set them the example of spending a certain time every day on spinning and weaving
Indian cotton by hand, in the old-fashioned Indian way,
for Indian bodies to wear, because he saw that this
severance of the germinal economic ties between India
and the West was the only sure means of saving the
Hindu society from going Western, body and soul.

There was no flaw in the Mahatma Gandhi's insight.
The Westernization of India that he foreboded and sought
to avert was, and is, fast developing out of that one
original grain of cotton-seed; and Gandhi's remedy for
India's Western infection was the right one. Only the
prophet failed to induce his disciples to follow him in
preserving India's cultural independence at this price in
economic austerity. The wearing of machine-made cotton
goods could not have been renounced by the Indian people
in Gandhi's generation without lowering the Indian peasantry's already intolerably low standard of living, and
without putting out of business altogether the new classes
of Indian cotton operatives and Indian mill-owners that
had already sprung up from India's soil in Bombay and
in Gandhi's own native city, Ahmadabad. Gandhi has
made an immense and perhaps permanent mark on the
history of India and of the world; but the irony of history
has condemned him to make this mark, not by saving
India from economic Westernization, but by speeding her
along the path of political Westernization through leading
her triumphantly to the Western political goal of national
self-government. Even Gandhi's genius was no match
for the remorseless working of a social "law." In a cultural

encounter, one thing inexorably goes on leading to another when once the smallest breach has been made in the assaulted society's defences.

Our inquiry will have made it evident that the reception of a foreign culture is a painful as well as a hazardous undertaking; and the victim's instinctive repugnance to innovations that threaten to upset his traditional way of life makes the experience all the worse for him; for, by kicking against the pricks, he diffracts the impinging foreign culture-ray into its component strands; he then gives a grudging admission to the most trivial, and therefore least upsetting, of these poisonous splinters of a foreign way of life, in the hope of being able to get off with no further concessions than just that; and then, as one thing inevitably leads to another, he finds himself compelled to admit the rest of the intruding culture piecemeal. No wonder that the victim's normal attitude towards an intrusive alien culture is a self-defeating attitude of opposition and hostility.

In the course of our survey we have had occasion to notice some of the statesmen in non-Western countries hit by the West who have had the rare vision to see that a society which is under fire from the radiation of a more potent foreign culture must either master this foreign way of life or perish. The figures of Peter the Great, Selīm III, Mahmūd II, Mehmed 'Alī, Mustafā Kemāl, and "the Elder Statesmen" of Japan in the Meiji Era have passed before our eyes. This positive and constructive response to the challenge of cultural aggression is a proof of statesmanship because it is a victory over natural inclinations. The natural response is the negative one of the oyster who closes his shell, the tortoise who withdraws into his carapace, the hedgehog who rolls himself up into a spiky ball, or the ostrich who hides his head in the sand, and there are classical examples of this alternative reaction in the histories of both Russia's and Islam's encounters with the West.

The policy of learning how to fight an aggressive alien civilization with its own weapons will arouse deep misgivings in conservative minds. Are not your Peters and your Mustafā Kemāls really selling the fort under pretex

of bringing its defences up to date? Is not the right retort
to the intrusion of an alien culture a resolute determina-
tion to boycott the accursed thing? If we scrupulously
obey every jot and tittle of the holy law that has been
laid upon us by the God of our fathers, will He not be
moved to put forth the almighty power of His right arm
for our defence against our infidel enemies? In Russia
this was the reaction of the Old Believers, who suffered
martyrdom for the sake of minute, and in foreign eyes
trifling, points of ecclesiastical ritual; and in the Islamic
world this was the reaction of the Wahhābīs, Sanūsīs,
Idrīsīs, Mahdists, and other puritanical sects who came
charging out of the desert on God's war-path against
apostate 'Osmanlis, who, in the fanatics' eyes, had betrayed Islam by going the Western way.

Muhammad Ahmad, the Sudanese fanatic, is the antithesis of Peter the Russian technocrat; but neither the
mastering of a new-fangled alien technology nor a zeal
for the preservation of a traditional way of life is the
last word in reply to the challenge of an assaulting alien
civilization. If we are to read what this last word is, we
must look ahead to a chapter of the story which, in the
unfinished history of the world's encounter with the West,
is today still hidden in the future. We can supply this
missing chapter if we turn to the history of the world's
encounter with the Greeks and Romans; for, in the record
of this episode, the scroll of history has already been un-
rolled from beginning to end, so that the whole of this
older book now lies open for our inspection. Our future
can perhaps be deciphered in this record of a Graeco-
Roman past. Let us see what we can make of this Graeco-
Roman record.

6

THE WORLD AND THE GREEKS AND ROMANS

One of the besetting infirmities of living creatures is egotism, as we all know from personal experience; and in self-conscious creatures this self-centredness generates an illusion. Every soul, tribe, and sect believes itself to be a chosen vessel; and the falsity of our belief in our own unique value does not easily become apparent to us. We can see the fallacy readily, though, when it is a case of somebody else hugging this illusion about himself. We Westerners, being human, are inclined to feel that what we have done to the world within the last few centuries is something unprecedented. An effective cure for this Western illusion of ours is to glance back at what, not so very long ago, was done to the world by the Greeks and Romans. We shall find that they too overran the world in their day, and that they too believed for a time that they were not as other men are. We shall also find, before we come to the end of this story of the world's encounter with the Greeks and Romans, that, in this episode, a temporarily dominant Graeco-Roman society's estimate of its own value broke down under the test of being weighed in the truth-finding balance of history.

The expansion of the West over the world which began with our dramatically sudden conquest of the oceans at the end of the fifteenth century has its counterpart in Graeco-Roman history in the expansion of the Greek world overland in and after the generation of Alexander the Great in the fourth century B.C. Alexander's march across Asia from the Dardanelles to the Panjab made as revolutionary a change in the balance of power in the world as the voyages of Da Gama and Columbus; and, like these, it was followed up by wider conquests in later generations. In the second century B.C. the Greeks conquered India right across to Bengal, and in the same century the Romans won for the Graeco-Roman world a frontage on the Atlantic Ocean in what are now Southern Spain and Portugal. The Basic Greek in which the New Testament was written in the first century of the Christian Era was spoken and understood from Travancore to the hinterland of Marseilles. At the same date Britain was being annexed to the Graeco-Roman world by force of Roman arms, while Greek art in the service of an Indian religion—Buddhism—was travelling peacefully north-eastwards from Afghanistan along a road that was eventually to carry it across China and down Korea to Japan. Thus, in sheer physical range, the Graeco-Roman culture, in its day, spread as widely in the Old World as our Western culture has spread in its day; and, in an age which has not yet seen the emergence of the indigenous civilizations of the Americas, the Greeks could boast, as we can today, that every contemporary civilization on the face of the planet (whose shape and size the Greeks had accurately calculated) had been reached and penetrated by the radiation of their world-conquering culture.

This impact of a Greek culture on the world in and after the fourth century B.C. gave the world as sharp a shock as the impact of our modern Western culture has been giving it since the fifteenth century of our era; and, as human nature has not undergone any perceptible change within the last few thousand years, it is not surprising to find the standard alternative psychological reactions to a cultural assault, which we have observed in the history of the world's encounter with ourselves, making their appearance likewise in the history of the world's earlier encounter with the Greeks and Romans.

This passage of history, too, can muster its intransigent mahdis and its adaptable Peter the Greats. In Peter's line,

for example, there was Mithradates the Great, an Iranian
king in Asia Minor, who very nearly got the better of
the Romans by arming and drilling his troops in the
Greek and Roman style and by taking the field against
Rome as a rival patron and champion of the Greeks and
their culture. And there was Herod the Great, the Edo-
mite King of Judaea, who was worsted by Psyche's task.
Herod's self-assigned mission was to educate his stiff-
necked Palestinian Jewish subjects into acquiescing in the
minimum compromises with Greek civilization and with
Roman power which, for a small Oriental people in a
predominantly Graeco-Roman world, were the only
practical alternatives to the desperate course of provoking
and incurring annihilation. The Herodian policy of prudent accommodation to imperious historical facts was
defeated by the obstinacy of a long line of Palestinian
Jewish mahdis. This militant movement had begun in the
second century B.C. in a fierce revolt against the Helleni-
zing policy of a Greek King of south-west Asia. Anyone
re-reading the First and Second Books of Maccabees will
almost certainly be struck by the family likeness between
the Maccabees' insurrection in Palestine in 166-165 B.C.
and the Mahdi Muhammad Ahmad's insurrection in the
Egyptian Sudan in A.D. 1881. After flickering up again
in the insurrections of a Theudas and a Judas whose
signal failures are cited by Gamaliel in the Acts of the
Apostles, the flame of this fanatical Palestinian Jewish
resistance to Hellenism rose to its final flare in the second
century of the Christian Era in the revolt of Bar Kōkabā,
who proclaimed himself the Messiah and was crushed by
the Roman Emperor Hadrian.

These Palestinian Jewish leaders of an Oriental resistance movement to the Graeco-Roman civilization were
not the only representatives of their kind. Already before
the end of the third century B.C. there had been some-
think like an "Indian Mutiny" among native Egyptian
troops who had been armed and drilled in the Greek style
by a Greek King of Egypt for the defence of his dominions against an invasion by a South-West Asian Greek
contemporary of his. The Greek-drilled Egyptians routed
the full-blooded Greek troops in the invading army; and

their astonishing victory over descendants of Alexander's invincible soldiers went to these native Egyptian soldiers' heads. And then there were outbreaks among the most ill-fated of all the Orientals who had fallen under Greek or Roman rule—the Syrians who had been kidnapped and been deported overseas to work as slaves in chain-gangs on Greek plantations in Sicily. Before the end of the second century B.C. these Syrian slaves in Sicily had made two desperate insurrections against their Greek masters and these masters' Roman protectors.

This grim tale of cruel oppression and savage revolt in the earlier chapters of the history of the world's encounter with the Greeks and Romans has found echoes in familiar chapters of the parallel history of the world's encounter with the West. In a Westernized world the slave-trade that once disgraced the Mediterranean has been revived in the Atlantic; the insurrection of plantation-slaves that was crushed in Sicily has been victorious in Haiti; the mutiny of the Ptolemies' Greek-drilled native Egyptian troops has been matched by the mutiny of a British East India Company's Western-drilled sepoys; and militant Oriental resistance movements against an alien ascendancy, that are reminiscent of the unsuccessful anti-Hellenic insurrections of the Palestinian Jews and the successful anti-Hellenic insurrections of the contemporary Iranian peoples, are in full swing at this moment in Indo-China and Malaya and are threatening to break out at three places in Africa. Up to this point we can read the story in our own record without needing to consult the Greeks' and Romans' dossier. But now we are reaching and passing the point where, on the open page of our book, the moving finger is writing in the latest entries in our still unclosed account; and, beyond this point, where the curtain veils our own future, the Graeco-Roman account is our best source of potential information about what may be in store for us.

Of course I am not meaning to suggest that we can cast a horoscope of our own future by observing what happened in Graeco-Roman history beyond this point, where our own record breaks off, and then mechanically translating this Graeco-Roman record into modern Western terms. History does not automatically repeat itself; and the most that any Graeco-Roman oracle can do for us is to reveal one among a number of alternative possible future denouements of our own drama. In our case the chances may well be against the plot's working out to its Graeco-Roman conclusion. It is conceivable that we Westerners and our non-Western contemporaries may give the course of our encounter with each other some quite different turn which has no counterpart in Graeco-Roman history. In peering into the future we are fumbling in the dark, and we must be on our guard against imagining that we can map out the hidden road ahead. All the same, it would be foolish not to make the most of any glimmer of light that hovers before our eyes; and the light reflected upon our future by the mirror of past Graeco-Roman history is at any rate the most illuminating gleam that is visible to us.

With these counsels of caution in our minds, let us now go on turning the pages of the book of Graeco-Roman history till we come to the picture of the Graeco-Roman world half-way through the second century after Christ. When we compare this with the picture of the same world two hundred years earlier, we shall perceive at once that in the interval there has been a change for the better here which unfortunately has had no parallel in our Western history up to date. In the last century B.C. the Graeco-Roman world had been racked by revolutions, wars, and rumours of wars, and had been seething with tumult and violence, quite as feverishly as our Western world is today; but midway through the second century after Christ we find peace reigning from the Ganges to the Tyne. The whole of this vast area, stretching from India to Britain, through which the Graeco-Roman civilization has been propagated by force of arms, is now divided between no more than three states, and these three are managing to live side by side with a minimum of friction. The Roman Empire round the shore of the Mediterranean, the Parthian Empire in 'Irāq and Iran, and the Kushan Empire in Central Asia, Afghanistan and Hindustan, cover the whole of the Graeco-Roman world between them; and, though the makers and masters of these three empires are all non-Greek in origin, they are nevertheless all "Phil-hellenes," as they are proud to call themselves: that is to say, they consider it to be their duty and their privilege to foster the Greek form of culture and to cherish the self-governing municipalities in which this Greek way of life is being kept alive.

Let us look into the hearts and minds of the millions of Greeks and Romans and the many more millions of Hellenized and semi-Hellenized ex-Orientals and ex-barbarians who are living under the shelter of a second-century Roman-Parthian-Kushan peace. The waters of war and revolution which had gone over the souls of this generation's great-great-grandparents have now ebbed away, and the nightmare of that time of troubles has long since ceased to be a living memory. Social life has been stabilized by constructive statesmanship; and, though the settlement has fallen far short of the ideals of social justice, it is tolerable even for the peasantry and the proletariat, while for all classes it is indisputably preferable to the Ishmaelitish anarchy to which it has put a long overdue end. Life now is more secure than it was in the preceding age; but for this very reason it is also more dull. Like humane anaesthetists, a Caesar and an Arsaces and a Kanishka have taken the sting out of those once burning economic and political questions that, in a now already half-forgotten past, were the salt as well as the bane of human life. The benevolent action of efficient authoritarian governments has undesignedly created a spiritual vacuum in human souls.

How is this spiritual vacuum going to be filled? That is the grand question in the Graeco-Roman world in the second century after Christ; but the sophisticated civil servants and philosophers are still unaware that any such question is on the agenda. The people who have read the signs of the times and have taken action in the light of these indications are the obscure missionaries of half-a-dozen Oriental religions. In the long-drawn-out encounter between the world and the Greeks and Romans, these preachers of strange religions have gently stolen the initiative out of Greek and Roman hands—so gently that those hard hands have felt no touch and, so far, have taken no alarm. Yet, all the same, the tide has turned in the Greeks' and Romans' trial of strength with the world. The Graeco-Roman offensive has spent its force; a counter-offensive is on its way; but this counter-movement is not yet recognized for what it is, because it is being launched on a different plane. The offensive has been military, political, and economic; the counter-offensive is religious. This new religious movement has before it a prodigious future, as time is going to show. What are the secrets of its coming success? There are three on which we can put our finger.

One factor that, in the second century after Christ, is favouring the rise and spread of the new religions is a weariness of the clash of cultures. We have watched the Orientals responding to the challenge of a radioactive Greek culture along two antithetical lines. There have been statesmen of Herod the Great's school, whose prescription for living in a Graeco-Roman cultural climate has been to acclimatize oneself, and there have been fanatics whose prescription has been to ignore the change of climate and to go on behaving as though this change had not occurred. After an exhaustive trial of both these strategies, fanaticism has discredited itself by turning out to be disastrous, while the Herodian policy has discredited itself by turning out to be unsatisfying. Whichever of the two alternative strategies has been followed, this cultural warfare has led nowhere; and the moral of this anticlimax is that no single human culture can make good its conceited claim to be a spiritual talisman. Disillusioned minds and disappointed hearts are now ready for a gospel that will rise above these barren cultural claims and counter-claims. And here is the opportunity for a new society, in which there shall be neither Scythian nor Jew nor Greek, neither bond nor free, neither male nor female, but in which all shall be one in Christ Jesus—or in Mithras, Cybele, Isis, or one of the bodhisattvas, an Amitabha or perhaps an Avalokita.

An ideal of human fraternity that will overcome the clash of cultures is thus the first secret of the new religions' success, and the second secret is that these new societies, which are open to all human beings, with no discrimination between cultures, classes, or sexes, also bring their human members into a saving fellowship with a superhuman being; for the lesson that human nature without God's grace is not enough has by now been graven deep on the hearts of a generation that has seen the tragedy of a time of troubles followed by the irony of an oecumenical peace.

At least two breeds of human gods have now been tried and found wanting. The deified militarist has been a flagrant scandal. Alexander, as the Tyrrhenian pirate told him to his face in the story as we have it from Saint Augustine, would have been called not a god but a gangster if he had done what he did with a couple of accomplices instead of doing it with a whole army. And what about the deified policeman? Augustus, now, has made himself into a policeman by liquidating all his fellow gangsters, and we are grateful to him for that; but, when we are required to register our gratitude by worshipping this reformed gangster as a god, we cannot comply with much conviction or enthusiasm; and yet our hearts are hungry for a divinity that we can worship in spirit and in truth.

In the gods who have made their epiphany in the new religions, we are at last in the presence of divinities to whom we can devote ourselves with all our heart and mind and strength. Mithras will lead us as our captain. Isis will nurse us as our mother. Christ has emptied Himself of His divine power and glory to become incarnate as a man and to suffer death upon the cross for our sake. And for our sake likewise a bodhisattva who has reached the threshold of Nirvāna has refrained from taking the last step into bliss. This heroic pathfinder has deliberately condemned himself to go on haunting the sorrowful treadmill of existence for aeons upon aeons more; and he has made this extreme sacrifice for the love of fellow sentient beings whose feet he can guide into the way of salvation so long as he pays the huge price of himself remaining sentient and suffering.

These were the appeals of the new religions to a majority of mankind who, in the Graeco-Roman world in the age of the imperial peace, were weary and heavy laden— as indeed they are at all times and places. But what about the Greek and Roman dominant minority that had devastated the world by conquering and plundering it, and were now patrolling the ruins as self-commissioned gendarmes? "They make a desert and call it peace" is the verdict on their handiwork that one of their own men of letters has put into the mouth of one of their barbarian victims. How were sophisticated and cynical Greek and Roman masters of the world going to respond to the challenge of the world's counter-offensive on the religious plane which was the world's answer to its rulers' previous offensive on the plane of war and politics?

If we look into these Greek and Roman hearts in the generation of Marcus Aurelius, we find a spiritual vacuum here also; for these earlier conquerors of the world, like us their present Western counterparts, had long ago discarded their ancestral religion. The way of life which they had chosen for themselves, and had been offering to all Orientals and barbarians whom they had brought within the range of Greek cultural influence, was a secular way in which the intellect had been conscripted to do duty for the heart by working out philosophies that were to take religion's place. These philosophies, which were to have set the mind free, had bound the soul to the sorrowful wheel of natural law. "Up and down, to and fro, round and round: this," the philosopher-emperor Marcus confessed to himself, "is the monotonous and meaningless rhythm of the Universe. A man of average intelligence who has arrived at the age of forty years will have experienced everything that has been and is and is to come."

This disillusioned Greek and Roman dominant minority was, in fact, suffering from the same spiritual starvation as the majority of contemporary mankind, but the new religions which were now being offered to all men and women without respect of persons would have stuck in a philosopher's throat if the missionary had not sugared the strange pill for him; and so, for the sake of accomplishing their last and hardest task of converting a Greek-educated die-hard core of a pagan public, the new religions did clothe themselves in divers forms of Greek dress. All of them, from Buddhism to Christianity inclusive, presented themselves visually in a Greek style of art, and Christianity took the further step of presenting itself intellectually in terms of Greek philosophy.

This, then, was the last chapter in the history of the world's encounter with the Greeks and Romans. After the Greeks and Romans had conquered the world by force of arms, the world took its conquerors captive by converting them to new religions which addressed their message to all human souls without discriminating between rulers and subjects or between Greeks, Orientals, and barbarians. Is something like this historic denouement of the Graeco-Roman story going to be written into the unfinished history of the world's encounter with the West? We cannot say, since we cannot foretell the future. We can only see that something which has actually happened once, in another episode of history, must at least be one of the possibilities that lie ahead of us.

THE ARGUMENT OF
A STUDY OF HISTORY

by D. C. Somervell

1. INTRODUCTION

I. THE UNIT OF HISTORICAL STUDY

The intelligible units of historical study are not nations or periods but "societies." An examination of English history, chapter by chapter, shows that it is not intelligible as a thing-in-itself but only as a part of a larger whole. This whole contains parts (e.g. England, France, the Netherlands) that are subject to identical stimuli or challenges but react to them in different ways. An example from Hellenic history is introduced to illustrate this. The "whole," or "society," to which England belongs is identified as Western Christendom; its extension in space at different dates is measured, and its origins in time. It is found to be older, but only slightly older, than the articulation of its parts. Exploration of its beginnings reveals the existence of another society which is now dead, namely the Graeco-Roman or Hellenic society, to which ours is "affiliated." It is also obvious that there are a number of other living societies—the Orthodox Christian, the Islamic, the Hindu and the far Eastern societies—and also certain "fossilized" relics of, at this stage, unidentified societies such as the Jews and the Parsees.

II. THE COMPARATIVE STUDY OF CIVILIZATIONS

The purpose of this chapter is to identify, define, and name all the societies—or, rather, civilizations, for there are also primitive or non-"civilized" societies—which have come into existence so far. The first method of search to employ is to take the existing civilizations already identified, examine their origins, and see if we can find civilizations now extinct to which these are affiliated as Western Christendom has been found to be affiliated to the Hellenic civilization. The marks of this relationship are (*a*) a universal state (e.g. the Roman Empire), itself the outcome of a time of troubles, followed by (*b*) an interregnum, in which appear (*c*) a Church and (*d*) a Völker-

301

wanderung of barbarians in an heroic age. The Church and the Völkerwanderung are the products, respectively, of the internal and external "proletariats" of a dying civilization. Employing these clues we find that:

The Orthodox Christian society is, like our own Western society, affiliated to the Hellenic society.

Tracing the Islamic society back to its origins we find that it is itself a fusion of two originally distinct societies, the Iranic and the Arabic. Tracing these back to their origin we find, behind a thousand years of "Hellenic intrusion," an extinct society, to be called the Syriac society.

Behind the Hindu society we find an Indic society.

Behind the Far Eastern society we find a Sinic society.

The "fossils" are found to be survivals from one or other of the extinct societies already identified.

Behind the Hellenic society we find the Minoan society, but we observe that the Hellenic society, unlike the other affiliated societies so far identified, did not take over a religion discovered by the internal proletariat of its predecessor. It might therefore be regarded as being not strictly affiliated to it.

Behind the Sinic society we find a Shang culture.

Behind the Indic society we find an Indus culture that stands in some relation to a contemporary Sumeric society.

As offspring of the Sumeric society we find two more societies, a Hittite and a Babylonic.

The Egyptian society had no predecessor and no successor.

In the New World we can identify four societies: the Andean, the Yucatec, the Mexic, and the Mayan.

Thus we have, in all, twenty-one specimens of "civilizations"; and, if we divide the Orthodox Christian society into Orthodox-Byzantine (in Anatolia and the Balkans) and Orthodox-Russian, and the Far Eastern into Chinese and Japanese-Korean, we have twenty-three.

III. THE COMPARABILITY OF SOCIETIES

(1) *Civilizations and Primitive Societies*

Civilizations have at any rate one point in common, that they are a separate class from primitive societies. These latter are very much more numerous but also very much smaller individually.

(2) *The Misconception of "the Unity of Civilization"*

The erroneous idea that there is only one civilization, namely our own, is examined and dismissed; also the "Diffusionist" theory that all civilization had its origin in Egypt.

(3) *The Case for the Comparability of Civilizations*

Civilizations are, relatively speaking, a very recent phenomenon in human history, the earliest of them having originated no more than six thousand years ago. It is proposed to treat them as "philosophically contemporaneous" members of a single "species." The half-truth "History does not repeat itself" is exposed as constituting no valid objection to the procedure proposed.

(4) *History, Science, and Fiction*

These are "three different methods of viewing and presenting the objects of our thought and, among them, the phenomena of human life." The differences between these three techniques are examined and the uses of Science and Fiction in the presentation of the theme of History are discussed.

2. THE GENESES OF CIVILIZATIONS

IV. THE PROBLEM AND HOW NOT TO SOLVE IT

(1) *The Problem Stated*

Of our twenty-three "civilized" societies sixteen are affiliated to previous civilizations, but six have emerged direct from primitive life. Primitive societies existing today are static, but it is clear that they must originally have been dynamically progressive. Social life is older than the human race itself; it is found among insects and animals, and it must have been under the aegis of primitive societies that sub-man rose to the level of man—a greater advance than any civilization has as yet achieved. However, primitive societies, as we know them, are static. The problem is: why and how was this primitive "cake of custom" broken?

(2) *Race*

The factor that we are looking for must be some special quality in the human beings who started civilizations or some special features of their environment at the time or some interaction between the two. The first of these views, namely, that there is some innately superior race, e.g. the Nordic Race, in the world, which is responsible for the creation of civilizations, is examined and rejected.

(3) *Environment*

The view that certain environments, presenting easy and comfortable conditions of life, provide the key to an explanation of the origin of civilizations is examined and rejected.

V. CHALLENGE AND RESPONSE

(1) *The Mythological Clue*

The fallacy in the two views already examined and rejected is that they apply the procedure of sciences which deal with material things to a problem that is really spiritual. A survey of the great myths in which the wisdom of the human race enshrined suggests the possibility that man achieves civilization, not as a result of superior biological endowment or geographical environment, but as a response to a challenge in a situation of special difficulty which rouses him to make a hitherto unprecedented effort.

(2) *The Myth applied to the Problem*

Before the dawn of civilization the Afrasian Steppe (the Sahara and the Arabian Desert) was a well-watered grassland. The prolonged and progressive desiccation of this grassland presented its habitants with a challenge to which they responded in various ways. Some stood their ground and changed their habits, thus evolving the Nomadic manner of life. Others shifted their ground southwards, following the retreating grassland to the tropics, and thus preserved their primitive way of life—which they are still living today. Others entered the marshes and jungles of the Nile Valley and—faced with the challenge that it presented—set to work to drain it, and these evolved the Egyptian civilization.

The Sumeric civilization originated in the same way and from the same causes in the Tigris-Euphrates Valley, and the Indus culture in the Indus Valley.

The Shang culture originated in the Yellow River Valley. The nature of the challenge which started it is unknown, but it is clear that the conditions were severe rather than easy.

The Mayan civilization arose in answer to the challenge of a tropical forest; the Andean in answer to that of a bleak plateau.

The Minoan civilization arose in answer to the challenge of the sea. Its founders were refugees from the desiccating coasts of Africa who took to the water and settled in Crete and other Aegean islands. They did not, in the first instance, come from the nearer mainlands of Asia or Europe.

In the cases of the affiliated civilizations the challenge that brought them into existence must have come primarily not from geographical factors but from their human environment, i.e. from the "dominant minorities" of the societies to which they are affiliated. A dominant minority is, by definition, a ruling class that has ceased to lead and has become oppressive. To this challenge the internal and external proletariats of the failing civilization respond by seceding from it and thereby laying the foundations of a new civilization.

VI. THE VIRTUES OF ADVERSITY

The explanation of the geneses of civilization given in the last chapter rests on the hypothesis that it is difficult rather than easy conditions that produce these achievements. This hypotheses is now brought nearer to proof by illustrations taken from localities where civilization once flourished but subsequently failed and where the land has reverted to its original condition.

What was once the scene of the Mayan civilization is now again tropical forest.

The Indic civilization in Ceylon flourished in the rainless half of the island. This is now entirely barren, though the ruins of the Indic irrigation system remain as evidence of the civilization that once flourished here.

The ruins of Petra and Palmyra stand on small oases in the Arabian Desert.

Easter Island, one of the remotest spots in the Pacific, is proved by its statues to have been once a centre of the Polynesian civilization.

New England, whose European colonists have played a predominant part in the history of North America, is one of the bleakest and most barren parts of that continent.

The Latin townships of the Roman Campagna, till recently a malarial wilderness, made a great contribution to the rise of the Roman Power. Contrast the favourable situation and poor performance of Capua. Illustrations are also drawn from Herodotus, the Odyssey, and the Book of Exodus.

The natives of Nyasaland, where life is easy, remained primitive savages down to the advent of invaders from a distant and inclement Europe.

VII. THE CHALLENGE OF THE ENVIRONMENT

(1) *The Stimulus of Hard Countries*

A series of pairs of contiguous environments is adduced. In each case the former is the "harder" country and has also had the more brilliant record as an originator of one form or other of civilization: The Yellow River Valley and the Yangtse Valley; Attica and Boeotia; Byzantium and Calchedon; Israel, Phoenicia, Philistia; Brandenburg and the Rhineland; Scotland and England; the various groups of European colonists in North America.

(2) *The Stimulus of New Ground*

We find that "virgin soil" produces more vigorous responses than land which has already been broken in and thus rendered "easier" by previous "civilized" occupants. Thus, if we take each of the affiliated civilizations, we find that it has produced its most striking early manifestations in places outside the area occupied by the "parent" civilization. The superiority of the response evoked by new ground is most strikingly illustrated when the new ground has to be reached by a sea-passage. Reasons for this fact are given, and also for the phenomenon that the drama develops in homelands and epic in overseas settlements.

(3) *The Stimulus of Blows*

Various examples from Hellenic and Western history are given to illustrate the point that a sudden crushing defeat is apt to stimulate the defeated party to set its house in order and prepare to make a victorious response.

(4) *The Stimulus of Pressures*

Various examples show that peoples occupying frontier positions, exposed to constant attack, achieve a more brilliant development than their neighbours in more sheltered positions. Thus the 'Osmanlis, thrust up against the frontier of the East Roman Empire, fared better than the Qaramanlis to the east of them; Austria had a more brilliant career than Bavaria thanks to being exposed to the prolonged assault of the Ottoman Turks. The situation and fortunes of the various communities in Britain between the fall of Rome and the Norman Conquest are examined from this point of view.

(5) *The Stimulus of Penalizations*

Certain classes and races have suffered for centuries from various forms of penalization imposed upon them by other classes or races who have had the mastery over them. Penalized classes or races generally respond to this challenge of being excluded from certain opportunities and privileges by putting forth exceptional energy and showing exceptional capacity in such directions as are left open to them—much as the blind develop exceptional sensitiveness of hearing. Slavery is perhaps the heaviest of penalizations, but out of the hordes of slaves imported into Italy from the Eastern Mediterranean during the last two centuries B.C. there arose a "freedmen" class which proved alarmingly powerful. From this slave world, too, came the new religions of the internal proletariat, among them Christianity.

The fortunes of various groups of conquered Christian peoples under 'Osmanli rule are examined from the same standpoint—particularly the case of the Phanariot Greeks. This example and that of the Jews are used to prove that so-called racial characteristics are not really racial at all but are due to the historical experiences of the communities in question.

VIII. THE GOLDEN MEAN

(1) *Enough and Too Much*

Can we say simply: the sterner the challenge the finer the response? Or is there such a thing as a challenge too severe to evoke a response? Certainly some challenges which have defeated one or more parties that have encountered them have ultimately provoked a victorious response. For example, the challenge of expanding Hellenism proved too much for the Celts but was victoriously answered by their successors the Teutons. The "Hellenic intrusion" into the Syriac world evoked a series of unsuccessful Syriac responses—the Zoroastrian, the Jewish (Maccabaean), the Nestorian, and the Monophysite—but the fifth response, that of Islam, was successful.

(2) *Comparisons in Three Terms*

None the less, it can be proved that challenges can be too severe: i.e. the *maximum* challenge will not always produce the *optimum* response. The Viking emigrants from Norway responded splendidly to the severe challenge of Iceland but collapsed before the severer challenge of Greenland. Massachusetts presented European colonists with a severer challenge than "Dixie" and evoked a better response, but Labrador, presenting a severer challenge still, proved too much for them. Other examples follow: e.g. the stimulus of blows can be too severe, especially if prolonged, as in the effect of the Hannibalic War on Italy. The Chinese are stimulated by the social challenge involved in emigrating to Malaya but are defeated by the severer social challenge of a white man's country, e.g. California. Finally, varying degrees of challenge presented by civilizations to neighbouring barbarians are reviewed.

(3) *Two Abortive Civilizations*

This section is a continuation of the argument of the last example in the preceding section. Two groups of barbarians on the frontiers of Western Christendom in the first chapter of its history were so stimulated that they began to evolve rival civilizations of their own which were, however, nipped in the bud, namely the Far Western Celtic Christians (in Ireland and Iona) and the Scandinavian Vikings. These two cases are considered, as are consequences that might have ensued if these rivals had not been swallowed and absorbed by the Christian civilization radiating from Rome and the Rhineland.

(4) *The Impact of Islam on the Christendoms*

On Western Christendom the effect of this impact was wholly good, and Western culture in the Middle Ages owed much to Muslim Iberia. On Byzantine Christendom the impact was excessive and evoked a crushing re-erection of the Roman Empire under Leo the Syrian. The case of Abyssinia, a Christian "fossil" in a fastness encircled by the Muslim World, is also noticed.

3. THE GROWTHS OF CIVILIZATIONS

IX. THE ARRESTED CIVILIZATIONS

(1) *Polynesians, Eskimos, and Nomads*

It might seem that, once a civilization had been brought into existence, its growth would be a matter of course; but this is not so, as is proved by the record of certain civilizations which have achieved existence but then failed to grow. The fate of these arrested civilizations has been to encounter a challenge on the border-line between the degree of severity which evokes a successful response and the greater degree which entails defeat. Three cases present themselves in which a challenge of this kind has come from the physical environment. The result in each case has been a *tour de force* on the part of the respondents which has so engrossed the whole of their energies that they have had none left over for further development.

The Polynesians achieved the *tour de force* of inter-insular voyaging between Pacific islands. It eventually defeated them and they relapsed into primitive life on their several now isolated islands.

The Eskimos achieved an extraordinarily skilled and specialized annual cycle adapted to life on the shores of the Arctic.

The Nomads achieved a similar annual cycle as herdsmen on the semi-desert Steppe. The ocean with its islands and the desert with its oases have many points in common. The evolution of Nomadism during periods of desiccation is analysed. It is noted that hunters become agriculturists before taking the further step of becoming Nomads. Cain and Abel are types of the agriculturist and the Nomad. Nomad incursions into the domains of civilizations are always due either to increased desiccation "pushing" the Nomad off the Steppe or to the breakdown of a civilization creating a vacuum which "pulls" the Nomad in as a participant in a Völkerwanderung.

(2) *The 'Osmanlis*

The challenge to which the Ottoman system was a response was the transference of a Nomad community to an environment in which they had to rule sedentary communities. They solved their problem by treating their new subjects as human flocks and herds, evolving human equivalents of the sheep-dogs of the Nomad in the form of a slave "household" of administrators and soldiers. Other examples of similar Nomad empires are mentioned, the Mamlūks for instance; but the 'Osmanli system surpassed all others in efficiency and duration. It suffered, however, like Nomadism itself, from a fatal rigidity.

(3) *The Spartans*

The Spartan response to the challenge of over-population in the Hellenic World was to evolve a *tour de force* which in many respects resembles that of the 'Osmanlis, with the difference that in the Spartan case the military caste was the Spartan aristocracy itself; but they too were "slaves," enslaved to the self-imposed duty of holding down permanently a population of fellow-Greeks.

(4) *General Characteristics*

Eskimos and Nomads, 'Osmanlis and Spartans have two features in common: specialization and caste. (In the former pair, dogs, reindeer, horses, and cattle supply the place of the human slave castes of the 'Osmanlis.) In all these societies the human beings are degraded by specialization as boat-men, horse-men, or warrior-men to a subhuman level in comparison with the all-round men, the ideal of Pericles' funeral speech, who alone are capable of achieving growth in civilization. These arrested societies resemble the societies of bees and ants, which have been stationary since before the dawn of human life on Earth. They also resemble the societies portrayed in "Utopias." A discussion of "Utopias" follows, in which it is shown that "Utopias" are generally the products of civilizations in decline and are attempts, in so far as they have a practical programme, to arrest the decline by pegging the society at its actual level at the moment.

X. THE NATURE OF THE GROWTHS OF CIVILIZATIONS

(1) *Two False Trails*

Growth occurs when the response to a particular challenge is not only successful in itself but provokes a further challenge which again meets with a successful response. How are we to measure such growth? Is it to be measured by an increasing control over the society's external environment? Such an increasing control can be of two kinds: increasing control over the human environment, which normally takes the form of conquest of neighbouring peoples, and increasing control over the physical environment, which is expressed in improvements in material technique. Examples are then adduced to show that neither of these phenomena—neither political and military expansion nor improvement in technique—is a satisfactory criterion of real growth. Military expansion is normally a result of militarism, which is itself a symptom of decline. Improvements in technique, agricultural or industrial, show little or no correlation with real growth. In fact, technique may well be improving at a time when real civilization is declining, and vice versa.

(2) *Progress towards Self-determination*

Real progress is found to consist in a process defined as "etherialization," an overcoming of material obstacles which releases the energies of the society to make responses to challenges which henceforth are internal rather than external, spiritual rather than material. The nature of this etherialization is illustrated by examples from Hellenic and modern Western history.

XI. AN ANALYSIS OF GROWTH

(1) *Society and the Individual*

Two traditional views are current as to the relation of society to the individual: one represents a society as simply an aggregate of "atomic" individuals, and the other regards the society as an organism and the individuals as parts of it, inconceivable except as members or "cells" of the society to which they belong. Both these views are shown to be unsatisfactory, and the true view is that a society is a system of relations between individuals. Human beings cannot be themselves without interacting with their fellows, and a society is a field of action common to a number of human beings. But the "source of action" is in the individuals. All growth originates with creative individuals or small minorities of individuals, and their task is twofold: first the achievement of their inspiration or discovery, whatever it may be, and secondly the conversion of the society to which they belong to this new way of life. This conversion could, theoretically, come about in one or other of two ways: either by the mass undergoing the actual experience which has transformed the creative individuals, or by their imitation of its externals—in other words, by *mimesis*. In practice the latter is the only alternative open in the case of all but a small minority of mankind.

Mimesis is "a short cut," but it is a route by which the rank and file, *en masse,* can follow the leaders.

(2) *Withdrawal and Return: Individuals*

The action of the creative individual may be described as a twofold motion of withdrawal-and-return: withdrawal for the purpose of his personal enlightenment, return for the task of enlightening his fellow men. This is illustrated from Plato's parable of the Cave, from Saint Paul's analogy of the seed, from the Gospel story and from elsewhere. It is then shown in practical action in the lives of great pioneers: Saint Paul, Saint Benedict, Saint Gregory the Great, the Buddha, Muhammad, Machiavelli, Dante.

(3) *Withdrawal and Return: Creative Minorities*

Withdrawal followed by Return is also characteristic of the sub-societies which form the constituent parts of "societies" in the proper sense. The period in which such sub-societies make their contributions to the growth of the societies to which they belong is preceded by a period in which they are markedly withdrawn from the general life of their society: for example, Athens in the second chapter of the growth of the Hellenic Society; Italy in the second chapter of the growth of the Western Society; and England in its third chapter. The possibility that Russia may be going to play a similar role in the fourth chapter is considered.

XII. DIFFERENTIATION THROUGH GROWTH

Growth as described in the foregoing chapter clearly involves differentiation between the parts of a growing society. At each stage some parts will make an original and successful response; some will succeed in following their lead by mimesis; some will fail to achieve either originality or mimesis, and succumb. There will also be increasing differentiation between the histories of different societies, and it is obvious that different societies have different predominating characteristics, some excelling in art, some in religion, others in industrial inventiveness. But the fundamental similarity in the purposes of all civilizations is not to be forgotten. Each seed has its own destiny, but the seeds are all of one kind, sown by the same Sower, in the hope of the same harvest.

4. THE BREAKDOWNS OF CIVILIZATIONS

XIII. THE NATURE OF THE PROBLEM

Of twenty-eight civilizations that we have identified (including the arrested civilizations in the list) eighteen are dead and nine of the remaining ten—all, in fact, except our own—are shown to have already broken down. The nature of a breakdown can be summed up in three points: a failure of creative power in the creative minority, which henceforth becomes a merely "dominant" minority; an answering withdrawal of allegiance and mimesis on the part of the majority; a consequent loss of social unity in the society as a whole. Our next task is to discover the causes of such breakdowns.

XIV. DETERMINISTIC SOLUTIONS

Some schools of thought have maintained that the breakdowns of civilizations are due to factors outside human control.

(i) During the decline of the Hellenic Civilization writers, both pagan and Christian, held that the decay of their society was due to "cosmic senescence"; but modern physicists have relegated cosmic senescence to an unbelievably distant future, which means that it can have had no effect on any past or present civilizations.

(ii) Spengler and others have maintained that societies are organisms, with natural transitions from youth and maturity to decay, like living creatures; but a society is not an organism.

(iii) Others have held that there is something inevitably dysgenic in the influence of civilization on human nature, and that after a period of civilization the race can only be restored by an infusion of barbaric "new blood." This view is examined and dismissed.

(iv) There remains the cyclic theory of history, as found in Plato's *Timaeus,* Virgil's Fourth Eclogue, and elsewhere. This probably originated in Chaldaean discoveries concerning our own solar system, and the vastly wider vision of modern astronomy has deprived the theory of its astronomical basis. There is no evidence in favour of the theory and much against it.

XV. LOSS OF COMMAND OVER THE ENVIRONMENT

The argument of this chapter is the converse of that in chapter X (1), where it was shown that an increase in control over the physical environment, as measured by improvement in technique, and an increase in control over the human environment, as measured by geographical expansion or military conquest, are not the criteria or causes of growth. Here it is shown that the decline of technique and the geographical contraction caused by military aggression from outside are not the criteria or causes of breakdowns.

(1) *The Physical Environment*

Several examples are adduced to show that the decay of technical achievement has been a result, not a cause, of breakdown. The abandonment of the Roman roads and of the Mesopotamian irrigation system was a result, not a cause, of the breakdowns of the civilizations that had formerly maintained them. The oncoming of malaria which is said to have caused breakdowns of civilizations is shown to have been a result of the breakdowns.

(2) *The Human Environment*

Gibbon's thesis that "the Decline and Fall of the Roman Empire" was due to "Barbarism and Religion" (i.e. Christianity) is examined and rejected. These manifestations of the external and internal proletariats of the Hellenic society were consequences of a breakdown of the Hellenic society that had already taken place. Gibbon does not begin his story far enough back; he mistakes the Antonine period for a "golden age" when it was really an "Indian summer." Various examples of successful aggression against civilizations are passed in review, and it is shown that in every case the successful aggression occurred *after* the breakdown.

(3) *A Negative Verdict*

Aggression against a society still in process of growth normally stimulates it to greater effort. Even when a society is already in decline, aggression against it may galvanize it into activity and give it a further lease of life. (The editor adds a note on the meaning of "breakdown" as a technical term used in this Study.)

XVI. FAILURE OF SELF-DETERMINATION

(1) *The Mechanicalness of Mimesis*

The only way in which the uncreative majority can follow the leadership of the creative leaders is by mimesis, which is a species of "drill," a mechanical and superficial imitation of the great and inspired originals. This unavoidable "short cut" to progress entails obvious dangers. The leaders may become infected with the mechanicalness of their followers, and the result will be an arrested civilization; or they may impatiently exchange the Pied Piper's pipe of persuasion for the whip of compulsion. In that case the creative minority will become a "dominant" minority and the "disciples" will become a reluctant and alienated "proletariat." When this happens the society enters on the road to disintegration. The society loses capacity for self-determination. The following sections illustrate ways in which this comes about.

(2) *New Wine in Old Bottles*

Ideally each new social force released by creative minorities should beget new institutions through which it can work. Actually it works more often than not through old institutions designed for other purposes. But the old institutions often prove unsuitable and intractable. One of two results may follow: either the breakup of the institutions (a revolution) or their survival and the consequent perversion of the new forces working through them (an "enormity"). A revolution may be defined as a delayed and consequently explosive act of mimesis; an enormity as a frustration of mimesis. If the adjustment of institutions to forces is harmonious, growth will continue; if it results in a revolution, growth becomes hazardous; if it results in an enormity, breakdown may be diagnosed. Then follow a series of examples of the impact of new forces upon old institutions, the first group being impacts of the two great new forces at work in the modern Western Society:

the impact of Industrialism on slavery, e.g. in the Southern States of the U.S.A.;

the impact of Democracy and Industrialism on war, as seen in the intensification of warfare since the French Revolution;

the impact of Democracy and Industrialism on the parochial state, as shown in the hypertrophy of nationalism and the failure of the free trade movement in the Modern Western World;

the impact of Industrialism on private property, as illustrated by the rise of Capitalism and Communism;

the impact of Democracy on education, as illustrated by the rise of the Yellow Press and of Fascist dictatorships;

the impact of Italian efficiency on Transalpine governments, as illustrated (except in England) by the emergence of despotic monarchies;

the impact of the Solonian revolution on the Hellenic city-states, as illustrated by the phenomena of *tyrannis, stasis,* and *hegemony*;

the impact of Parochialism on the Western Christian Church, as illustrated by the Protestant Revolution, the "Divine Right of Kings," and the eclipse of Christianity by patriotism;

the impact of the Sense of Unity on Religion, as illustrated by the rise of bigotry and persecution;

the impact of Religion on Caste, as shown in the Hindu Civilization;

the impact of Civilization on the Division of Labour, showing itself as esotericism in the leaders (who become ἰδιῶται) and lop-sidedness in the followers (who become βάναυσοι). The latter defect is illustrated from cases of penalized minorities, e.g. the Jews, and from aberrations of modern athleticism;

the impact of Civilization on Mimesis, which is directed no longer, as in primitive societies, towards the traditions of the tribe, but towards pioneers. Too often the pioneers selected for imitation are not creative leaders but commercial exploiters or political demagogues.

(3) *The Nemesis of Creativity: Idolization of an Ephemeral Self*

History shows that the group which successfully responds to one challenge is rarely the successful respondent to the next. Various examples are given, and it is shown that this phenomenon corresponds with certain fundamental postulates of both Greek and Hebrew thought. Those who have succeeded once are apt, on the next occasion, to be found "resting on their oars." The Jews, having responded to the challenges of the Old Testament, are worsted by the challenge of the New. The Athens of Pericles dwindles into the Athens of Saint Paul. In the Italian *Risorgimento* the centres which have responded in the Renaissance prove ineffective, and the lead is taken by Piedmont, which has had no part in previous Italian glories. South Carolina and Virgina, leading states of the U.S.A. in the first and second quarters of the nineteenth century, have failed to make a recovery from the Civil War comparable with that of the previously undistinguished North Carolina.

(4) *The Nemesis of Creativity: Idolization of an Ephemeral Institution*

Idolization of the city-state proved, in the later stages of Hellenic history, a snare into which the Greeks fell but not the Romans. A "ghost" of the Roman Empire caused the breakdown of the Orthodox Christian society. Illustrations are also given of the hampering effects of the idolization of kings, parliaments, and ruling castes, whether bureaucracies or priesthoods.

(5) *The Nemesis of Creativity: Idolization of an Ephemeral Technique*

Illustrations from biological evolution show that perfect "technique" or perfect adaptation to an environment often proves an evolutionary "cul de sac," and that the less specialized and more "tentative" organisms show greater survival power. The amphibians are contrasted favourably with the fishes, and the rat-like ancestors of man with their contemporaries, the giant reptiles. In the industrial sphere the success of a particular community in the first stages of a new technique, e.g. in the invention of the paddle-steamer, makes that community slower than others to adopt the more efficient screw-propeller. A brief review of the history of the art of war from David and Goliath to the present day shows that, at each stage, the inventors and beneficiaries of one innovation proceed to rest on their oars and allow the next innovation to be made by their enemies.

(6) *The Suicidalness of Militarism*

The three previous sections have presented illustrations of "resting on one's oars," which is the passive way of succumbing to the nemesis of creativity. We now pass on to the active form of aberration, summarized in the Greek formula κόρος ὕβρις, ἄτη (surfeit, outrageous behaviour, and destruction). Militarism is an obvious example. The reason why the Assyrians brought ruin on themselves was not because, like the victors reviewed at the end of the previous chapter, they allowed their armour to "rust." From a military standpoint they were continuously and progressively efficient. Their ruin came because their aggressiveness exhausted them—besides rendering them intolerable to their neighbours. The Assyrians are an example of a military frontier province turning its arms against the interior provinces of its society. The similar cases of the Austrasian Franks and Timur Lenk are also examined, and other examples are cited.

(7) *The Intoxication of Victory*

A theme similar to that of the preceding paragraph is illustrated from a non-military sphere by the example of the Hildebrandine Papacy, an institution which failed after raising itself and Christendom from the depths to the heights. It failed because, intoxicated by its own success, it was tempted to make illegitimate use of political weapons in pursuit of inordinate aims. The controversy over Investiture is examined from this standpoint.

5. THE DISINTEGRATION OF CIVILIZATIONS

XVII. THE NATURE OF DISINTEGRATION

(1) *A General Survey*

Is disintegration a necessary and invariable consequence of breakdown? Egyptian and Far Eastern history show that there is an alternative, namely petrifaction, which was also nearly the fate of the Hellenic civilization and may be the fate of our own. The outstanding criterion of disintegration is the schism of the body social into three fractions: dominant minority, internal proletariat, and external proletariat. What has already been said about these fractions is recapitulated, and the plan of the following chapters is indicated.

(2) *Schism and Palingenesia*

The apocalyptic philosophy of Karl Marx proclaims that the class war will be followed, after the Dictatorship of the Proletariat, by a new order of society. Apart from Marx's particular application of the idea, this is what actually happens when a society falls into the tripartite schism already noticed. Each of the fractions achieves a characteristic work of creation: the dominant minority a universal state, the internal proletariat a universal church, and the external proletariat barbarian war-bands.

XVIII. SCHISM IN THE BODY SOCIAL

(1) *Dominant Minorities*

Though militarists and exploiters are conspicuous among the characteristic types in dominant minorities, there are also nobler types: the legists and administrators who maintain the universal states, and the philosophic inquirers who endow societies in decline with their characteristic philosophies, e.g. the long chain of Hellenic philosophers from Socrates to Plotinus. Examples are cited from various other civilizations.

(2) *Internal Proletariats*

The history of the Hellenic society shows an internal proletariat recruited from three sources: citizens of the Hellenic states disinherited and ruined by political or economic upheavals; conquered peoples; victims of the slave-trade. All alike are proletarians in feeling themselves "in" but not "of" the society. Their first reactions are violent, but these are followed by "gentle" reactions culminating in the discovery of "higher religions" such as Christianity. This religion, like Mithraism and its other rivals in the Hellenic world, originated in one of the other "civilized" societies conquered by Hellenic arms. The internal proletariats of other societies are examined and similar phenomena observed: e.g. the origins of Judaism and Zoroastrianism in the internal proletariat of the Babylonic society were similar to those of Christianity and Mithraism in the Hellenic society, though, for reasons given, their later development was different. The transformation of the primitive Buddhist philosophy into the Mahāyāna provided a "higher religion" for the Sinic internal proletariat.

(3) *The Internal Proletariat of the Western World*

Abundant evidence can be adduced of the existence of an internal proletariat here—among other things, the existence of an "intelligentsia" recruited from the proletariat as an agent of the dominant minority. The characteristics of an intelligentsia are discussed. The internal proletariat of the modern Western society has, however, shown itself markedly unfertile in the production of new "higher religions," and it is suggested that this is due to the continued vitality of the Christian Church from which Western Christendom was born.

(4) *External Proletariats*

So long as a civilization is growing, its cultural influence radiates into and permeates its primitive neighbours to an indefinite distance. They become a part of the "uncreative majority" which follows the creative minority's lead. But when a civilization has broken down the charm ceases to act, the barbarians become hostile, and a military frontier establishes itself which may be pushed far afield but ultimately becomes stationary. When this stage has been reached, time works on the side of the barbarians. These facts are illustrated from Hellenic history. Violent and gentle responses by the external proletariat are pointed out. The pressure of a hostile civilization transforms primitive fertility religions of the external proletariat into religions of the Olympian "divine warband" type. The characteristic product of triumphant external proletariats is epic poetry.

(5) *External Proletariats of the Western World*

Their history is reviewed and violent and gentle responses of the external proletariats are illustrated. Owing to the overwhelming material efficiency of the modern Western society, barbarism of the historic type has almost disappeared. In two of its remaining strongholds, Afghanistan and Sa'udi Arabia, native rulers are protecting themselves by adopting imitations of Western culture. However, a new and more atrocious barbarism has become rampant in the ancient centres of Western Christendom itself.

(6) *Alien and Indigenous Inspirations*

Dominant minorities and external proletariats are handicapped if they have an alien inspiration. For example, universal states founded by alien dominant minorities (such as British India) are less successful in making themselves acceptable than indigenous universal states like the Roman Empire. Barbarian war-bands provoke much more stubborn and passionate opposition if, like the Hyksos in Egypt and the Mongols in China, their barbarism is tinged with the influence of an alien civilization. On the other hand the "higher religions" produced by internal proletariats generally owe their attractiveness to an alien inspiration. Nearly all the "higher religions" illustrate this fact.

The fact that the history of a "higher religion" cannot be understood unless two civilizations are taken into account—the civilization from which it has derived its inspiration and the civilization in which it has taken root—shows that the assumption on which this Study has hitherto been based—the assumption that civilizations, taken in isolation, are "intelligible fields of study"—begins at this point to break down.

XIX. SCHISM IN THE SOUL

(1) *Alternative Ways of Behaviour, Feeling, and Life*

When a society begins to disintegrate, the various ways of behaviour, feeling, and life characteristic of individuals during the growth stage are replaced by alternative substitutes, one (the former in each pair) passive, the other (the latter) active.

Abandon and self-control are alternative substitutes for creativity; truancy and martyrdom for the discipleship of mimesis.

The sense of drift and the sense of sin are alternative substitutes for the *élan* which accompanies growth; the sense of promiscuity and the sense of unity for the "sense of style" which is the subjective counterpart of the objective process of differentiation which accompanies growth.

On the plane of life there are two pairs of alternative variations upon the movement towards a transfer of the field of action from the macrocosm to the microcosm which underlies the process previously described as etherialization. The first pair of alternatives—archaism and futurism—fail to achieve this transfer and breed violence. The second pair—detachment and transfiguration—succeed in making the transfer and are characterized by gentleness. Archaism is an attempt to "put back the clock," futurism an attempt at a short cut to an impossible millennium on Earth. Detachment, which is a spiritualization of archaism, is a withdrawal into the fortress of the soul, and abandonment of "the world." Transfiguration, which is a spiritualization of futurism, is the action of the soul which produces the "higher religions." Examples of all four ways of life and of their relations to each other are given. Finally, it is shown that some of these ways of feeling and life are primarily characteristic of souls in dominant minorities, others of souls in proletariats.

(2) *"Abandon" and Self-control* are defined, with examples.

(3) *Truancy and Martyrdom* are defined, with examples.

(4) *The Sense of Drift and the Sense of Sin*

The sense of drift is due to a feeling that the whole World is ruled by Chance—or Necessity, which is shown to be the same thing. The wide range of the belief is illustrated. Certain predestinarian religions, e.g. Calvinism, are productive of remarkable energy and confidence, and the cause of this, at first sight, curious fact is considered.

Whereas the Sense of Drift normally acts as an opiate, the Sense of Sin should be a stimulus. The doctrines of *Karma* and "Original Sin" (which combine the ideas of sin and determinism) are discussed. The Hebrew Prophets furnish the classic case of the recognition of sin as being the true, though not the obvious, cause of national misfortunes. The teaching of the Prophets was taken over by the Christian Church and was thus introduced to a Hellenic world which for many centuries had been unconsciously preparing itself to receive it. The Western society, though inheriting the Christian tradition, seems to have discarded the sense of sin, which is an essential part of that tradition.

(5) *The Sense of Promiscuity*

This is a passive substitute for the sense of style characteristic of civilizations in course of growth. It manifests itself in various ways. (*a*) *Vulgarity and Barbarism in Manners*. The dominant minority shows itself prone to "proletarianization," adopting the vulgarities of the internal and the barbarisms of the external proletariat, until, in the final stage of dissolution, its way of life has become indistinguishable from theirs. (*b*) *Vulgarity and*

Barbarism in Art is the price commonly paid for the abnormally wide diffusion of the art of a disintegrating civilization. (*c*) *Lingue Franche.* The intermingling of peoples leads to confusion and mutual competition of languages; some of them spread as "lingue franche," and in every case their expansion entails a corresponding debasement. Many examples are examined as illustrations. (*d*) *Syncretism in Religion.* Three movements are to be distinguished: the amalgamations of separate schools of philosophy; the amalgamations of separate religions, e.g. the dilution of the religion of Israel by combination with the neighbouring cults, which was opposed with ultimate success by the Hebrew Prophets; and the amalgamation or syncretism of philosophies and religions with one another. Since philosophies are a product of dominant minorities and "higher religions" a product of internal proletariats, the interaction here is comparable with that illustrated in (*a*) above. Here, as there, the proletarians move some way towards the position of the dominant minority, but the dominant minority moves a far greater distance towards the position of the internal proletariat. For example, the Christian religion employs for its theological exegesis the apparatus of Hellenic philosophy, but this is a small concession compared with the transformation undergone by Greek philosophy between the ages of Plato and of Julian. (*e*) *Cuius regio eius religio?* This section is a digression arising out of the case of the philosopher-emperor Julian considered at the end of the previous section. Can dominant minorities make up for their spiritual weakness by using political force to impose the religion or philosophy of their choice? The answer is that, subject to certain exceptions, they will fail, and the religion which seeks the support of force will grievously injure itself thereby. The one apparently striking exception is the case of the spread of Islam, and this is examined and shown to be not really as much of an exception as it at first appears to be. An opposite formula, *religio regionis religio regis,* is nearer the truth: a ruler who, from cynicism or conviction, adopts the religion of his subjects prospers thereby.

(6) *The Sense of Unity*

This is the "active" antithesis of the passive feeling of
promiscuity. It expresses itself materially in the creation
of universal states, and the same spirit inspires the concepts of an omnipotent law or an omnipresent godhead
pervading and ruling the Universe. These two concepts
are examined and illustrated. In the latter connexion the
career of Yahweh, the "jealous god" of the Hebrews, is
traced from his beginnings as the "jinn" of a Sinaitic
volcano to his eventual sublimation as the historic vehicle
for a purified and exalted conception of the One True
God who is worshipped by the Christian Church, and an
explanation is offered of his triumph over all his rivals.

(7) *Archaism*

This is an attempt to escape from an intolerable present
by reconstructing an earlier phase in the life of a disintegrating society. Ancient and modern examples are given,
the modern including the Gothic Revival and the artifical
revival, for nationalistic reasons, of a variety of more or
less extinct languages. Archaizing movements generally
either prove sterile or transform themselves into their opposite, namely:

(8) *Futurism*

This is an attempt to escape the present by a leap into
the darkness of an unknown future. It involves a scrapping
of the traditional links with the past, and is in fact revolu-
tionism. In art it expresses itself as iconoclasm.

(9) *The Self-transcendence of Futurism*

As archaism may fall into the gulf of futurism, so
futurism may rise to the heights of transfiguration. In
other words, it may abandon the forlorn attempt to find
its Utopia on the terrestrial plane and may seek it in the
life of the soul, untrammelled by time and space. In this
connexion the history of the post-Captivity Jews is examined. Futurism expressed itself in a series of suicidal
attempts to create a Jewish Empire on Earth, from

Zerubbabel to Bar Kōkabā; transfiguration, in the establishment of the Christian religion.

(10) *Detachment and Transfiguration*

Detachment is an attitude which finds its most uncompromising and exalted expression in a philosophy professing to represent the teaching of the Buddha. Its logical conclusion is suicide, for real detachment is possible only for a god. The Christian religion, on the other hand, proclaims a God who has voluntarily abandoned a detachment which it was clearly within His power to enjoy. "God so loved the World. . . ."

(11) *Palingenesia*

Of the four ways of life here examined, transfiguration is the only one which presents a thoroughfare, and it does so by a transference of the field of action from the macrocosm to the microcosm. This is true also of detachment, but, whereas detachment is only a withdrawal, transfiguration is a withdrawal and return: a palingenesia, not in the sense of a rebirth of another example of an old species but in the sense of a birth of a new species of society.

XX. THE RELATION BETWEEN DISINTEGRATING SOCIETIES AND INDIVIDUALS

(1) *The Creative Genius as a Saviour*

In the growth stage creative individuals lead successful responses to successive challenges. In the disintegration stage they appear as saviours *of* or *from* the distintegrating society.

(2) *The Saviour with the Sword*

These are the founders and maintainers of universal states, but all the works of the sword prove ephemeral.

(3) *The Saviour with the Time Machine*

These are the archaists and futurists. These, too, take to the sword and suffer the swordsman's fate.

(4) *The Philosopher masked by a King*

This is Plato's famous remedy. It fails on account of the incompatibility between the detachment of a philosopher and the coercive methods characteristic of political potentates.

(5) *The God incarnate in a Man*

Various imperfect approximations fall by the way and Jesus of Nazareth alone conquers death.

XXI. THE RHYTHM OF DISINTEGRATION

Disintegration proceeds not uniformly but by an alternation of routs and rallies. For example, the establishment of a universal state is a rally after the rout of a time of troubles, and the dissolution of a universal state is the final rout. As there is found to be usually one rally followed by a rout in the course of a time of troubles and one rout followed by a rally in the course of a universal state, the normal rhythm seems to be rout–rally–rout–rally–rout–rally–rout: three-and-a-half beats. This pattern is exemplified in the histories of several extinct societies, and then applied to the history of our own Western Christendom with a view to ascertaining what stage in its development our society has reached.

XXII. STANDARDIZATION THROUGH DISINTEGRATION

As differentiation is the mark of growth, so standardization is the mark of disintegration. The chapter concludes with an indication of the problems standing over for examination in the forthcoming volumes.

As differentiation is the mark of growth, so standardization is the mark of disintegration. The chapter concludes with an indication of the problems standing over for examination in the forthcoming volumes.

6. UNIVERSAL STATES

XXIII. ENDS OR MEANS?

The course of the work down to the present point is summarized, and reasons are given for proceeding to a further examination, in successive Parts, of universal states, universal churches, and barbarian war-bands. Are universal states to be regarded simply as the final phases of civilizations or as prologues to further developments?

XXIV. THE MIRAGE OF IMMORTALITY

The citizens of universal states not only, in most cases, welcome their establishment but believe them to be immortal, and continue in this belief, not only when the universal state is obviously on the verge of dissolution but after it has disappeared, with the result that the institution reappears as a "ghost" of its former self, e.g. the Roman Empire of the Graeco-Roman world as the Holy Roman Empire in the affiliated society of Western Christendom. An explanation may be found in the fact that a universal state marks a rally after a time of troubles.

XXV. SIC VOS NON VOBIS

The institutions of a universal state fail in the long run to preserve its existence, but at the same time serve the purposes of other institutions, more particularly, the purposes of the higher religions of the internal proletariats.

(1) *The Conductivity of Universal States*

The universal state, by imposing order and uniformity, provides a medium of high conductivity, not only geographically between what had previously been separate parochial states, but also socially between the different classes of society.

(2) *The Psychology of Peace*

The tolerance which the rulers of universal states find necessary for their own maintenance favours the spread of higher religions, as is illustrated by the common idea (expressed, for example, in Milton's Nativity Ode) that the Roman Empire was providentially ordained for the benefit of the Christian Church. Such toleration is not, however, universal or absolute. At the same time this tolerance, in the form of anti-militarism, will prove advantageous to aggressive outsiders—barbarians or neighbouring civilizations.

(3) *The Serviceability of Imperial Institutions*

Communications. Roads, sea routes, and their orderly maintenance serve others beside the Government, e.g. Saint Paul's use of Roman roads. Will the higher religions of the present day make similar use of the world-wide system of communications provided by modern technology? If so, they will encounter problems which can be illustrated by the histories of Christian missions in non-Christian worlds at earlier dates.

Garrisons and Colonies serve purposes of civilization as well as of government, but also contribute to the pammixia and proletarianization which mark disintegrating societies. The most obvious beneficiaries are the barbarian war-bands, but the higher religions profit also. Illustration from the development of Islam. Mithraism spread from garrison to garrison along the frontier of the Roman Empire and Christianity from colony to colony, e.g. the significance of Corinth and Lyons, both of them colonies founded by the Roman Government, in the early history of the Christian Church.

Provinces. Contrasted policies illustrated from the history of the Sinic universal state, and the use of provincial organization by a higher religion illustrated from the development of the Christian Church.

Capital Cities. Various factors influence their location. The original capital of the conquerors who found the universal state may not prove permanently suitable. A survey of capitals and their migrations follows. Some capitals which have lost their political significance remain memorable as headquarters of religions.

Official Languages and Scripts. The problems confronting the rulers of universal states in the choice of official languages and their various solutions. The currency of some languages, e.g. Aramaic and Latin, has extended, in time and space, far beyond the empires in which they originally prevailed.

Law. Here again the rulers of universal states have differed greatly from one another in the extent to which they have imposed their own systems on their subjects. The legal systems of universal states have been utilized by communities for which they were not designed, e.g. the use of Roman Law by the Muslims and by the Christian Church, and the use of the Code of Hammurabi by the authors of the Mosaic law.

Calendars; Weights and Measures; Money. The problems of calendar-making and the close association of calendars with religion. Our methods of measuring time are still part Roman, part Sumerian, and the French Revolution failed to revolutionize them. Weights and measures: the battle of the decimal and duodecimal systems. Money: its significance, and origin in Greek cities; its subsequent spread through the absorption of these cities into the Lydian and Achaemenian empires. Paper money in the Sinic world.

Standing Armies. The Roman Army a source of inspiration to the Christian Church.

Civil Services. Civil service problems illustrated by a comparison of the policies of Augustus, Peter the Great, and the British Rāj in India. Civil service *êthos* in the Sinic and British Indian services. The Roman Civil Service training of three great churchmen founders of Western Christendom.

Citizenship. Extension of citizenship a privilege conferred by the rulers of universal state; it helps to produce the egalitarian conditions in which the higher religions flourish.

7. UNIVERSAL CHURCHES

XXVI. ALTERNATIVE CONCEPTIONS OF THE RELATIONS BETWEEN UNIVERSAL CHURCHES AND CIVILIZATIONS

(1) *Churches as Cancers*

Since churches grow in the decaying bodies social of universal states, they are naturally regarded as cancers, both by their contemporary opponents and by a school of modern historians. Reasons are given for regarding this view as mistaken; religions tend to quicken rather than destroy the sense of social obligation in the votaries.

(2) *Churches as Chrysalises*

Each of the civilizations of the third generation alive to-day has as its background a church, through which it is affiliated to a civilization of the second generation. The indebtedness of the Modern Western civilization to the Christian Church is analysed. By contrast, the civilizations of the second generation were affiliated to their predecessors by other links, and this fact suggests a revision of our hitherto accepted plan of the course of history.

(3) *Churches as a Higher Species of Society*

(a) *A New Classification*

The rises and falls of civilizations compared with the revolutions of a wheel whose purpose is to carry forward the chariot of Religion. The steps in religious progress represented by the names of Abraham, Moses, the Hebrew Prophets, and Christ are to be seen as products, respectively, of the disintegrations of the Sumeric, Egyptiac, Babylonic, and Hellenic societies. Does the forthcoming unification of the World today offer a prospect of a further advance? If so, the higher religions now existing have difficult lessons to learn.

(b) *The Significance of the Churches' Past*

An admission that the record of the Churches hitherto seems to disqualify them for the role here assigned to them.

(c) *The Conflict between Heart and Head*

The impact of Modern Science on Religion was not the first conflict of its kind. The conflict between the early Christian Church and Hellenic philosophy had ended in a compromise, in which the philosophers accepted the "Truth" of Christian Revelation provided that that Revelation clothed itself in the language of the philosophers. These outworn Hellenic garments have long since become a source of embarrassment, enlisting the Christian Church in a number of non-religious lost causes with which Christianity had no concern. Religion must surrender to Science every province of intellectual knowledge to which Science can establish a title. Religion and Science are concerned with different kinds of truth, and the modern psychology of the Subconscious Psyche throws a profound light on the nature of the difference.

(d) *The Promise of the Churches' Future*

The distinguishing mark of the Churches is that they all have as a member the One True God. This differentiates them from all other types of societies, and the consequences of this difference are elucidated.

XXVII. THE ROLE OF CIVILIZATIONS IN THE LIVES OF CHURCHES

(1) *Civilizations as Overtures*

An examination of the vocabulary of technical terms which the Christian Church took over from the Hellenic civilization and transformed to new uses is an example of "etherialization" and suggests that the Hellenic civilization served as an overture to Christianity.

(2) *Civilizations as Regressions*

The subsequent degradation of these same technical terms when taken over for secular use by the Western society which has emerged from, and emancipated itself from, the Christian Church.

XXVIII. THE CHALLENGE OF MILITANCY ON EARTH

The break-away of the affiliated civilization from the Church is due to false steps on the part of the Church, and these are an inevitable consequence of the embodiment of the spirit of religion in an ecclesiastical institution for the purpose of "militancy on Earth." Three types of false step are noted: (i) a political imperialism gives reasonable cause for offence to secular authorities as an interference with the proper discharge of their own duties; (ii) the economic success which inevitably attends the discharge of economic duties "heartily, as to the Lord and not unto men"; (iii) the idolization by a Church of its corporate self.

Can Religion promise no Golden Age ahead at the end of the journey? In an Other World perhaps, but not in this one. Original Sin presents an unsurmountable obstacle. This World is a province of the Kingdom of God, but it is a rebellious province, and, in the nature of things, it will always remain so.

8. HEROIC AGES

XXIX. THE COURSE OF THE TRAGEDY

(1) *A Social Barrage*

An heroic age is the social and psychological consequence of the crystallization of a *limes,* or military frontier, between the universal state of a distintegrating civilization and the trans-frontier barbarians. It may be likened to a barrage or dam across a valley, creating a reservoir above it, and the implications of this simile are elaborated in this and the following sections of the chapter.

(2) *The Accumulation of Pressure*

The pressure on the *limes,* or barrage, increases as the trans-frontier barbarians learn the military techniques of the civilization that they are "up against." The guardians of the civilization find themselves reduced to employing barbarians themselves, and these mercenaries turn against their employers and strike at the heart of the empire.

(3) *The Cataclysm and its Consequences*

The triumphant barbarians are inevitably ruined by their own success, being totally unfitted to cope with the crisis that they have created. None the less, in their agony, they give birth to heroic legends, and ideals of conduct such as are expressed in the Homeric *Aidôs* and *Nemesis* and the Umayyad *Hilm*. The heroic age of disorder ends with surprising suddenness, and is followed by a "dark age" in which the forces of law and order gradually reassert themselves. The "interregnum" ends, and a new civilization begins.

(4) *Fancy and Fact*

Hesiod's curious scheme of "Ages"—Gold, Silver, Bronze, and Iron, in which an "Age of Heroes" is inserted between the Bronze and the Iron Ages. The "Age of Heroes" is, in fact, the Age of Bronze described over again, in terms not of historic fact but of Homeric fancy. The glamour of the epic poetry produced by triumphant barbarism deceived Hesiod, the poet of the "dark age" following. It also deceived, for example, the forerunners of the Third Reich who glorified the "blond beasts" of "Nordic" barbarism. Yet the barbarians served as a link through which those civilizations of the second generation that produced higher religions were affiliated to civilizations of the first generation.

NOTE: *"The Monstrous Regiment of Women"*

An explanation of how demonic women came to play so conspicuous a part in the tragedies of heroic ages, not only in legend but also in fact.

9. CONTACTS BETWEEN CIVILIZATIONS IN SPACE

XXX. AN EXPANSION OF THE FIELD OF STUDY

Civilizations, which can be studied adequately in separation from each other in their phases of genesis, growth, and breakdown, cease to be intelligible fields of study in their final phase of disintegration. Their contacts in this phase have now to be studied. Certain geographical areas —Syria and the Oxus-Jaxartes Basin—have been conspicuous in the histories of these contacts, and it is no accident that these same areas and their immediate surroundings also contain the birthplaces of the higher religions.

XXXI. A SURVEY OF ENCOUNTERS BETWEEN CONTEMPORARY CIVILIZATIONS

(1) *A Plan of Operations*

We propose to begin by examining the encounters between the Modern West and all the other contemporary civilizations. The modern period of the history of the Western society can be dated from two events, one just before the close of the fifteenth century of our era, and the other just after the beginning of the sixteenth. The first was the mastering of the technique of oceanic navigation; the second was the break-up of the "medieval" Western Christian Commonwealth which had been put together and held together by the Papacy. "The Reformation" was, of course, a stage in a long process of evolution which had begun in the thirteenth century and was not completed till the seventeenth. But "the Reformation" itself overtook the same generation as had witnessed the voyages of Columbus and da Gama. We shall next step backward in time and examine the contacts of the West in its "medieval" phase with the two rival societies which it encountered; and then the contacts of the Hellenic society, concluding with a glance at some earlier contacts of the same order.

In dealing with the contacts of the Modern West, we shall find that these chapters of history, though known to us in detail up to date, are most of them—perhaps all of them—unfinished, and leave off on a note of interrogation.

(2) *Operations according to Plan*

(a) *Encounters with the Modern Western Civilization*

(i) *The Modern West and Russia.* The original patrimony of Russian Orthodox Christendom had suffered from invasions and conquests at the hands of the Western parochial state of Poland-Lithuania from the fourteenth century onwards—losses not fully retrieved until A.D. 1945. The radiation of the Western culture received a welcoming ("Herodian") response from Peter the Great, but, after two centuries of Westernization on lines approved in the West itself, the Petrine régime was tried and found wanting in the ordeal of the First World War, and was supplanted by an heretical Westernizing régime: Communism.

(ii) *The Modern West and the Main Body of Orthodox Christendom.* In this society, which had been politically clamped together under the rule of an alien universal state, the Ottoman Empire, modern Western culture penetrated, not from above downwards, as in Russia, but from below upwards, from the seventeenth century onwards. This might have led to the Westernizing of the Pādishāh's empire under Phanariot Greek influence. Unfortunately nationalist movements prevailed and led to the break-up of the empire into parochial states. Russia failed to secure the leadership of these peoples, either on Pan-Orthodox or on Pan-Slav lines, though a Russian Pan-Communist régime has now been imposed upon some of them.

(iii) *The Modern West and the Hindu World*. Here the West imposed itself in the form of an alien universal state, replacing another alien universal state, the Muslim Mughal Rāj, which had already gone into liquidation. The British Rāj employed an Indian élite, much as the Ottoman Pādishāh had employed an Eastern Orthodox Christian élite. This Indian élite eventually succeeded (where the Phanariots had failed) in Indianizing the Rāj while preserving it intact, with the large exception of the secession of Pakistan. The strong and weak points of the British Indian Civil Service are discussed, and the population problem indicated as the cloud on the horizon of India's future.

(iv) *The Modern West and the Islamic World*. At the opening of the Modern Western period the two sister Islamic societies, Arabic and Iranic, blocked all the overland lines of access to other parts of the World from the domains of the Western and Russian societies, but a sensational reversal of fortune to Islam's disadvantage was about to follow. Since this change in the balance of power the rulers of a number of Muslim states have been pursuing policies of Petrine "Herodianism" with varying degrees of success. The Islamic world embraces the homelands of three out of the four primary civilizations of the Old World, and the natural agricultural wealth of these areas has now been reinforced by the discovery that they are rich in oil. In consequence they have become the "Naboth's Vineyard" of a twentieth-century World in which the West and Russia are in conflict.

(v) *The Modern West and the Jews*. The Jewish Diaspora did not fit into the Western system of homogeneous territorial states. In an historical survey starting, not from the opening of the Modern Age of Western history, but from the beginnings of the Western Christian society itself, three phases may be noted. In the first phase (e.g. in the history of Visigothia) the Jews, though unpopular and ill-treated, were found useful, since, in that age, the Western Christians were (as Cecil Rhodes said of the Oxford dons) "children in finance." In the next phase, the Western Christians had learnt to "be their own Jews," and the Jews were expelled (e.g. from England in A.D. 1291). In the third phase, the Western society was financially competent enough to allow the Jews back again (e.g. to England in A.D. 1655) and to welcome their *expertise* in business. The Liberal age which then ensued unhappily did not prove to be the end of the story. The section concludes with examinations of Anti-Semitism and of Zionism.

(vi) *The Modern West and the Far Eastern and Indigenous American Civilizations.* These civilizations had had no previous contact with the West before it presented itself in its Modern phase. To all appearance (though this may be deceptive) the American civilizations were completely obliterated. The stories of the impact of the Modern West on China and on Japan run curiously parallel. In both cases there is a reception of Western culture in its Early Modern religious form, followed by rejection; and, at a later date, an impact of Late Modern Western technology. The differences between the two histories are largely accounted for by the fact that China is a vast and sprawling empire and Japan a close-knit insular community. Both societies were, at the time of writing, in eclipse: China under Communism and Japan under American control. Both, like India, were facing a population problem.

(vii) *Characteristics of the Encounters between the Modern West and its Contemporaries.* "Modern Western" civilization is "middle-class" civilization. Those non-Western societies which had developed a middle class welcomed the Modern Western êthos. If a ruler of a non-Western civilization that had no indigenous middle class wished to "Westernize," he had to create an artificial middle class for his purpose in the form of an intelligentsia. These intelligentsias ultimately turn against their masters.

(b) *Encounters with Medieval Western Christendom*

(i) *The Flow and Ebb of the Crusades.* Medieval Western Christendom entered on a period of expansion in the eleventh century, followed by a period of collapse and withdrawal on some frontiers, though not on others, two centuries later. The causes of this expansion and subsequent retreat are analysed.

(ii) *The Medieval West and the Syriac World.* The Crusaders and their Muslim adversaries had much in common. Norman "Franks" and Saljūq Turks were, both alike, ex-barbarians recently converted to the higher religion of the society which they had entered and, in many respects, dominated. The cultural radiation of the Syriac civilization into the less advanced Western Christian society affected poetry, architecture, philosophy, and science.

(iii) *The Medieval West and Greek Orthodox Christendom.* There was a greater antipathy between these two Christian Societies than between either of them and its Muslim neighbours. This mutual antipathy is illustrated by citations, on the one side, from the Lombard Bishop Liutprand's account of his mission to Constantinople and, on the other side, from the picture of the Crusaders in Anna Comnena's *History.*

(c) *Encounters between Civilizations of the first two Generations*

(i) *Encounters with the post-Alexandrine Hellenic Civilization.* The Hellenic civilization in this phase had encounters with every contemporary civilization in the Old World, and the results of the consequent Hellenic radiation were not worked out and completed until several centuries after the Hellenic society itself had gone into dissolution. The Hellenic culture spread far beyond the conquests of Hellenic armies, e.g. into the Sinic world.

The career of Alexander marks an expansion in Hellenic history comparable with the conquest of the Ocean in the history of Western Christendom; but, whereas the West, in its Modern phase, was emancipating itself from its chrysalis religion, Christianity, the Hellenic civilization, having had no such religious chrysalis, was becoming increasingly hungry for religion.

(ii) *Encounters with the pre-Alexandrine Hellenic Civilization.* A conflict between three antagonists for mastery of the Mediterranean Basin, the rivals of the pre-Alexandrine Hellenic society being the Syriac society and a fossilized remnant of the Hittite society, namely, the Etruscans. The Syriac society manifested itself both in the Phoenician sea-power and, in the later stages of the story, in the Achaemenian Empire. The most important cultural conquest of the Greeks in this period turned out to be the Hellenization of Rome, which was achieved indirectly through a previous Hellenization of the Etruscans.

(iii) *Tares and Wheat.* The only fruitful results of encounters between civilizations are the works of peace. A glance at contacts between civilizations of the first generation, Indic and Sinic, Egyptiac and Sumeric, follows.

XXXII. THE DRAMA OF ENCOUNTERS
BETWEEN CONTEMPORARIES

(1) *A Concatenation of Encounters*

On the military level, a challenge from one side leads to a challenge from the other, and this, after redressing the balance, passes over into a counter-aggression and provokes a retort in turn. A chain of such encounters between "East" and "West" is traced from the Achaemenian Empire's assault on Greece down to the twentieth-century reactions of non-Western peoples against Western imperialism.

(2) *Diversities of Responses*

A military response is not the only one possible. Communist Russia reinforces armaments with ideological warfare. Where a military response has been impossible, or has been tried and failed, some conquered peoples have reacted by maintaining their identity as communities by an intensive cultivation of their religion. A classic case of this response is that of the Jews since their dispersion. The supreme response is the creation of a higher religion which in due course takes the conquerors captive.

XXXIII. THE CONSEQUENCES OF ENCOUNTERS BETWEEN CONTEMPORARIES

(1) *Aftermaths of Unsuccessful Assaults*

The result of the successful repulse of an assault may be the militarization of the victor, with ultimately disastrous results. Thus a victory over the Achaemenian invader led, within fifty years, to the breakdown of the Hellenic civilization.

(2) *Aftermaths of Successful Assaults*

(*a*) *Effects on the Body Social.* The social price that a successfully aggressive civilization has to pay is a seepage of its alien victims' culture into its own life-stream. The effect on the victims of assault is of the same order, but more complex. The introduction of Western ideals and institutions into non-Western societies often produces disconcerting results, for "one man's meat is another man's poison." The attempt to introduce one element of an alien culture, while excluding the rest, is doomed to failure.

(*b*) *Responses of the Soul*

(i) *Dehumanization.* The successful assailant succumbs to *hubris* and regards the conquered as "under-dogs." Thus the brotherhood of Man is denied. When "under-dog" is regarded as a "heathen" he may recover human status by conversion; when regarded as a "barbarian" he may recover human status by passing an examination; but when he is regarded as a "native" he has no hope, short of the overthrow or the conversion of his master.

(ii) *Zealotism and Herodianism.* The terms imply a clear-cut distinction between rejection and acceptance of the conqueror's êthos, but a closer examination suggests that the distinction is not as clearcut as it looks at first.

The point is illustrated by a consideration of modern Japan, and of the careers of Gandhi and Lenin.

(iii) *Evangelism*. The self-defeat of the original Zealots and Herodians is set against the achievement of St. Paul.

NOTE. *"Asia" and "Europe": Facts and Fantasies*

"Asia" and "Europe" originated as names of the opposite mainland coasts confronting Hellenic mariners on a voyage from the Aegean to the Black Sea. The attribution of political and cultural significance to the terms has led to nothing but confusion. "Europe" is a sub-continent, with an ill-defined frontier, of the continent of "Eurasia."

10. CONTACTS BETWEEN CIVILIZATIONS IN TIME

XXXIV. A SURVEY OF RENAISSANCES

(1) *Introduction—"the Renaissance"*

The origin of the term "renaissance" is stated, and the meaning given to it in this *Study* explained.

(2) *Renaissances of Political Ideas and Institutions*

The late Medieval Italian renaissance began earlier, and exercised a more enduring influence on the political plane than on the literary or the artistic. City states; secular monarchies; the Holy Roman Empire. Ecclesiastical coronation a renaissance of an Old Testament rite.

(3) *Renaissances of Systems of Law*

The revivals of Roman Law in Eastern Orthodox Christendom and in Western Christendom, and their consequences for Church and State.

(4) *Renaissances of Philosophies*

The revivals of the Sinic Confucian philosophy in the Far Eastern society in China and of the Hellenic Aristotelian philosophy in Medieval Western Christendom were paralleled events in several respects. The former survived until worsted by an intruding Modern Western êthos at the beginning of the twentieth century. The latter was shaken by the Hellenic literary renaissance of the fifteenth century and was finally worsted by the "Baconian" scientific movement of the seventeenth century.

(5) *Renaissances of Languages and Literatures*

A conspicuous part was played by dynastic rulers in launching renaissances in this department, e.g. the prodigious libraries assembled by certain Chinese emperors. The Italian renaissance of Hellenic languages and literatures had an abortive forerunner in the "Carolingian renaissance," which, in turn, had its roots in a renaissance in Northumbria. Renaissances cannot succeed until the society seeking to call up the "ghost" of a dead civilization has itself reached the appropriate stage of development for performing the act of necromancy.

(6) *Renaissances of the Visual Arts*

A number of examples are cited, besides the Western instance popularly known as "the Renaissance." The course of this last is traced in architecture, sculpture, and painting. In all three departments the ultimate result was to sterilize originality.

(7) *Renaissances of Religious Ideals and Institutions*

The contemptuous attitude of Judaism to its successful Christian offspring, and the uneasy and ambiguous attitude of the Christian Church towards the Jewish ideals of monotheism and aniconism, are discussed. The Sabbatarianism and bibliolatry of the Protestant movement from the sixteenth century onwards furnish a clear example of a powerful and popular renaissance of Judaism within the Western Christian fold.

11. LAW AND FREEDOM IN HISTORY

XXXV. THE PROBLEM

(1) *The Meaning of Law*

The "Law of Nature" distinguished from the "Law of God."

(2) *The Antinomianism of Modern Western Historians*

The notion that History reveals the workings of a Divine Providence, as maintained down to the time of Bossuet, has since been discredited. But the men of science, whose Law of Nature has replaced the Law of God in most departments of inquiry, have felt constrained to leave History in a state of lawlessness where anything may be expected to follow from anything else, as in the view of H. A. L. Fisher.

XXXVI. THE AMENABILITY OF HUMAN AFFAIRS TO "LAWS OF NATURE"

(1) *A Survey of the Evidence*

(*a*) *The Private Affairs of Individuals.* Insurance companies rely on a calculable regularity in human affairs.

(*b*) *The Industrial Affairs of a Modern Western Society.* Economists find themselves able to calculate wavelengths of trade cycles.

(*c*) *Rivalries of Parochial States: the Balance of Power.* The fairly regular recurrences of war and peace cycles in the histories of several civilizations.

(*d*) *The Disintegrations of Civilizations.* Regularities in the rout-and-rally alternations, with suggested explanations.

(*e*) *The Growths of Civilizations.* The regularity traceable in breakdown and disintegration phases is here absent.

(*f*) *"There is no armour against Fate."* Further illustrations are given of the persistence with which a tendency, thwarted first at one point and then at another, sometimes ultimately wins through.

(2) *Possible explanations of the currency of Laws of Nature in History*

The uniformities that we have discerned may be due to the working either of laws current in Man's non-human environment or of laws inherent in the psychic structure of Man himself. These alternatives are examined, and it is found that Man's dependence on the laws of non-human Nature diminishes with Man's progress in technology. The succession of human generations is found to have great significance, three generations being the time-span of several kinds of changes in mental habit. The laws of the Sub-conscious Psyche, which psychologists were only just beginning to discover at the time of writing, are next considered as an influence on the course of history.

(3) *Are Laws of Nature current in History inexorable or controllable?*

As regards the laws of non-human Nature, Man cannot alter them, but he can harness them to his own purposes. As regards the laws affecting human nature itself, a more cautious answer seems to be called for. The result will depend on Man's relations, not just with his fellow men and himself, but above all with God his Saviour.

XXXVII. THE RECALCITRANCE OF HUMAN NATURE TO "LAWS OF NATURE"

This recalcitrance is illustrated by a number of examples of "challenge and response." Faced with a challenge, Man is free, within limits, to alter the pace of change.

XXXVIII. THE LAW OF GOD

Man does not live under the Law of Nature only, but also under the Law of God, which is Perfect Freedom. Contrasted views of the nature of God and His Law are examined.

12. THE PROSPECTS OF THE WESTERN CIVILIZATION

XXXIX. THE NEED FOR THIS INQUIRY

The ensuing inquiry marked a departure from the standpoint, adopted and hitherto maintained throughout this *Study,* of treating all the civilizations known to history synoptically. The departure is justified by the facts that the Western society is the only one surviving that is not manifestly in disintegration, that in many respects it had become world-wide, and that its prospects were, in fact, the prospects of a "Westernizing world."

XL. THE INCONCLUSIVENESS OF A PRIORI ANSWERS

There was no reason for supposing, on pseudo-scientific grounds, that, because all other civilizations had perished or were perishing, the West was bound to go the same way. Emotional reactions, such as "Victorian" optimism and "Spenglerian" pessimism, were equally void of cogency as evidence.

XLI. THE TESTIMONY OF THE HISTORIES OF THE CIVILIZATIONS

(1) *Western Experiences with Non-Western Precedents*

What light do our previous studies of breakdowns and disintegrations throw on our present problem? We have noted war and militarism as being the most potent cause of the breakdown of a society. The West has so far wrestled unsuccessfully with this disease. On the other hand it has achieved unprecedented successes in other directions: e.g. the abolition of slavery; the growth of democracy and education. The West also now displays the ominous division into dominant minority and internal and external proletariats. On the other hand, some remarkable successes have been achieved in coping with the problems of a diversity of internal proletariats within the Westernizing world.

(2) *Unprecedented Western Experiences*

The mastery of Man over non-human nature and the accelerating rapidity of social change are both without parallel in the histories of earlier civilizations. The plan of the following chapters is indicated.

XLII. TECHNOLOGY, WAR, GOVERNMENT

(1) *Prospects of a Third World War*

Characteristics of the United States of America and of the Soviet Union, and of the attitude of the rest of the human race towards each of them.

(2) *Towards a Future World Order*

The prospects of the human race compared with Heyerdahl's raft, *Kon-tiki*, on approaching the reef. A future World Order would inevitably be something very different from the present United Nations Organization. The qualifications of the American nation for leadership are discussed.

XLIII. TECHNOLOGY, CLASS-CONFLICT, AND EMPLOYMENT

(1) *The Nature of the Problem*

The triumphs of modern technology had led to an unprecedented demand for "freedom from want"; but would Mankind be prepared to pay the price required for the satisfaction of this demand?

(2) *Mechanization and Private Enterprise*

Modern technology had entailed a mechanization, or regimentation, not only of the manual workers, but also of their employers (nationalization, &c.), of the civil service ("red tape"), and of the politicians (party discipline). The working-class organs of resistance (trade unions) had required further regimentation. The authors of the Industrial Revolution, on the other hand, had come out of a non-regimented society.

(3) *Alternative Approaches to Social Harmony*

The American, the Russian, and the West European, especially the British, approaches analysed and compared.

(4) *Possible Costs of Social Justice*

Social life impossible without some measure both of personal liberty and of social justice. Technology tilts the balance in favour of the latter. What, in an age when the death-rate was being lowered by preventive medicine, were going to be the consequences of an uncontrolled "personal liberty" to propagate the human species? The prospects of a Great Famine ahead are discussed, and the conflicts that it seemed likely to engender.

(5) *Living happy ever after?*

Suppose that the World Society found a successful solution of all these problems, would the human race thenceforth "live happy ever after"? No, because "original sin" is born again in every child that comes into the World.

13. CONCLUSION

XLIV. HOW THIS BOOK CAME TO BE WRITTEN

The writer, born into the age of the Late Victorian optimism, and encountering the First World War in early manhood, was struck by the parallels between the experience of his own society in his own lifetime and those of the Hellenic society, a study of which had provided the staple of his education. This raised in his mind the questions: Why do civilizations die? Is the Hellenic civilization's fate in store for the Modern West? Subsequently his inquiries were extended to include the breakdowns and disintegrations of the other known civilizations, as further evidence for throwing light on his questions. Finally, he proceeded to investigate the geneses and growths of civilizations, and so this *Study of History* came to be written.

MERIDIAN BOOKS

12 East 22 Street, New York 10, New York

Titles listed here are not necessarily available in the British Empire

LIVING AGE BOOKS

published by MERIDIAN BOOKS, INC.

12 East 22 Street, New York 10, New York

Titles listed here are not necessarily available in the British Empire